MW00444222

Terrorism and Counter-Terrorism

Blackwell Public Philosophy
Edited by Michael Boylan, Marymount University

In a world of 24-hour news cycles and increasingly specialized knowledge, the Blackwell Public Philosophy series takes seriously the idea that there is a need and demand for engaging and thoughtful discussion of topics of broad public importance. Philosophy itself is historically grounded in the public square, bringing people together to try to understand the various issues that shape their lives and give them meaning. This 'love of wisdom' – the essence of philosophy – lies at the heart of the series. Written in an accessible, jargon-free manner by internationally renowned authors, each book is an invitation to the world beyond newsflashes and soundbites and into public wisdom.

Permission to Steal: Revealing the Roots of Corporate Scandal by Lisa H. Newton
Doubting Darwin? Creationist Designs on Evolution by Sahotra Sarkar
The Extinction of Desire: A Tale of Enlightenment by Michael Boylan
Torture and the Ticking Bomb by Bob Brecher
In Defense of Dolphins: The New Moral Frontier by Thomas I. White
Terrorism and Counter-Terrorism: Ethics and Liberal Democracy by Seumas Miller

Forthcoming:

Spiritual but Not Religious: The Evolving Science of the Soul by Christian Erickson
Evil On-Line: Explorations of Evil and Wickedness on the Web by Dean Cocking and Jeroen van den Hoven

For further information about individual titles in the series, supplementary material, and regular updates, visit www.blackwellpublishing.com/publicphilosophy

TERRORISM AND COUNTER-TERRORISM
Ethics and Liberal Democracy

Seumas Miller

Blackwell
Publishing

BLACKWELL PUBLISHING
350 Main Street, Malden, MA 02148-5020, USA
9600 Garsington Road, Oxford OX4 2DQ, UK
550 Swanston Street, Carlton, Victoria 3053, Australia

First published 2009 by Blackwell Publishing Ltd

1   2009

Library of Congress Cataloging-in-Publication Data

Miller, Seumas.
    Terrorism and counter-terrorism : ethics and liberal democracy / Seumas Miller.
        p.   cm.
    Includes bibliographical references and index.
    ISBN 978-1-4051-3942-7 (hardcover : alk. paper) – ISBN 978-1-4051-3943-4
(pbk. : alk. paper)   1. Terrorism.   2. Terrorism–Prevention.   3. Terrorism–Moral
and ethical aspects.   4. Terrorism–Prevention–Moral and ethical aspects.   I. Title.
    HV6431.M5735 2009
    363.325–dc22

                                                                    2007046036

A catalogue record for this title is available from the British Library.

Set in 10/13pt Galliard
by Graphicraft Limited, Hong Kong
Printed and bound in Singapore
by Markono Print Media Pte Ltd

For further information on
Blackwell Publishing, visit our website at
www.blackwellpublishing.com

For Professor Emeritus Ian Macdonald, former Head of the Department of Philosophy at Rhodes University, Grahamstown, South Africa: a committed liberal in troubled times

Contents

Acknowledgements

I wish to thank Andrew Alexandra, John Blackler, Michael Davis, Larry May, Thomas Pogge, Igor Primoratz, David Rodin and anonymous readers from Blackwell Publishing for comments on earlier versions of some of the chapters in this book. I especially wish to thank Michael Selgelid, who co-authored Chapter 7.I also thank Justin Dyer from Blackwell Publishing for his helpful copy-editing work.

Earlier versions of some of the material used in this book appeared in the following publications authored or co-authored by Seumas Miller:

Ethical Issues in Policing in India (with Sankar Sen, Prakash Mishra and John Blackler), Hyderabad: National Police Academy, 2007; 'Torture and terrorism', *Iyyun* 55, January 2006; 'Is torture ever morally justifiable?', *International Journal of Applied Philosophy* 9(2), 2005; 'Terrorism and collective responsibility: response to Narveson and Rosenbaum', *International Journal of Applied Philosophy* 18(2), 2004; 'Civilian immunity, forcing the choice and collective responsibility', in I. Primoratz (ed.), *Civilian Immunity*, Oxford: Oxford University Press, 2007; 'Torture', in E.N. Zalta (ed.), *Stanford Encyclopedia of Philosophy*, Spring 2006 Edition; 'Terrorism and collective responsibility', in G. Meggle (ed.), *Ethics of Terrorism and Counter-Terrorism*, Frankfurt: Ontos Verlag, 2005; 'Osama bin Laden, terrorism and collective responsibility', in C.A.J. Coady and M. O'Keefe (eds), *Terrorism and Justice: Moral Argument in a Threatened World*, Melbourne: Melbourne University Press, 2002; 'Just War theory: the case of South Africa', *Philosophical Papers* 9(2), 1990; 'On the morality of waging war against the state', *South African Journal of Philosophy* 10(1), 1991; *Ethical Consideration of the Dual-Use Dilemma in the Biological Sciences* (with Michael Selgelid) (Commissioned Report for the Department of The Prime Minister and Cabinet, Government of Australia, November 2006), *Science and Engineering Ethics* 13, December 2007.

Introduction

This book is a contribution to the literature on the ethics or morality – I use the terms interchangeably – of terrorism and counter-terrorism from the standpoint of applied philosophy. Accordingly, its focus is not terrorism or counter-terrorism *per se*; it is not a descriptive or explanatory account of instances and forms of terrorism, or of the various tactical and strategic responses available to security agencies seeking to combat terrorism. Rather, I deal with a number of the profound moral issues that terrorism and counter-terrorism give rise to, including the moral permissibility/impermissibility of terrorists using lethal force against non-combatants in the service of (possibly morally justifiable) political goals, the practices of assassinating and torturing terrorists, and the infringement of civil liberties by security agencies, e.g., detention without trial, intrusive surveillance, for the purpose of protecting the lives of citizens against terrorist attacks. More specifically, my focus is the moral problems that terrorism and counter-terrorism present for the contemporary liberal-democratic state.

Moreover, this book is philosophical or ethico-analytic in character; it does not simply seek to offer a descriptive account of the various moral problems that terrorism and counter-terrorism give rise to, much less to survey the various *de facto* moral attitudes that different groups might have to these problems and any proposed solutions. Rather, I seek to analyse these moral problems, and identify the moral considerations that ought to inform – albeit not fully determine – public policy and legislation in relation to terrorism and counter-terrorism. In so doing I apply specific philosophical theories and perspectives and, more generally, employ universally accepted procedures of human reasoning. So the book is an exercise in applied philosophy. Needless to say, as such, it helps itself to relevant empirical, public policy and legal literature on terrorism and counter-terrorism, as required.

Chapter 1 sets the stage for the ethico-philosophical analyses in Chapters 2 to 7 that constitute the essence of the book. Chapter 1 traverses the landscape of terrorism as it pertains to the contemporary liberal-democratic state by offering a brief account of five salient (real and alleged) terrorist groups and their associated campaigns. They are: (1) Al-Qaeda; (2) terrorism and counter-terrorism in the Israeli–Palestinian conflict; (3) the Irish Republican Army's (IRA) campaign of violence in the 1970s, 1980s and 1990s in Northern Ireland; (4) the African National Congress's (ANC) armed struggle against the apartheid state in South Africa; (5) terrorism and counter-terrorism in India in recent times.

Each of these five groups involves a contemporary liberal-democratic state, either as the *target* of terrorism, e.g., Al-Qaeda's attack on the World Trade Center in New York on September 11, 2001, the *perpetrator* of terrorism (a species of state terrorism), e.g., the Indian security forces' policy of torturing and killing ('disappearances') Sikh militants/separatists/terrorists in the Punjab in the 1980s, or as the *political goal* of the terrorist activity, e.g., the ANC's armed struggle to establish a liberal-democratic state in South Africa.

Note that in selecting these five groups I am not necessarily labelling all of them as terrorists. Al-Qaeda is self-evidently and quintessentially a terrorist group, but the ANC arguably was not. Nor am I seeking to ignore the manifest deficiencies of some of these nation-states as liberal democracies. Israel, for example, has since the Six Day War of 1967 been exercising *de facto* political control over the West Bank and (until recently) Gaza Strip (indirectly since the establishment of the Palestinian National Authority in 1994) while denying the Palestinian inhabitants their political and civil rights. Finally, it should be noted that the liberal-democratic states in question, i.e., the US, the UK, Israel and India, are, or have been at certain times, both the victims of terrorism and the perpetrators of terrorist acts.

Chapter 2 provides a discussion of the two most plausible kinds of definition of terrorism – albeit these two different kinds are often conflated – namely, those framed in terms of targeting innocents, and those framed in terms of targeting non-combatants. I argue for a third kind of definition, albeit a definition that builds on the strengths and weaknesses of the two identified defective kinds of definition. An important feature of my proposed definition is that it respects the conceptual distinction – as opposed to the exemplification in fact – between acts of terrorism *per se* and morally justified acts of terrorism. Even if in fact there are no acts of morally justified terrorism, it should not be part of the definition of terrorism that this be so. A further important feature of my proposed definition is that acts of terrorism (thus defined) could, pragmatically speaking, be criminalized under international law; the utility of any definition of terrorism consists in part in its potential for being accepted by many or most national governments, and enshrined in international law.

Chapter 3 addresses the question of the moral permissibility/impermissibility of targeting various categories of non-combatants by (alleged) terrorist groups. I take it to be self-evidently morally wrong for terrorists to target innocent civilians, such as children. However, there are other civilian groups in respect of which matters are not so clear. Specifically, I distinguish non-violent rights violators from combatants (the category of combatants is taken to include the leaders of combatants and those who assist combatants *qua* combatants). Within the former category I distinguish perpetrators of positive (non-violent) rights violations, e.g., those who dispossess a group of its territory by fraud, and perpetrators of culpable omissions, e.g., state officials who refuse to distribute medical supplies to disease-afflicted children with the consequence that the children die. I argue that under certain conditions it might be morally justifiable to use lethal force against non-violent rights violators. The implication of this is that *some* forms of terrorism might be morally justified under certain circumstances. It goes without saying that many, probably most, forms of terrorism, e.g., those perpetrated by Al-Qaeda, are not morally justifiable.

The principal focus of Chapter 4 is the infringement of human rights, e.g., freedom of speech, freedom of action, right to privacy, within the liberal-democratic state during peacetime as part of a counter-terrorism strategy. I argue that notwithstanding the need to give police additional specific powers in relation to intelligence/evidence gathering in particular, the morally legitimate actions of a liberal-democratic state are significantly constrained by the human rights of its individual citizens, specifically the various rights to freedom. Accordingly, there are a range of in-principle limits to counter-terrorism strategies adopted to protect the lives of citizens; it is not simply a matter of weighing up, or trading off, the right to life of some citizens against the rights to freedom of others in the abstract. To put matters somewhat crudely, there are significant in-principle limits on what a liberal-democratic state is entitled to do, even in order to protect the lives of its citizenry. Thus it is morally unacceptable, for example, to detain terrorist suspects indefinitely without trial.

Here, as elsewhere, I note the importance of not confusing the following three different contexts: (1) a well-ordered, liberal democracy at peace; (2) a liberal democracy under a state of emergency; and (3) a theatre of war. Confusing these contexts leads to a dangerous blurring of the distinctions, for example, between what is an appropriate police power of detention of suspects under a state of emergency, as opposed to normal peacetime conditions.

An important distinction in play here is that between a one-off action that is morally justified, all things considered, and a law, or lawful institutional practice, that is morally justified in the setting of a liberal-democratic state. A particular one-off action performed in a specific context might be morally justified, all things considered, without the action in question either being lawful, or being an action of a type that ought to be lawful, in a liberal democracy. In general, the law, especially the criminal law, tracks – and ought to track – morality; however, this is not necessarily or invariably the case. I make use of this distinction in a number of the chapters in this book.

Chapter 5 addresses a variety of moral issues that arise for a liberal-democratic state operating under a state of emergency or engaged in an armed conflict with a non-state actor in a theatre of war. A liberal democracy might justifiably be operating under a state of emergency because it is confronting a one-off disaster, e.g., the 9/11 attack on the World Trade Center, and/or because of a serious, ongoing, internal armed struggle, e.g., the IRA's campaign of violence in Northern Ireland in the 1970s.

If a state of emergency is to be morally justifiable, it must be comprehensively legally circumscribed, both in relation to the precise powers granted to the government and its security agencies, and in relation to the termination of those powers and their judicial oversight while in use.

A liberal democracy might be engaged in an armed conflict with a non-state actor in a theatre of war because of serious, ongoing, terrorist attacks on the part of an external, non-state actor, e.g., Hezbollah's rocket attacks on Israeli towns. In theatres of war, terrorists are *de facto* military combatants (terrorist-combatants). Moreover, since terrorist organizations are, or ought to be, unlawful, terrorist-combatants are unlawful combatants. Since the terrorism-as-war framework (as opposed to a terrorism-as-crime framework) applies to theatres of war, it is justifiable to implement (say) a shoot-on-sight policy in relation to known terrorists; moreover, it might be morally justifiable to deploy the practice of targeted killings (assassinations) of individual terrorists.

The terrorism-as-war framework should be applied only under the following general conditions:

1 The terrorism-as-crime framework cannot adequately contain serious and ongoing terrorist attacks.
2 The application of the terrorism-as-war framework is likely to be able adequately to contain the terrorist attacks.

3 The application of the terrorism-as-war framework is proportionate to the terrorist threat.

4 The terrorism-as-war framework is applied only to an extent, e.g., with respect to a specific theatre of war but not necessarily to all areas that have suffered, or might suffer, a terrorist attack, and over a period of time, that is necessary.

5 All things considered, the application of the terrorism-as-war framework will have good consequences security-wise and better overall consequences, e.g., in terms of loss of life, restrictions on freedoms, economic impact, institutional damage, than the competing options.

Notwithstanding the possible moral acceptability of such counter-terrorism measures in a theatre of war and/or under a state of emergency (but not otherwise during peacetime), fundamental moral principles concerning human rights must be respected. In particular, it is not morally permissible for a government to discount the lives of innocent non-citizens in favour of protecting the lives of its own non-combatant, let alone combatant, citizens (as has been argued by some theorists in relation to the Israeli counter-terrorism strategy). Nor is it morally permissible for a government to possess the legal power (say) intentionally to kill one cohort of its (innocent) citizens in the service of some (alleged) larger purpose, such as (say) the protection of a second, but larger, cohort of its (innocent) citizens. Someone might suggest that a government ought to have the legal power to order the mid-air destruction of an aircraft under the control of terrorists, but whose passengers were innocent civilians, if the government deemed this necessary to prevent the aircraft crashing into a large building and killing a much larger number of innocent civilians. Such scenarios raise the related questions of the moral permissibility of legalizing: (a) the unintended (but foreseen) killing of persons known to be innocent; and (b) the intentional killing of persons known to be innocent. I argue that the legalization of (a), but not (b), is (under certain circumstances) morally acceptable.

Chapter 6 concerns a specific counter-terrorism measure, namely, torture. The chapter is in four parts: the first part addresses the question, 'What is torture?'; the second, 'What is wrong with torture?'; the third, 'Is torture ever morally justifiable?'; and the fourth, 'Should torture ever be legalized or otherwise institutionalized?' I argue that in certain extreme circumstances, the torture of a person known to be a terrorist might be morally justifiable. Roughly speaking, the circumstances are that: (1) the terrorist is in the process of completing his action of attempting to (say) murder thousands of innocent people by detonating a nuclear device, and is refusing to provide the information necessary to allow it to be defused;

and (2) torturing the terrorist is necessary and sufficient to save the lives of the innocent people in question. However, I also argue that torture should not under any circumstances be legalized or otherwise institution-alized. Here I invoke again the above-mentioned distinction between a morally justified, one-off action and a morally justified law, or lawful institutional practice. The legalization of torture, including use of torture warrants, is unnecessary, undesirable and, indeed, a threat to liberal-democratic institutions; as such, it is not morally acceptable.

In the final chapter of this book I turn to the matter of the potential use of weapons of mass destruction (WMDs) by terrorists and, more specific-ally, to the so-called 'dual-use dilemma' confronted by researchers in the biological sciences, and by governments and policymakers. Techniques of genetic engineering are available to enhance the virulence, transmiss-ibility, and so on, of naturally occurring pathogens such as Ebola and smallpox; indeed, recent developments in synthetic genomics enable the creation of pathogens *de novo*. The unfortunate consequence of these scientific developments is that the means are increasingly available to enable terrorists to launch bioterrorist attacks on populations that they consider to be enemies. Accordingly, there is a dual-use dilemma. On the one hand, research in the biological sciences can, and does, do a great deal of good, e.g., by producing vaccines against viruses; on the other hand, the results of such research can potentially be used by terrorists to cause enormous harm by, for example, the weaponization of infectious diseases against which there is no vaccine.

This chapter attempts to steer a middle course between an irrespons-ibly permissive approach to the regulation of research in the biological sciences that would allow research to continue (more or less) unimpeded, and an unrealistic and probably counter-productive approach which would seek to subject it to the kind of heavy-handed, top-down, governmental regulation characteristic of nuclear research. It recommends, among other things, the setting up of an independent authority, mandatory physical safety, education and personnel security procedures, the licensing of dual-use technologies, and various censorship provisions.

Liberal-democratic societies tend to view terrorism, whether perpetrated by state or non-state actors, as both morally repugnant and deeply irrational. This is no doubt especially true of bioterrorism and other forms of politically motivated mass murder. However, as has often been pointed out, the counter-terrorist response of a liberal democracy needs to be governed by principles of morality and rationality if it is not to prove more damaging than the terrorist attacks themselves. Hence Goya's famous painting (reprinted on the cover of this book) is doubly salient: *The Sleep of Reason Produces Monsters.*

1

The Varieties of Terrorism

The September 11, 2001 attacks on the World Trade Center in New York and the Pentagon in Washington, DC catapulted terrorism to the top of the US political agenda and produced immediate and profound global consequences, not only politically and militarily, but also economically. There have been a number of subsequent specific terrorist bombings of civilians, including in Bali in 2002, Madrid in 2004, London in 2005, New Delhi in 2005 and Mumbai in 2006. In addition, there have been ongoing terrorist attacks in a number of theatres of internecine war, including in Iraq, Kashmir, Sri Lanka and in the Israeli–Palestinian conflict in the Middle East. In some of these contexts there appears to be a ratcheting up of a given terrorist group's lethal capability, e.g., in 2006 the Lebanon-based terrorist organization Hezbollah for the first time launched a series of rocket attacks on Israeli cities from Lebanon (to which the Israelis responded with bombing raids on Beirut and other cities in Lebanon). These specific and ongoing attacks have ensured that terrorism remains in the international media headlines and at the world's political centre stage.

No one denies the reality and impact of terrorism in the contemporary world. But when it comes to defining terrorism, and especially to combating terrorism, there is much disagreement. If Al-Qaeda is a paradigm of a terrorist network, what of the African National Congress (ANC) in the 1960s, 1970s and 1980s? The ANC was branded a terrorist organization by the South African apartheid government. However, the ANC and its supporters claimed that they were not a terrorist organization, but rather a liberation movement engaged in an armed struggle. State actors, e.g., the US government, often deny the existence of state terrorism.[1] Terrorism, they claim, is an activity only undertaken by sub-state groups. But was not the Soviet Union under Stalin a terrorist state? Certainly, it routinely used a great many of the methods of terrorism. Again, many Israelis will argue that when Israeli forces engage in targeted assassinations of members of Hamas and the like, they are not engaged in terrorism but rather are using morally justified counter-terrorist tactics. (See Chapter 5.) By contrast, Palestinians proclaim these and other acts of the Israeli state to be acts of terrorism perpetrated against the Palestinian people. Liberal humanists decry the use of some counter-terrorism measures, such as the indefinite detention without trial of alleged terrorists, as a violation of human rights. But many conservatives in liberal democracies hold such measures to be necessary in the so-called 'war against terrorism'.

Prior to attempting to provide answers to these and related questions, we need to traverse the landscape of terrorism, or at least what has been regarded as terrorism.[2] Historically, terrorist organizations and campaigns have typically been identified not so much by their political motivations as by their methods; the methods they use to achieve their political ends are ones deployed in order to instil fear, i.e., quite literally to terrorize. These methods include assassination, indiscriminate killing, torture, kidnapping and hostage taking, bombing civilian targets (including suicide bombing) and ethnic cleansing. Some of these methods are necessarily acts of terror, e.g., torture. However, some of them are not necessarily methods of terror. The attempted assassination of Hitler by elements of the German military, for example, was not undertaken to terrorize Hitler or anyone else, but simply to eliminate the person chiefly responsible for (among other things) continuing to prosecute a hugely destructive and unwinnable war. Further, some of these methods invariably instil fear, but this might not be a primary motivation for their use in all contexts. Ethnic cleansing, for example, might be undertaken simply to ensure that a population is relocated (albeit against their will), as was presumably the case in apartheid South Africa.[3] Nevertheless, ethnic cleansing invariably involves the instilling of high levels of fear. Again, genocide is invariably preceded by terror, e.g., the Hutu militias (Interahamwe) in Rwanda certainly terrorized the Tutsi population prior to slaughtering

---

[1]   US State Department definition quoted in D.J. Whittaker (ed.), *The Terrorism Reader*, 2nd edn, London: Routledge, 2003, p. 3.

[2]   For useful introductions see ibid., and C. Townshend, *Terrorism: A Very Short Introduction*, Oxford: Oxford University Press, 2002.

[3]   In some contexts, e.g., at Srebrenica in Bosnia in 1995, ethnic cleansing has meant mass slaughter, and not simply forcible removal.

approximately one million of its members.[4] However, conceptually speaking, the instilling of fear is not necessarily a primary motivation in genocide. And genocide goes beyond terrorism; the point is not simply to terrorize the target population, but to eliminate it.[5]

I will assume in what follows that terrorism, or at least the species under consideration in this book, is politically motivated. (This is not to say that it might not have additional motivations, e.g., religious ends.) Moreover, I will further assume that terrorism involves the methods mentioned above (at least), and that these methods are used with the intention of terrorizing or instilling fear in a target population.

So much by way of a preliminary description of the phenomenon of terrorism. Prior to offering a definition of terrorism, we need to try further to demarcate its boundaries by recourse to actual contemporary examples.

The approach to be taken here in relation to the further demarcation of terrorism is in large part empirical-comparative. In doing so I concede that terrorism is an essentially contested concept and that, therefore, there is inevitably a degree of stipulation involved in any definition on offer. I first provide a number of contemporary case studies of organizations and campaigns widely referred to as being terrorist in nature. I do so with a view to providing a set of descriptions of salient contemporary instances of terrorism – or what are widely alleged to be instances of terrorism – that are sufficiently rich to enable the derivation of the key defining features of modern terrorism, or at least of the key criteria of terrorism. However, I should make it clear that my main interest in this book is with the implications of terrorism for contemporary liberal democracy. Hence I will not focus much attention on the terrorist and counter-terrorist campaigns of totalitarian or authoritarian states, but rather concentrate on those campaigns either mounted against or by liberal-democratic states, or pursued by groups seeking to establish liberal-democratic states.

Here I use the notion of a liberal-democratic state somewhat loosely to mean representative democracies committed (in theory and to a large extent in practice) to the protection of basic political, civil and human rights for their citizens. I do not mean to imply that liberal democracies thus characterized are necessarily communal exemplars of moral rectitude, or even of human well-being broadly conceived. For example, gross economic inequality, domination and exploitation of other weaker nation-states, and an impoverished 'junk' culture are consistent with this

---

[4]   F. Keane, *Season of Blood: A Rwandan Journey*, London: Viking, 1995, p. 29.
[5]   On some definitions of genocide, mass murder of an ethnic or social group is not necessary; rather what is necessary is elimination of the identity of members of the group, e.g., by destruction of the group's language and culture.

notion of a liberal-democratic state; thus, although the US is the world's leading liberal democracy, arguably it also has just such an array of morally repugnant features. However, I do mean to imply the view that democracy and the protection of basic political, civil and human rights are, or ought to be, among the fundamental values embodied in contemporary nation-states, whatever their other ethical, cultural or religious commitments might be. Accordingly, I do not rule out the possibility of an Islamic liberal democracy any more than I rule out the possibility of a Christian one or a Jewish one.[6] Indeed, I note that a majority of the world's Muslims currently live in democracies committed (at least in theory) to individual rights, namely, India, Indonesia and Turkey.

I take the US, the UK, Israel, India and the post-apartheid South African state to be liberal-democratic states, albeit (in different ways) flawed ones.[7] These liberal-democratic states are flawed by virtue of the fact that, for example, their security agencies have at least on occasion, if not on a regular basis, resorted to terrorist tactics such as torture. I also take it that some of these states are closer to the liberal-democratic paradigm than others. It is self-evident, for example, that neither India-controlled Kashmir nor the West Bank (currently under *de facto*, albeit indirect, Israeli control) is governed in accordance with liberal-democratic principles.

The terrorist groups and campaigns that I have chosen are as follows: (1) Al-Qaeda; (2) terrorism and counter-terrorism in the Israeli–Palestinian conflict; (3) the Irish Republican Army's (IRA) campaign of violence in the 1970s, 1980s and 1990s; (4) the ANC's campaign of violence against the apartheid state in South Africa in the 1960s, 1970s and 1980s; and (5) terrorism and counter-terrorism in India in recent times.

Al-Qaeda

The terrorism practised by Osama bin Laden's Al-Qaeda is a species of non-state terrorism directed principally at non-Muslim western states, especially the US, the UK and Israel, that are alleged to be attacking Islam. While bin Laden and Al-Qaeda found a natural home and ally among the fundamentalist Islamist Taliban in Afghanistan (initially supported by Pakistan), his organization – and the ideological movement it has in part

---

[6]   On liberal democratic aspects of an Islamic state, namely, Iran post-Shah, see A. Saikal, *Islam and the West: Conflict or Cooperation?* London: Palgrave, 2003, pp. 84–8.

[7]   For a contrary view in relation to Israel, see B. Kimmerling, *Politicide: Ariel Sharon's War against the Palestinians*, London: Verso, 2003, p. 175.

spawned – is global in character.[8] Bin Laden's organization is an important element of a loose coalition of extremist Islamist groups based in a variety of locations, including Egypt, Algeria, Afghanistan, Indonesia, Sudan and Pakistan. Peter Bergen refers to it as 'Holy War Inc.'.[9] The global nature of this coalition is evidenced by such terrorist campaigns as that being waged in Algeria by the Al-Qaeda-linked Islamic Salvation Front (ISF), in which there have been over 100,000 victims of terrorism since 1992, as well as by the September 11, 2001 attacks on the World Trade Center in New York and the Pentagon (c. 3,000 deaths), by the Bali bombing in 2002, in which around 200 people, including 88 Australians (mainly tourists), were killed by terrorists almost certainly linked to Al-Qaeda, and by the London bombings in 2005, in which some 50 train commuters were killed by terrorists who were British citizens heavily influenced by, if not directly connected to, the Al-Qaeda movement.

It is important, however, to distinguish the brand of Islam propounded by bin Laden from the more moderate forms of Islam to be found throughout the Muslim world in places such as Indonesia, India and, for that matter, the Middle East and North Africa.[10] For example, bin Laden is anti-democratic, opposed to the emancipation of women, and opposed to the modern secular state with its division between religious institutions and the institutions of government. So bin Laden is opposed to secular governments operating in predominantly Muslim countries, such as is the case in Turkey and Indonesia. And he is implacably opposed to pro-western Muslim governments such as Saudi Arabia, no matter how religiously conservative they are. Indeed, on some accounts,[11] extremist Islamists such as bin Laden not only reject moderate forms of Islam, they also embrace a form of religious totalitarianism according to which all individuals in all aspects of their lives ought to be completely subjected to God-ordained laws as interpreted and applied by the Muslim vanguard. According to Berman,[12] one manifestation of this ideology is the religious fervour for martyrdom and, more specifically, for engaging in mass suicides such as the 'human wave' attacks orchestrated by Ayatollah Khomeini in the Iran–Iraq war. Another manifestation of this ideology is its alleged (e.g., by Berman) wholesale rejection of, and attacks on, liberal

[8]   K. Greenberg (ed.), *Al Qaeda Now: Understanding Today's Terrorists*, Cambridge: Cambridge University Press, 2005, p. xii.
[9]   P.L. Bergen, *Holy War Inc.: Inside the Secret World of Osama bin Laden*, New York: Free Press, 2001.
[10]   On this issue see, e.g., Saikal, *Islam and the West*, chap. 1.
[11]   P. Berman, *Terror and Liberalism*, New York: Norton, 2004, p. 99.
[12]   Ibid., p. 108.

values, especially individual freedom. By contrast with such accounts, other writers, such as Mohammad-Mahmoud Ould Mohamedou,[13] stress the 'hegemonic attitudes' of the US to Muslims and Arabs, and the corresponding increase in conflict between the two.[14] The issue is not, on this kind of view, Islamic fundamentalism or religious extremism, but rather US hegemony and injustice, including US support for Israel and the expanded US military role in the Middle East.

In light of these differences of viewpoint among commentators regarding, so to speak, the ideological essence of Al-Qaeda, it is pertinent to consider bin Laden's pronouncements concerning Al-Qaeda's military and political objectives. Bin Laden has stated that Al-Qaeda has as an aim not simply the self-defence of Muslim lands in the face of US hegemony, but also the destruction of the evil empire that the US constitutes, and the establishment of an Islamist caliphate (presumably) comprising the existing nation-states of North Africa, the Middle East, Afghanistan, Pakistan, Indonesia, and so on, and based on his particular brand of Islamic fundamentalism.[15] Accordingly, Al-Qaeda's political and military objectives are not restricted to mere self-defence. Moreover, these political and military objectives are far more ambitious than those of groups such as the PLO, the IRA or the ANC. The latter have, or had, essentially local, i.e., national, aims of a restricted and more or less feasible kind. By comparison, Al-Qaeda's ultimate aim appears to be grandiose in the extreme and, therefore, highly unlikely ever to be achieved.

The preparedness of bin Laden's followers to commit suicide, and thereby supposedly achieve martyrdom, is an enormous advantage for a terrorist organization. Moreover, Al-Qaeda's cause is greatly facilitated not only by

---

[13]   Mohammad-Mahmoud Ould Mohamedou, *Understanding Al-Qaeda: The Transformation of War*, London: Pluto Press, 2007.
[14]   Ibid., pp. 8–10.
[15]   Greenberg (ed.), *Al Qaeda Now*, p. 229:

> It is He Who has sent His Messenger (Muhammed peace be upon him) with guidance and the religion of truth (Islam) to make it victorious over all other religions. . . . The Islamic Nation that was able to dismiss and destroy the previous Evil empires like yourself; the Nation that rejects your attacks, wishes to remove your evils, and is prepared to fight you.

See also pp. 230–1:

> Since the fall of the Islamic Caliphate state, regimes that do not rule according to the Koran have arisen. If truth be told, these regimes are fighting against the law of Allah. . . . I say that I am convinced that thanks to Allah, this [Islamic] nation has sufficient forces to establish the Islamic state and the Islamic Caliphate but we must tell these forces that this is their obligation.

real and perceived injustices (including western economic and political domination, and – alleged – western disrespect for Islamic cultural and religious institutions), and already existing national, ethnic and religious conflict, but also by global financial interdependence and modern technology, such as the global communication system and the nuclear, chemical and biological weapons of mass destruction that bin Laden has been seeking to develop. Perhaps Al-Qaeda's success is not ultimately dependent on widespread political and popular support for its goals, although it is certainly reliant on a widely accepted core set of ideological commitments and disaffection with corrupt and authoritarian Arab governments, and with US policies in the Middle East, e.g., US support for an authoritarian government in Saudi Arabia in order to secure US strategic interests in oil, ongoing economic and military assistance to Israel in the context of the Israel–Palestinian conflict, and the US-led invasion and occupation of Iraq. Rather, Al-Qaeda's success might largely be a function of its psychological preparedness and logistical capacity to perpetrate acts of terror, coupled with the technological capacity to communicate those acts worldwide, and thereby wreak havoc in a globally economically interdependent world. Its methods have proved extremely effective in relation to the goal of destabilization.

That said, Al-Qaeda's methods clearly involve the intentional killing of the innocent, and are not constrained by principles of the proportional use of force or minimally necessary force; principles enshrined not only in the Christian-based Just War Theory, but also in mainstream Islamic teachings.[16] Indeed, bin Laden's aim is to maximize the loss of human life in populations he regards as enemies, i.e., western and other non-Muslim communities. In short, bin Laden's terrorist campaign is essentially a form of mass murder. Accordingly, there is some reason to fear the possibility of Al-Qaeda acquiring and deploying weapons of mass destruction, whether they be nuclear, radiological, chemical or biological.[17] Al-Qaeda is known to have such intentions, and the acquiring and weaponization of biological agents, in particular, is apparently becoming relatively easy. (See Chapter 7.) In this respect there is an important difference between Al-Qaeda and most other terrorist groups, such as the PLO and the IRA, who do not have mass murder as a strategy.

Notwithstanding the murderous nature of the September 11 attacks, they were performed in the name of moral righteousness by people prepared to give up their own lives, as well as the lives of those whom they

---

16 Saikal, *Islam and the West*, p. 27.

17 See Paul Wilkinson, for example (*Terrorism versus Democracy: The Liberal State Response*, 2nd edn, London: Routledge, 2006, p. xv).

murdered. Osama bin Laden and like-minded religious extremists have managed to mobilize Muslim moral outrage at western – especially US – political and military intervention in the Middle East and elsewhere to their cause, and they have done so on a significant scale. Indeed, here they appear to be tapping into a rich vein of long held, and deeply felt, Muslim resentment and suspicion of the US and its western allies. Doubtless, given the history of British and (later) US intervention in, and domination of, the Middle East, in particular, such feelings are not entirely without justification.[18] At any rate, in this respect Al-Qaeda is, of course, not unique among terrorist groups. Terrorist groups typically come into existence because of, and are sustained by, some real or imagined injustice.

Moreover, in order for Osama bin Laden and his group to mobilize moral sentiment they have had to overcome, at least in the minds of their followers, what might be regarded as more or less universally held – including in Muslim societies – principles of moral acceptability, including the principle according to which only those responsible for injustice or harm should be targeted. Yet the majority of those killed, and intended to be killed, by the September 11 terrorists were – according to more or less universally held principles of moral responsibility – innocent victims. They included not only civilians, but also children, visiting foreign nationals, and so on. This being so, what moral justification is offered by the terrorists and their supporters?

Bin Laden at one point offers a retaliatory justification for the killing of innocents: if you kill our innocents, we are entitled to kill yours. This argument is, of course, spurious. The killing of one set of innocents does not morally justify the killing of another set of innocents; it merely compounds the evil. (I discuss these, and related issues, more fully in Chapter 3.)

At any rate, in response to this kind of question from al Jazeera correspondent, Tayseer Alouni, bin Laden had this to say:

> I agree that the Prophet Mohammed forbade the killing of babies and women. That is true, but this is not absolute. There is a saying, 'If the infidels kill women and children on purpose, we shouldn't shy way from treating them in the same way to stop them from doing it again'. The men that God helped [attack, on September 11] did not intend to kill babies; they intended to destroy the strongest military power in the world, to attack the Pentagon that houses more than 64,000 employees, a military center that houses the strength and the military intelligence. . . . The towers are an economic power

---

[18]   See Edward Said's work (e.g., *Orientalism*, New York: Vintage Books, 1979) for a generalized critique of western domination in this regard.

and not a children's school. Those that were there are men that supported the biggest economic power in the world. They have to review their books. We will do as they do. If they kill our women and our innocent people, we will kill their women and their innocent people until they stop.[19]

In other places bin Laden denies, at least implicitly, that so-called 'innocent' victims of his terrorist attacks are in fact innocent. For example, on 22 February 1998 in announcing the formation of the World Islamic Front for Jihad against the Jews and the Crusaders he said:

> All those crimes and calamities are an explicit declaration by the Americans of war on Allah, His Prophet, and Muslims. . . . Based upon this and in order to obey the Almighty, we hereby give Muslims the following judgment: The judgment to kill and fight Americans and their allies, whether civilians or military, is an obligation for every Muslim who is able to do so in any country.[20]

Accordingly, perhaps bin Laden believes that his brand of terrorism is both likely to succeed and morally acceptable by virtue of the guilt of its victims; it is essentially self-defence against terrorism. The former belief is false by virtue of the fact that many of the victims of the September 11 attacks on the Twin Towers were, on any rational account of the matter, innocent, e.g., children, visitors, members of ordinary civilian occupational groups. What are his grounds for the latter belief?

Osama bin Laden and thousands of other Arab Muslims went to Afghanistan in the 1980s to join the Afghans in their fight against the (so-called) godless, Communist invaders from Russia. According to bin Laden, Islam won a great victory against the Russian superpower. He apparently thinks that he can repeat the same feat in relation to the US. Certainly, Afghanistan (and nearby Pakistan) has provided a breeding ground for terrorism specifically directed at the US and its allies, as well as for the terrorism exported to other Muslim states. As far as the latter is concerned, militant Muslims from many nations came to fight the Afghanistan war (often using bases in Pakistan), and then returned to their home countries, including Algeria, Egypt and the like, to wage terrorist campaigns against their own governments. In doing so they have had an overall destabilizing effect in the Middle East and elsewhere, and greatly enhanced the global influence of Al-Qaeda.

Now bin Laden claims that Al-Qaeda is fighting the US in order to defend Islam against the threats to its existence posed by America,

---

[19]   Greenberg, ed., *Al Qaeda Now*, p. 200.
[20]   Quoted in Bergen, *Holy War Inc.*, p. 105.

specifically through the latter's ongoing support of Israel, its military bases in Saudi Arabia (where the two most holy Islamic sites, Mecca and Medina, are located) and its invasion and occupation of Iraq. Whatever the rights and wrongs of the generalized self-defence claim, and of associated specific claims, there is no doubt that the US role in the Middle East is susceptible to pejorative moral critique.[21] The US regards the oil-rich Middle East as of great strategic importance, and has historically been prepared to intervene politically and militarily to promote its strategic interests as it views them, including by taking a one-sided, pro-Israeli stand in the Israel–Palestinian conflict, and by supporting corrupt and authoritarian governments when it suits, e.g., Saddam Hussein prior to his invasion of Kuwait.

The counter-terrorist response to Al-Qaeda on the part of the US and its allies has taken place at a number of levels.[22] (See Chapters 4 and 5.) There has been increased resourcing and restructuring of security forces, e.g., the new Department of Homeland Security in the US. There has been a ramping up of security measures and an increase in police powers. For example, airport security has been tightened, there has been an increase in data collection and in monitoring and surveillance (some of it apparently unlawfully undertaken by the National Security Agency after being authorized by President Bush in breach of the Foreign Intelligence Surveillance Act which prohibits warrantless domestic wiretappings[23]), and police have been given wider powers to detain without trial suspects or even non-suspects who might have information. In addition, foreign nationals suspected of being terrorists have been incarcerated indefinitely, e.g., at Guantánamo Bay in Cuba. At a strategic military level, meanwhile, the US has invaded Iraq and sent armed forces into Afghanistan to combat Al-Qaeda and its supporters in the Taliban.

The overall effects of these measures are difficult to determine (with some notable exceptions). It now seems clear that the US has exacerbated, rather than reduced, the problem of global Islamic terrorism by invading and occupying Iraq. At the time of writing, the anti-US insurgency

---

[21] For a sustained, if somewhat one-sided, critique see N. Chomsky, *Power and Prospects: Reflections on Human Nature and the Social Order*, Sydney: Allen and Unwin, 1996, chap. 6.

[22] Some have argued it has been an incompetent response. For example, James Risen (*State of War: The Secret History of the CIA and the Bush Administration*, New York: Free Press, 2006) details a long list of sins of omission – e.g., lack of CIA understanding of Iraq prior to the US-led invasion, failure to pursue Al-Qaeda connections with the Saudi power elite (p. 179) – and of commission – such as rogue operations, e.g., torture and rendition, or the episode in which virtually the entire CIA spy network in Iran was in effect inadvertly disclosed to the Iranian security agencies (p. 193).

[23] First reported in the *New York Times* in December 2005.

is far from being under control and Iraqi security forces are far from being in a position to provide law and order without very substantial US assistance; indeed, Iraq has become a potent symbol of the US–Islam confrontation as expressed by bin Laden and a breeding ground for terrorists. Second, liberal-democratic values have been compromised to an extent by these measures. For example, the absolute ban on torture has been questioned by the Bush administration and, indeed, torture has been practised by the US military in Abu Ghraib prison in Iraq. In the UK there is provision for indefinite detention of suspects without bringing them to trial if they do not have British citizenship and expelling them would present a real risk of their being tortured.[24] In Australia, new anti-terrorist legislation (ASIO Bill [No. 2]) permits ASIO (the Australian Security Intelligence Organization) to detain and question persons who are not even suspects, if it is believed these innocents could provide relevant information.[25]

Terrorism and Counter-Terrorism in the Israeli–Palestinian Conflict

The Israeli–Palestinian conflict is in large part a struggle over land.[26] A century ago the population of Palestine was less than 10 per cent Jewish. However, the Jews had an historical claim to occupancy since biblical times. At any rate, in the early part of the twentieth century the British rulers of Palestine acceded to the establishment of a national Jewish home in Palestine, and the population of Jews increased to one third of the two million people in Palestine in 1948 (the last year of British rule). Official Zionism proclaimed the view that Jews and Arabs could live side by side in Palestine. However, David Ben-Gurion (Israel's first Prime Minister)

---

[24] Sections 21 to 32 of the Anti-Terrorism, Crime and Security Emergency Bill 2001 now allow detention without trial where the option of deportation is not available. Article 3 of the European Convention on Human Rights, to which the UK is a signatory, forbids torture and inhuman treatment. See D. Haubrich, 'September 11, anti-terror laws and civil liberties: Britain, France and Germany compared', *Government and Opposition* 38(1), 2003, p. 15.

[25] A. Lynch and G. Williams, *What Price Security? Taking Stock of Australia's Anti-Terror Laws*, Sydney: University of New South Wales Press, 2006, pp. 33–4.

[26] See (including for factual material used here) T. Kapitan, 'Terrorism in the Arab–Israeli conflict', in I. Primoratz (ed.), *Terrorism: The Philosophical Issues*, London: Palgrave Macmillan, 2004; and I. Primoratz, 'Terrorism in the Israeli–Palestinian conflict: a case study in applied ethics', *Iyyun: The Jerusalem Philosophical Quarterly* 55, 2006, pp. 27–48. For a detailed historical account of a journalistic kind, see R. Fisk, *The Great War for Civilisation: The Conquest of the Middle East*, London: HarperCollins, 2005.

and others embraced the concept of forcible removal (ethnic cleansing) as the solution to the problem of one land and two peoples. Moreover, the Arabs themselves were opposed to Zionism and, in particular, to the creation of a Jewish state in Palestine. A policy of forcible removal was clearly going to trigger a violent response, as in fact happened.

Inter-communal violence took place in Palestine during the period of British rule, as did acts of terrorism, e.g., planting of bombs in Arab marketplaces by Irgun (a Jewish underground group). Arab groups responded in kind, bombing Jewish civilians. In 1939 Britain abandoned its policy of establishing a Jewish state. This met with Jewish opposition, including terrorist attacks, e.g., the bombing of the King David Hotel in Jerusalem. In 1947 the United Nations General Assembly recommended partition of Palestine into two states, and inter-communal violence and terrorism between Jews and Arabs increased. However, the Jewish forces were better armed and organized and ended up controlling most of Palestine and expelling most of the Arabs from what, just two years later, was to become the Jewish state of Israel. The Palestinians outside Israel ended up for the most part in refugee camps. The parts of Palestine not comprising Israel were taken over by Jordan (the West Bank) and Egypt (Gaza Strip). Some 700,000 Palestinians were ethnically cleansed from what is now Israel.[27]

In the 1967 war, Israel conquered the West Bank and Gaza Strip and some 200,000 Palestinians were expelled or fled. Israel began settling Jews in these territories. Arabs within Israel are an ethnic minority with the status of second-class citizens. Post-1967 Israel has exercised political control over the West Bank and Gaza Strip (indirectly since 1994) and yet denied Palestinians living in these areas their political rights.[28]

As mentioned above, both Arabs and Israelis have resorted to terrorism. Since the 1960s, armed and organized resistance on the part of the Palestinians has taken place on a significant scale. Organizations such as the PLO (Palestine Liberation Organization) and especially Hamas have undertaken a systematic campaign of bombings of Israeli civilian targets, such as buses, restaurants and marketplaces. Notable here has been the use of so-called 'suicide bombers' (more aptly called 'homicide-suicide bombers'). They have also engaged in plane hijacking and hostage taking. The Munich Olympic Games in 1972 witnessed the taking of Israeli athletes as hostages.

For their part, the Israelis have responded with extra-judicial killing of suspected terrorists (see Chapter 5), and bombing raids on suspected

---

[27] Kimmerling, *Politicide*, p. 25.

[28] Ibid., p. 39. Evidently, the setting up of the Palestinian Authority in 1994 only relinquished Israeli *direct* control. As of June 2007, Gaza is under the control of Hamas.

terrorist-occupied buildings in civilian areas. Two methods of terror deployed by the Israelis are torture (see Chapter 6) and bombing of civilian areas, e.g., of Beirut in 1982.[29] In addition, there have been several massacres of civilians, notably in 1982, when the Israeli Defence Minister Ariel Sharon sanctioned and facilitated the slaughter of over 2,000 civilian Palestinians in the Sabra and Shatilla refugee camps in Beirut; Israeli tanks surrounded the camps and provided flares at night while Lebanese militia carried out the massacre.[30]

Terrorism and Counter-Terrorism and the IRA in Northern Ireland

In 1969 the Irish Republican Army (IRA) commenced a campaign of violence that did not end until a peace agreement was signed in 1998.[31] The IRA's protagonists were rival Protestant groups, e.g., the Ulster Defence Association (UDA), Northern Ireland's police force, the Royal Ulster Constabulary (RUC), and the occupying British army. The IRA campaign included targeted assassinations, punishment beatings and civilian bombings not only in Northern Ireland, but also in the Republic of Ireland and in mainland Britain. The IRA also engaged in robberies and kidnappings to finance their activities. During this thirty-year period 3,500 civilians lost their lives, and 300 RUC officers were killed – a high total considering the IRA's membership was only several hundred. The IRA's practice of bombing pubs and the like in which innocent lives were lost was a quintessentially terrorist method. On the other hand, the IRA typically issued a warning immediately prior to a bombing attack, thereby lessening the scale of deaths; in this respect they were unlike, say, Al-Qaeda.

The political context of this is as follows. The whole of Ireland was under British rule until it was partitioned into north and south (1922). The north (Northern Ireland) remained within Great Britain, the south emerged as the Republic of Ireland. The north had its own parliament (Stormont); however, direct British rule was imposed on a number of occasions, e.g., 1974, in the context of insurrectionary activity. The north

---

[29]   Ibid., p. 91.

[30]   Ibid., p. 94.

[31]   See (including for factual material used here) Whittaker (ed.), *The Terrorism Reader*, chap. 8; P. Simpson, 'Violence and terrorism in Northern Ireland', in Primoratz (ed.), *Terrorism: The Philosophical Issues*, and also M.L.R. Smith, *Fighting for Ireland: Military Strategy of the Irish Republican Movement*, London: Routledge, 1995.

was dominated politically and economically by Protestants, the south by Catholics.

Irish nationalists, such as the IRA, had never accepted the partition of Ireland and British rule in any part of Ireland. On the other hand, Protestants in the north sought to protect their political and economic interests by constructing an enclave in Ireland under British protection. In this enclave, Protestants dominated political and economic life, and Catholics were largely excluded from it, e.g., elections were gerrymandered, the RUC was largely Protestant, Catholics were discriminated against in employment (including in Belfast shipyards), education and housing; hence there was an issue of socio-economic rights of Catholics in Northern Ireland, as well as the religious divide and the issue of nationalism.

Like many terrorist groups, the IRA presented itself as engaged in a war and argued that its members were political and military personnel, and should not be treated as common criminals. The British sought to treat them as criminals, and the issue came to a head in the famous hunger strikes in the early 1980s on the part of Bobby Sands and others held in gaols.

Criminalizing the IRA was problematic from the point of view of some of the counter-terrorist operations mounted by the British and the RUC. For example, the latter on occasion (unlawfully) ambushed and killed IRA members when they arrived at an arms cache. Such an ambush would be regarded as an acceptable military tactic in time of war; however, it is not an acceptable police practice in relation to suspected criminals. Other (unlawful) counter-terrorist responses included targeted assassination and torture.

The African National Congress's Armed Struggle in Apartheid South Africa

The armed struggle of the ANC against the apartheid government in South Africa commenced in 1961 when it abandoned its commitment to a principle of non-violence.[32] The armed struggle continued until the early 1990s. The key events here were the 1990 release from prison of Nelson Mandela and his election in 1994 as South Africa's first black President. The context for the ANC's armed struggle was the failure of non-violent strategies in the face of systematic, ongoing and widespread human rights violations. The latter took the following form.

---

[32] Material here is taken from S. Miller, 'Just War theory: the case of South Africa', *Philosophical Papers* 19(2), 1990, pp. 143–61.

There was unequal, racially based segregation in the Republic of South Africa (as distinct from the so-called 'Independent States'). In accordance with the Group Areas Act, blacks were required by law to live in black-only areas, whites in white-only areas, coloureds in coloured-only areas, Indians in Indian-only areas, and so on. State schools were by law either blacks only, or whites only, etc., and hospital wards were racially segregated. Moreover, the facilities and living areas provided for blacks were inferior to those provided for whites. The so-called 'Independent States' (Ciskei, Transkei, etc.) should have been – and in fact were, internationally – regarded as (partially autonomous) racially segregated areas of South Africa, rather than as distinct countries resulting from genuine and legitimate political division. Their creation involved the forcible removal (ethnic cleansing) of millions of people; they were hugely overcrowded, poverty-stricken and dependent on South Africa for handouts; and their continued existence depended on the South African government.

Social and economic goods are notoriously difficult to measure. However, it is clear that: black unemployment was very high in South Africa and the so-called 'homelands', and most of these unemployed people did not have the safety net of unemployment benefits; many black workers – especially those outside industries served by strong unions – received wages below the minimum level required to keep themselves and their families above what advanced western countries consider to be the poverty line; the majority of blacks did not receive adequate primary and secondary education, and had to take the lowest paid and most menial jobs; there was a massive housing shortage for blacks; and millions of blacks did not receive basic services such as water, electricity, and sewerage. In short, in general social and economic terms the majority of blacks were essentially in a third world situation. Whites, by contrast, earned wages, received education and experienced general living conditions comparable with people in advanced western countries. Moreover – and this was one of the most striking features of the South African situation – that this degree of inequality existed, and largely continues to this day, is to a significant extent due not simply to cultural differences, or even neglect, but to the deliberate policies of the apartheid South African government over many decades. These policies included: the dumping of millions of people onto areas that the government's own investigative commissions had told them could not possibly sustain even the existing population; an official policy of not educating black people beyond primary school level; and policies of job reservation for whites so that blacks were left to perform only the most menial tasks at very low wage levels.

Political control rested firmly in the hands of the white-minority government. Blacks in particular – and they constituted 75 per cent of the population – had no political rights in the central government; they could not vote or hold office. Moreover, this political control, underwritten by economic power and, in the last analysis, military power, was used to maintain the system under which whites were hugely socially, economically and politically advantaged at the expense of blacks.

From its formation in 1912 up until it was banned in 1960, the ANC, an organization that was entitled to claim the support of the majority, or at least a very large minority, of black South Africans, pursued certain non-violent strategies. In 1961 in the face of evident failure – if anything, violation of rights increased over this period, particularly with the coming to power of the Nationalist Party in 1948 – the strategy of violent resistance was adopted. This consisted initially of bombing strategic installations, and then widened to include military and police personnel, together with certain other categories of civilian personnel. On the face of it a strategy that restricted itself to non-violent resistance alone had been tried and had failed. Now this is not to say that non-violent means of resistance, including strikes and boycotts, were not necessary. The claim is rather that they had not been sufficient, for the South African state had responded ruthlessly and effectively whenever such non-violent resistance had begun to look as though it might challenge the basic power structure of the status quo.

It might be claimed that in fact it was certain sorts of non-violent strategies deployed by external countries, especially economic sanctions, that were the most effective in the struggle against the apartheid system, and ultimately in bringing the South African government to the negotiating table. Such strategies did not operate in a vacuum, however. Concerning economic sanctions, in the first place, the drying up of the capital inflow, the divestment, and so on, were to a considerable extent caused by a perception of political instability, which in turn was largely due to internal insurrectionary activity, and especially internal violence. In the second place, these sanctions would hardly have been imposed if internal insurrectionary activity had not riveted the world's attention on South Africa.

Here we can distinguish three sorts of violence. Firstly, there is the more or less spontaneous violence of mass action, crowds of people out of control, killing, burning, etc. Secondly, there is premeditated, disciplined terrorism. This involves tactics such as bombing civilian areas, torture, etc. Thirdly, there is premeditated, disciplined violence which is not terrorism.

Violence can be directed at property or at persons. Presumably, the ANC was entitled to destroy buildings and installations, as distinct from their occupants, in so far as they were used by personnel performing tasks that constituted violations of the rights of ANC members and supporters. What of violence directed at persons? Here we need to distinguish between types of violence and types of persons at whom violence is directed. Certain forms of violence such as 'necklacing' (burning someone to death by placing a burning car tyre around his or her neck) and bombing civilian areas clearly count as instances of terrorism. Moreover, some of these forms were employed at times by the ANC, or at least by persons trained by, and supporters of, the ANC. (There was for a period some dispute in respect of *de facto* ANC policy in this regard. In fact the ANC on a number of occasions dissociated itself from such acts. And historically it demonstrated a concern in respect of loss of innocent life.)

A final mention should be made of violence directed by the apartheid South African state at members of the ANC and ordinary black South Africans. This included numerous instances of torture, assassination, shooting protesters in the back as they fled, and forcible removal.

Terrorism and Counter-Terrorism in India

India experienced terrorism in the Punjab state in the 1980s and early 1990s at the hands of Sikh separatist/militants, and is continuing to face the problem in Jammu and Kashmir.[33] Both of these states share borders with Pakistan, and terrorists have operated from bases in Pakistan with the tacit support (at times) of the Pakistani government (or at least of elements of the Pakistan security agencies, e.g., the Inter-Services Intelligence Agency (ISI)). There has been terrorism of a different nature in various states of the northeast, namely, Nagaland, Manipur, Assam and Mizoram. All these states have borders with either Myanmar or Bangladesh. A further kind of terrorism is that of Naxalism (Maoist revolutionary groups). In March 2007, for example, Naxalites shot dead some 60 security personnel in Chattisgarh. Having originated in West Bengal, Naxalism has since spread to the states of Bihar, bordering Nepal, and to some interior states, such as Andhra Pradesh, Madhya Pradesh, Chattisgarh, Jharkhand, Maharastra and Orissa.

Apart from these major movements, there have been terrorist attacks of a sporadic nature in different parts of the country. Most of these have been expressions of religious fundamentalism. These include the explosions in Mumbai on March 1993, which killed about 250 civilians, and again in Mumbai in October 2006, and explosions in Coimbatore, Tamil

---

[33] The material in this section is derived in large part from S. Miller, S. Sen, P. Mishra and J. Blackler, *Ethical Issues in the Policing of India*, Hyderabad: National Institute for Policing, 2007; and K. Dhillon, *Police and Politics in India: Colonial Concepts, Democratic Compulsions: Indian Police 1947–2002*, New Delhi: Manohar, 2005.

Nadu, in February 1998. There have also been the activities of the LTTE in Tamil Nadu, which culminated in the assassination of Sri Rajiv Gandhi in 1991.

There are various underlying causes for these forms of terrorism. The major causes can be categorized under the following headings:

- *Ethnic causes*: These causes are evident in Nagaland, Mizoram and Manipur, and have led to movements to establish separate homeland states.
- *Religious fundamentalism*: Religious fundamentalism played a major role in the terrorist activities in Punjab and in Jammu and Kashmir in the initial phase. This manifested itself in selective killings of members of particular religious communities, leading to migration of members of that particular community to other safer places.
- *Political causes*: Political reasons played a significant role in terrorist activities in Assam and Tripura. Large-scale migration from Bangladesh led to a change in the composition of the population in these states. The segment of the population that lost out politically as well as eco-nomically because of this altered ratio reacted with violence. The conflict in Jammu and Kashmir is also in part politically motivated, with rival groups supporting the status quo against those who want a separate state or incorporation into Pakistan. Moreover, some of the terrorist groups operating in Jammu and Kashmir are linked to Al-Qaeda and, in recent times, have carried out terrorist attacks beyond the region in New Delhi and Mumbai, e.g., Lashkar-e-Toiba.
- *Economic causes*: Andhra Pradesh, Madhya Pradesh, Chattisgarh Orissa, Jharkhand and Bihar are prime examples of economically based ter-rorism. Economic inequality, lack of development, non-implementation of land reforms, and atrocities by the police and other government functionaries are all reasons for the alienation of various groups of (especially) lower caste people in these states. In this context, an altern-ative political and social system being put forward by leftist-Maoist organizations, generally termed 'Naxalites', has gained acceptance in some quarters.

Most of the terrorist incidents leading to the deaths of innocent civil-ians have been the consequence of religious terrorism. Terrorism has involved the use of sophisticated improvised explosive devices (IEDs), suicide bombings, as well as hand-held weapons, and has involved resort to hijacking, hostage taking, and the like. Terrorists have engaged in kidnapping for ransom or for the release of fellow terrorists being held prisoner. However, it is security personnel who are the main targets of terrorist attacks in India.

- *Counter-terrorism agencies*: Under India's Federal Constitution, the principal responsibility for policing and maintenance of law and order lies with the individual states. The central government gives the states advice, financial help, training, intelligence and other assistance. Moreover, there are a number of central police agencies that assist the states. These include the following:
- *Physical security agencies*: These include: the Central Industrial Security Force, responsible for physical security at airports and sensitive establishments; the National Security Guards, a specially trained intervention force to deal with terrorist situations, such as hijacking, hostage taking, etc.; and the Special Protection Group, responsible for the security of the Prime Minister, former Prime Ministers and other VIPs.
- *Paramilitary forces*: These include the Central Reserve Police Force and the Border Security Force, which assist the police in counter-terrorism operations when called upon to do so.
- *The army*: Their assistance is sought as a last resort when the police and paramilitary forces are not able to cope with a terrorist threat or attack.

All these agencies have to work in close coordination and mount special operations. This aspect of policing is very different from normal day-to-day policing. All such operations have to be strongly supported by a sound intelligence back-up.

In the course of anti-terrorism operations there have been many police excesses, including torture and 'disappearances'. Consider torture. Scientific methods of interrogation take time and require a lot of patience. Terrorists are themselves the perpetrators of heinous crimes. Hence, the police frequently have (unlawfully) employed torture. While mounting a special operation, either to apprehend terrorists or to deter them from doing certain acts, excessive force leading to death is not unusual. In particular, fake encounters (ambushes in which terrorists are unlawfully killed when they could have been captured) have become an issue in Indian policing.

These excesses are in part a function of the view held by the security forces that lawful policing methods are quite ineffective in dealing with the threat of terrorism. In most of the terrorist-affected areas, courts do not function normally, witnesses are terrified and will not provide sworn evidence, and, more generally, people are unwilling to cooperate with the security agencies for fear of reprisals. All this makes the task of the security agencies difficult. In this context, police have come to rely on the use of unlawful methods.

In India, as elsewhere, some special laws to combat terrorism have been enacted from time to time. For example, the Terrorist and Disruptive

Activities Prevention Act (TADA) was in use for quite a few years. However, strong and vociferous criticism of its draconian provisions and misuse in some cases led to it being repealed. The Prevention of Terrorist Activities Act (POTA) was introduced in its place. But that Act is no longer in force either, and at the time of writing there is no special law to deal with terrorist activities in India.

Conclusion

While all terrorist groups have (by definition) political and military aims, there are important differences between the aims of terrorist groups. Some are essentially ethno-nationalist groups engaged in a struggle for land and self-determination, e.g., the PLO. Others have religious aims: e.g., Hezbollah is seeking to establish an Islamic state in Lebanon. Still others are essentially secular and nationalist, e.g., the IRA, or socialist-revolutionary, e.g., Naxalites in India.[34] Notwithstanding Marxist and eth-nically focused elements in its ranks, the ANC is perhaps best understood as having the aim of establishing a liberal-democratic state in place of an authoritarian apartheid state; certainly, this was the outcome of its efforts. Al-Qaeda is different from most other contemporary terrorist groups in terms of the scope of its aims; the establishment of a pan-Islamic caliphate is a far more ambitious aim than, say, the establishment of a Palestinian state.

Given the diverse political aims of terrorist groups, the search for a definition of terrorism might be thought to be more usefully focused on the methods of terrorist groups rather than their aims. (The definition of terrorism is discussed in Chapter 2.) As we have seen, these methods include indiscriminate killings, assassination and hostage taking. A particular fea-ture of terrorist groups is their targeting of innocent people. Here one thinks of bombs placed on buses or in marketplaces. However some, perhaps most, terrorist groups have also – indeed, principally – targeted individuals and groups that are not innocent in the required sense, e.g., politicians responsible for the injustices (real or imagined) the terrorist group is seeking to redress, or police and military personnel enforcing these 'unjust' policies. This was true of the IRA, for example. Moreover, a small number of so-called 'terrorist' groups, notably the ANC, have eschewed the policy of targeting innocents (in the above sense). This has led many to dispute the proposition that the ANC was in fact a terrorist organization at all. The ANC did, however, employ violence to instil fear,

---

[34] I say 'essentially', because many of these secular groups, nevertheless, have religious aspects, e.g., the IRA; many nationalist groups have a strong class-based ideological gloss, e.g., Naxalites.

e.g., targeting apartheid officials. To this extent it employed a strategy of terror. In response it might reasonably be claimed that the fact that a group makes limited use of a strategy of terror – especially one that is relatively morally discriminating by, for example, refraining from targeting innocents – does not make it a terrorist organization *per se*.

Some terrorist groups, e.g., Al-Qaeda, seek to maximize the loss of innocent life of the populations of 'enemy' states or groups: that is, they have a policy of mass murder, unlike most terrorist groups. Accordingly, and notwithstanding the commonality of methods used by terrorists, there are differences between terrorist groups with respect to the methods that they employ.

These differences between terrorist groups have implications for counter-terrorism measures. In the case of those terrorist groups pursuing politically feasible and manifestly just causes (albeit using morally unacceptable *methods*), the most important counter-terrorist measure – if I can use this mode of description for political solutions to terrorism – is simply to rectify the injustice or otherwise address the grievance that is motivating their terrorist activities. The most obvious recent example of this is South Africa, albeit the ANC might not – depending on one's definition – be regarded as a terrorist organization. However, there are a number of other national liberation struggles that could be pointed to here in which the armed forces of liberation engaged in terrorism on anyone's definition of the term, e.g., the EOKA in Cyprus, or the Mau Mau in Kenya.

Let us assume that the cases of Northern Ireland, Kashmir and the Israeli–Palestinian conflict are more complex in that there is far more disagreement about the justice or reasonableness of the causes being pursued by the terrorist groups in question, i.e., by the IRA, Lashkar-e-Toiba (et al.) and the PLO (et al.), respectively. (Here I am bracketing the issue of the putative terrorist tactics deployed as counter-terrorism measures against these terrorist groups by the nation-states in question.) Nevertheless, it is evident that what is called for in each of these cases – and in the case of Northern Ireland, appears at the time of writing to have been provided – is a political solution that addresses the real (as well as, perhaps, some of the imagined) injustices motivating these terrorist groups and their supporters. In short, it is not simply a matter of holding the line against terrorism – 'we don't negotiate with terrorists' – much less of winning 'the war against terrorism', for sometimes there are real grievances motivating terrorists that need to be addressed. To be effective, counter-terrorism measures need to address the real grievances that provide an important motivation for some, indeed many, terrorist groups. In the case of the Israel–Palestine conflict, presumably what is called for is the establishment of a Palestinian state (and recognition by it of the existing Israeli state) and agreement on the difficult and complex matter of partition of territory. At the very least, counter-terrorism measures need to avoid exacerbating the problem that they are seeking to redress or, indeed, creating a problem in the first place. Arguably, the Israeli counter-terrorist responses to terrorism perpetrated by Palestinian groups have, cumulatively and in the longer term, simply exacerbated the problem: consider, for example, the current and apparently growing strength of Hamas in the Gaza Strip. As for the US-led invasion of Iraq – presented in part as a counter-terrorist response to an (alleged) connection between Al-Qaeda and Saddam Hussein's regime – it appears to be an instance of creating a terrorist problem where none existed (or, at least, where none existed for the US – there were many Iraqis being subjected to the state terrorism of Saddam Hussein).

It goes without saying that accepting the justice of the cause pursued by a particular terrorist group, or the reality for political solutions to conflicts involving terrorism, is not to condone terrorism as a method; far from it, as will become evident in my detailed discussions of these matters in the chapters following this one. Moreover, it needs to be stressed that some terrorist groups are not actually pursuing just causes; even their goals (let alone their methods) are morally repugnant. Al-Qaeda, as we have seen, is a case in point. Here there is no question of acknowledging the morality of their ends, let alone seeking to assist in the implementation of their political goals. However, even in such cases as these there may well be a need to address underlying grievances and injustices that are exacerbating matters by providing fertile soil for the inculcation of the ideology of these forms of terrorism, e.g., jihad, martyrdom, etc., and that are, as a consequence, facilitating the establishment of terrorist recruitment and training programmes, financial support bases, and the like.

The general point I want to insist on here is that in so far as some particular terrorist campaign is underpinned by real or imagined injustices, it constitutes a moral problem calling for moral input into its (presumably political) solution. It is not simply a matter of calibrating and exercising power in the service of one's strategic interests within an overarching conceptual framework of Realpolitik. Indeed, it is becoming increasingly clear that in the contemporary globalizing world, at least, Realpolitik does not even serve one's narrow, national self-interest in the relatively short term, let alone provide morally justifiable, long-term solutions to terrorism. Is not the US now experiencing 'blowback' as a consequence of its one-sided support of Israel, its large-scale covert CIA funding of extremist fundamentalist groups in Afghanistan via the Inter Services Intelligence Agency (ISI) – the Pakistani Secret Service – during the Soviet invasion of Afghanistan in the 1980s, and its policy of supporting and then invading Saddam Hussein's Iraq? More generally, is not the US experiencing blowback in part as a consequence of its longstanding and unprincipled policy in the Middle East and Central Asia of supporting authoritarianism and religious extremism when it suited its own narrow, national self-interest, e.g., in relation to Middle East oil, and promoting liberal-democratic values only sporadically, e.g., in post-Saddam Hussein Iraq, and (again) only when it suited its own narrow, national self-interest (or was believed to do so), rhetoric notwithstanding? In an increasingly globalizing and, therefore, economically, politically and communicatively interdependent world, moral principles and values, rather than simply Realpolitik, need to be emphasized, including in relation to combating international terrorism. Nor is an emphasis on moral principle and values simply an exercise in so-called 'ideological warfare'. For example, it is now evident that the radicalization of Muslim youth is a key tactic within the overall strategic framework of extremist Islamist groups, such as Al-Qaeda. Accordingly, countering radicalization is of fundamental importance.[35] However, the process of countering radicalization ought to consist in an attempt to educate and to address real practical problems rather than to set in train a competing process of indoctrination and manipulation (albeit one in the service of one's own favoured ends).

Notwithstanding the validity of these above points concerning political solutions and addressing underlying grievances and injustices, terrorism, if it is to be successfully combated, requires specific military and policing counter-terrorism measures. These will vary from one context to another, but might involve military interventions of the sort undertaken by the US in Afghanistan, and will certainly include addressing the issue of terrorist recruitment, increases in intelligence and evidence-gathering activities (e.g., building and accessing of databases, profiling, communication interception, surveillance and use of informants), additional checks and controls in relation to border security (e.g., at airports), greater scrutiny and control over financial (including international) transactions, enhanced physical security of key installations, and the like. If, and under what circumstances, these measures might need to involve infringements of basic moral rights are matters to be discussed in detail in the following chapters.

I have described a number of salient terrorist groups and settings, and identified a number of features of these groups. I have also introduced the issue of counter-terrorism. However, I have not yet explicitly discussed the definition of terrorism. To this task I now turn.

---

[35] See, for example, T.H.J. Joustra, *Radicalisation in Broader Perspective*, National Coordinator for Counterterrorism, The Hague, 2007.

2

Defining Terrorism

Listening to most of the world's media, one might easily form the view that terrorism is *always*, even perhaps *necessarily*, morally wrong. Moreover, according to many theorists of terrorism, e.g., Igor Primoratz, Jan Narveson and David Rosenbaum, terrorism is morally indefensible.[1] However, whether terrorism is *never* morally justified turns at least in part on one's definition of terrorism, and there are a number of competing definitions.[2] Some of these, such as those of Primoratz and Rosenbaum, define terrorism in such a way that only the harming or threatening to harm of innocent persons can count as terrorism. On this kind of definition it is highly likely that terrorism can never, or almost never, be morally justified. However, as with other definitions, this definition is contestable and indeed contested.

In this chapter I consider and reject, firstly, definitions of terrorism couched in terms of innocents and, secondly, definitions in terms of non-combatants (sometimes conflated with definitions in terms of innocents). I also provide my own definition, building on the strengths and weaknesses of the two defective kinds of definition.

Irrespective of their definition of terrorism, most theorists (including myself) adhere to what might be regarded as versions of the standard view of the moral justification for self-defence. According to the standard view

---

[1] I. Primoratz, 'What is terrorism?', in I. Primoratz (ed.), *Terrorism: The Philosophical Issues*, New York: Palgrave Macmillan, 2004, p. 24; J. Narveson, 'Pacifism and terrorism: why we should condemn both', *International Journal of Applied Philosophy* 17(2), 2003, p. 14; A.S. Rosenbaum, 'On terrorism and the just war', *International Journal of Applied Philosophy* 17(2), 2003, p. 180.

[2] For an early and influential definition, see C. Wellman, 'On terrorism itself', *Journal of Value Inquiry* 13(4), 1979, pp. 250–8.

of justified self-defence, a person is morally permitted to kill an attacker if: (1) the attacker is unjustifiably trying to kill the defender, and will succeed if the defender does not intervene; (2) the only way for the defender to intervene successfully is for the defender to kill the attacker.

Here we need to distinguish between self-defence in the context of civil society or, more specifically, self-defence in the context of a well-ordered, liberal-democratic society during peacetime, and self-defence in the context of war. Let us now consider the latter context. However, in doing so let us not lose sight of the fact that conditions of war are very different from ordinary peacetime conditions. In particular, the notion of a military combatant is tied to (actual or potential) conditions of war. So the fact, for example, that in a well-ordered, liberal-democratic state at peace some citizens, or police officers, are armed does not make these people combatants (in the military sense). I return to this issue below.

Civilian immunity is an element of Just War Theory and an element of the so-called '*ius in bello* condition'. (Just War Theory is a theory that applies to the waging of war and comprises the *ius ad bellum* and the *ius in bello*. The *ius ad bellum* specifies the conditions under which it is morally permissible to embark on a war; the *ius in bello* the conditions under which war should be conducted once embarked upon.) According to the *ius in bello* condition, only combatants (roughly speaking, soldiers, airmen, etc.) and their leaders are legitimate targets. Civilians, or at least innocent civilians, ought to enjoy immunity in wars. This is because civilians are (by and large) non-attackers.

The standard view of justified self-defence and the *ius in bello* condition of Just War Theory are linked in that (arguably) in the context of a war combatants are engaged in self-defence: the enemy is trying to kill them and will do so unless they intervene by killing the enemy.[3] On this view, combatants are, as Narveson says,[4] designated fighters in the context of a division of labour which excludes civilians from fighting and thus from being legitimate targets.

In fact this linkage between self-defence and *ius in bello* is problematic, given that at least one side in a war is not fighting a *just* war; surely combatants fighting an unjust war – say, a war of conquest – are at some level not engaged in *justifiable* self-defence, and indeed not even engaged in *self-defence*. Accordingly, combatants engaged in fighting an unjust war are not, *contra* the standard view, in a morally equivalent situation to the

---

[3] See M. Walzer, *Just and Unjust Wars: A Moral Argument with Historical Illustrations*, New York: Basic Books, 1977.

[4] Narveson, 'Pacifism and terrorism', p. 160.

combatants on the opposite side fighting a just war. As is the case with an individual engaged in defending his life against an unjustified attack, the justifiability or otherwise of the cause – in the case of war, the *ius ad bello* – is a very important moral consideration. That said, it may well be that there are important considerations in favour of conferring *legal* immunity on combatants who have been fighting an unjust war (as opposed to their leaders). (I am assuming that the combatants in question have been fighting that war in accordance with the principles of *ius in bello*.) Here, as elsewhere, law and morality may need to be decoupled. But I will leave these complexities aside and simply note that the justice or otherwise of the cause is a morally important consideration, both in the case of combatants engaged in a conventional war and in the case of revolutionary wars, wars of national liberation and (so-called) terrorists engaged in armed struggles. (Here I note that it might be that some [so-called] terrorists are not in reality combatants as such, but merely civilians engaged in violent acts; more on this below.)

Narveson is at pains to argue that justified self-defence and civilian immunity are inconsistent with both pacifism and terrorism. Certainly, these views are inconsistent with *some* forms of pacifism and *some* forms of terrorism. As it happens, I am not convinced that these views are inconsistent with various moderate forms of pacifism, such as that espoused by Andrew Alexandra.[5] But since pacifism is not my concern here, I will not pursue the matter. As will become clear, I hold that the standard view of justified self-defence, and (in the context of war) especially the *ius in bello* condition (properly understood), are not necessarily inconsistent with *some* forms (and contexts) of terrorism, depending on how terrorism is defined.

But let us now turn directly to definitions of terrorism. I do so in the context of the following assumptions:

1   Terrorism consists of violent actions directed at persons.
2   Terrorism is a strategy that involves such methods as assassination (targeted killings), indiscriminate killing, torture, hostage taking, kidnapping, ethnic cleansing and the use of chemical, biological or nuclear weapons.
3   Terrorism involves terrorizing or instilling great fear in one group in order to cause some other group to do what they otherwise might not have done.
4   Terrorism is a means to achieve political or military ends.
5   Terrorism relies on a degree of publicity.

[5]   A. Alexandra, A. 'Political pacifism', *Social Theory and Practice* 29(4), 2003, pp. 589–606.

The first assumption is essentially a matter of standard linguistic usage and, therefore, meaning: the term 'terrorism' is standardly used to refer to violence directed at persons, and refers to violent actions, such as bombings, killings and the like.[6] There is a residual issue as to whether or not violent actions directed solely at property, e.g., blowing up an empty building or unmanned electricity station, could count as acts of terrorism. Since this is controversial and marginal to my concerns here, I will assume that such acts are not integral to the meaning of the term 'terrorism'. Accordingly, I will restrict terrorist acts to violent actions directed at persons.

The second assumption is in part an empirical claim based on a consideration of the violent methods actually employed by those groups generally agreed to be terrorists. It is also in part based on a conceptual connection between these methods and the activity of terrorizing. The prospect of being killed or tortured, for example, is inherently fearful.

The third assumption is in large part a conceptual claim. For an activity to count as terrorism, someone has to be trying to terrorize someone else, and for terrorism to be a strategic activity – as opposed to, for example, an expressive activity – it has to be in the service of some further end, i.e., changing the attitudes and/or behaviour of some group.[7]

The fourth assumption is largely stipulative, albeit not unmotivated. Terrorism in the target sense of this book is an activity directed to political or military ends. This is not to say that criminals, for example, do not use the methods of terror to achieve their criminal ends: clearly some criminals kidnap to extract a ransom, torture to instil fear and thereby extort money, and so on. Moreover, torture and other methods of terror can be, and have been, used for religious ends, e.g., the methods of torture used by the Spanish Inquisition in the Middle Ages. However, my concern here is with political or military ends. On the other hand, it needs to be noted that sometimes terrorism has multiple ends, e.g., Al-Qaeda's terrorist methods serve political as well as religious ends, Pablo Escobar's terrorist methods in Colombia, such as assassinating politicians, judges, police and journalists who opposed him, served political as well as criminal ends.

The fifth assumption is in part stipulative and in part conceptual. If fear is to be instilled in some group as a consequence of the harm done to some other group, then the first group needs to know that the second group has in fact been harmed. Accordingly, the terrorist strategy relies on a degree of publicity. Indeed, it might well be that, other things being equal, the higher the level of publicity, the more successful the

---

[6] Robert E. Goodin disputes this in his *What's Wrong with Terrorism?* Cambridge: Polity, 2006.
[7] I don't mean to imply that terrorism is not often an expressive activity (in addition to being a strategic activity).

terrorist strategy is. This certainly was the case with Al-Qaeda's terrorist attack on the World Trade Center on September 11, 2001.

These five assumptions are summarized in the following set of propositions that, as a result, constitute a (albeit, as will emerge, not the only) constraint on any acceptable definition of terrorism:[8]

1   Terrorism is a political or military strategy that consists in deliberately using violence against civilians.
2   Terrorism is a means of terrorizing the members of some social or political group in order to achieve political or military purposes.
3   Terrorism relies on the violence receiving a high degree of publicity, at least to the extent necessary to engender widespread fear in the target political or social group.

The first proposition is problematic with respect to its use of the term 'civilians'. Civilian contrasts with military, and the implication here is that terrorism is a strategy deployed in the context of *war*. But when Timothy McVeigh bombed the Alfred P. Murrah Federal Building in Oklahoma City in 1995, killing 168 people, he performed an act of terrorism, but he did not do so in the context of a war. McVeigh might have been under the illusion that there was a war and he was a combatant; but, if so, he was deluded. Similarly, Aum Shinrikyo's sarin gas attack on the Tokyo Underground in 1995 that killed twelve people was an act of terrorism, but not one carried out in the context of war.

The definition of war is itself inherently problematic, and no doubt especially when it comes to wars involving a non-state actor as one of the protagonists. Nevertheless, non-state actors can engage in war, e.g., revolutionary war. However, a well-ordered liberal-democratic state is not in a condition of war merely because a non-state actor performs an isolated act of violence against the state by killing ordinary office-workers and other citizens going about their day-to-day lives. Rather, such acts are crimes of murder and, specifically, crimes of murder that are also acts of terrorism (given the aim of terrorizing people in the service of political purposes).

The general point to be made here is that an act of terrorism is not necessarily performed in the context of war. Accordingly, terrorists are not necessarily (military) combatants – even combatants guilty of war crimes – and the combatant/non-combatant distinction (in its military sense) might not relevantly apply to the victims of terrorists. A person killed in the

---

[8]   For material on definitions of terrorism, see D.J. Whittaker (ed.), *The Terrorism Reader*, 2nd edn, London: Routledge, 2003, chap. 1.

Oklahoma bombing or in the Tokyo Underground attack, and who happened to be a member of the police service, or indeed of the armed services, has not been killed by an enemy combatant in a war; rather, he or she has been murdered by fellow civilians in peacetime, just as his or her fellow civilians were murdered. McVeigh and the members of Aum Shinrikyo are terrorists but not combatants. Moreover, police officers who appear on the scene and seek to apprehend such terrorists – or shoot them in self-defence or to prevent further acts of killing – are not combatants (in the required military sense); rather, they are police seeking to enforce the law. Hence the actions of the police in question are not governed by rules of engagement for military combat; rather, their actions are governed by police procedures the point of which is to uphold the law and, as far as is possible, preserve life. (See Chapter 4.)

This is not to say that some so-called 'armed struggles' conducted by terrorist groups are not wars and that, therefore, some terrorist acts ought to be understood as acts of war performed by combatants. As is well known, many terrorists groups, such as the IRA, engaged in protracted campaigns of violence that generated a military response and significantly disrupted civil society for lengthy periods of time (unlike, say, the actions of Timothy McVeigh). This is so even if, as was the case in Northern Ireland, the military forces happen to be under police control, and therefore civilian authority. Moreover, many of these terrorist groups insisted that they were combatants fighting a war, or at least combatants fighting an armed struggle against enemy combatants. Whether or not the members of the IRA were, or ought to have been, regarded as combatants fighting a war is controversial. At any rate, my point here is that *in principle* there could be – and in fact there have been – armed struggles conducted by terrorist groups that are wars, and in such cases the terrorists are essentially combatants (irrespective of what their legal status might have been). The wars of national liberation conducted by terrorist groups in Algeria against the French and in Kenya against the British are cases in point. Accordingly, we need to distinguish between terrorists who are essentially combatants engaged in a war and terrorists who are not combatants, but merely civilians performing the ordinary crime of murder in peacetime (albeit in order to instil fear to secure political purposes). Naturally, this distinction is somewhat vague and, in many contexts, difficult to make; nonetheless, the distinction exists, as the McVeigh and Aum Shinrikyo examples demonstrate.

So the above proposition (proposition (1)) is misleading or, at least, incomplete. It fails to specify the meaning of 'civilians' and, relatedly, to distinguish between terrorism as a crime in peacetime and terrorism in the context of a war.

The question that now arises is whether or not the term 'civilian' in the above proposition ought to be replaced by the term 'innocents' in the context of constructing a definition of terrorism. After all, the notion of an innocent is, at least on the face of it, independent of whether or not the terrorist or his or her victims are combatants or non-combatants; so it promises to breach the divide between terrorism in war and terrorism in peacetime. A definition of terrorism in terms of innocents is recommended by a number of theorists, including Igor Primoratz and David Rosenbaum.[9]

The Definition of Terrorism in Terms of Innocents

Let me now present the definition of terrorism in terms of innocents. By definition, terrorism is a political or military strategy that:

1   consists in deliberately using violence against innocents;
2   is a means of terrorizing the members of some social or political group in order to achieve political or military purposes;
3   relies on the violence receiving a high degree of publicity, at least to the extent necessary to engender widespread fear in the target political or social group.

The definition in terms of innocents needs to offer an account of what counts as an innocent.[10] Here we need to make a threefold distinction between violent attackers, perpetrators of an injustice (other than violence) and revolutionaries (those seeking to overthrow a government, whether by violent means or otherwise). Let us assume that anyone belonging to

---

[9]   Rosenbaum, 'On terrorism and the just war', p. 6; Primoratz, 'What is terrorism?', p. 24.
[10]   According to Primoratz, 'terrorism is the deliberate use of violence, or threat of its use, against innocent people with the aim of intimidating some other people into a course of action they otherwise would not take' (Primoratz, 'What is terrorism?', p. 24). Here we need to know what counts as being innocent on Primoratz's account. According to Primoratz, the direct victims of terrorism are innocent in the sense that

> They have not done anything the terrorist could adduce as a justification of what he does to them. They are not attacking him, and thus he cannot justify his action as one of self-defence. They are not engaged in war against him, and therefore he cannot say that he is fighting in a war himself. They are not responsible, in any plausible sense of the word, for the (real or alleged) injustice, suffering, deprivation which is inflicted on him or on those whose cause he has embraced, and which is so enormous that it could justify a violent response. (Ibid., pp. 17–18)

any of these three categories of persons is not innocent in the required sense. But note that someone could belong to one or more of these three categories and yet their associated actions might be (all things considered) morally justifiable. For example, a person could be a combatant (violent attacker) fighting a morally justified war of national liberation. This combatant is not an innocent in the required sense, but his or her violent actions are (*ex hypothesei*) morally justified.

Let us refer to the first of these three categories as combatants.[11] As we have seen, the notion of a combatant (in its military sense) is tied to the condition of war. Assume there is a political group perpetrating acts of terror against the citizens of a well-ordered, liberal-democratic state in peacetime, e.g., Aum Shinrikyo releasing nerve gas in the Tokyo underground. Obviously, such terrorists are not attacking enemy combatants; there is no war in progress. Rather, they are attacking innocent civilians. Now imagine that there is a war. Assume that there is a military force perpetrating acts of terror against non-combatants, e.g., dropping an atomic bomb on Hiroshma in order to terrorize the Japanese leadership into surrendering. Such terrorists are attacking non-combatants who are also innocent civilians. So far so good for the definition of terrorism in terms of innocents.

Our second category consists of people who are responsible for some injustice, or other form of serious moral wrongdoing, but who are not combatants. For example, the slum dwellers who were the victims of the Bhopal gas disaster in India in 1984 rightly believe that Union Carbide is responsible for the death and sickness of hundreds of thousands of their number, and that the US and Indian governments are responsible for failing to ensure adequate compensation. Neither the Union Carbide management nor the members of the US or Indian government are combatants in this context. However, nor are they innocent; rather, they are morally responsible for injustice, suffering and/or deprivation.[12] By the lights of the definition of terrorism in terms of innocents, a political group that killed members of the Union Carbide management (in order to pressure the US or Indian government to intervene to redress the injustice), or directly killed members of the US or Indian government in order to cause their respective governments to redress the injustice of inadequate compensation, would not be a terrorist group; for these

---

[11]   We need to distinguish between combatants, the leaders of combatants and those who assist combatants *qua* combatants, e.g., munitions workers, spies. Here, for the purposes of simplification, I will ignore the latter two categories. However, many Just War theorists would treat all three categories as legitimate targets and, therefore, in effect as combatants.
[12]   To use Primoratz's descriptive terminology. See note 10, *supra*.

victims are not innocent. This consequence of the definition renders it implausible. A political group that seeks to redress injustices by perpetrating lethal attacks on corporate leaders and/or government officials and/or security personnel in a well-ordered, liberal-democratic state at peace is, other things being equal, a terrorist group by virtue of so doing. During the 1970s the Red Brigades in Italy and the Red Army Faction (Baader–Meinhof Group) in Germany are cases in point, albeit these groups also murdered persons who were innocents (in the required sense).[13]

(Naturally, other things might not be equal. Given the Israeli government's policy of the ethnic cleansing of Palestinians, lethal attacks by Palestinians on those Israeli leaders and security personnel who are responsible for this policy and its enforcement may well be morally justified, i.e., morally justified if other conditions obtain; crucially, the unavailability of non-violent methods. Of course, such policies on the part of the Israeli government would not morally justify Hamas murdering innocent children and the like by bombing marketplaces.[14])

Let us now consider a second, and rather different, kind of counter-example to the definition of terrorism in terms of innocents. Imagine a non-democratic, indeed highly authoritarian, government pursuing policies that are widening the gap between the rich and the poor. Assume that well-intentioned democrats with a social conscience attempt to mobilize opposition to the government; opposition in the form of non-violent protests, strikes, boycotts, dissemination of anti-government material, passive non-compliance, and so on. These opposition elements are seeking to overthrow the government, indeed the system of government, albeit by non-violent means. The ANC in its initial non-violent phase prior to the 1960s is a case in point. Accordingly, they are not innocents in the required sense. (Indeed, from the perspective of the authoritarian government, these opposition forces are engaged in attempting to overthrow the *legitimate* government of the country.) Moreover, they may well succeed if harsh counter-measures are not introduced. Accordingly, the government embarks on a campaign of killings ('disappearances') and torture of opposition elements in order to instil fear in the opposition forces as a whole, and thus put an end to the 'insurrection'. Surely this is state terrorism of the kind practised by the Argentinian generals in the

---

[13]   See Whittaker (ed.), *The Terrorism Reader*, pp. 206–7 and pp. 223–4.

[14]   Ted Honderich appears to think otherwise. T. Honderich, *After the Terror*, Edinburgh: Edinburgh University Press, 2002, p. 151: 'I myself have no serious doubt, to take the outstanding case, that the Palestinians have exercised a moral right in their terrorism against Israelis.'

1980s and (to a lesser extent) by the apartheid government in South Africa against the ANC. Nevertheless, it remains the case that the opposition forces are responsible for attempting to overthrow the government; and the government believes itself – and is believed by many, let us assume – to be legitimate. By the lights of the definition of terrorism in terms of innocents, the killings and torture perpetrated by the government are not terrorism, since the opposition forces are not innocent in the required sense.

What response is available to defenders of the definition? One such response to both of the above kinds of counter-example (i.e., examples involving killing public officials in liberal-democratic states and ones involving killing insurrectionary democrats in authoritarian states) is to add the further condition that unless the violent response is, objectively speaking, morally justified, then the violent response is terrorism, notwithstanding the fact that the target group is not, strictly speaking, innocent. If this condition is made then: (a) the killers of public officials in liberal democracies turn out to be terrorists (since their murderous actions are not morally justified); and (b) the insurrectionary democrats in our example turn out to be victims of terrorism after all (since it is completely morally unacceptable to kill and torture those who are simply using non-violent means to establish a democracy and implement policies of social justice).

The upshot of this manoeuvre is that there are now two (mutually exclusive) categories of terrorism: (1) terrorism in which the victims are innocent in the initial sense of the definition; and (2) terrorism in which the victims are not innocent in the initial sense, but in which the violent response of the terrorists is not morally justified.

The addition of this second category fatally compromises the definition of terrorism in terms of innocents. For, *contra* the definition, it turns out that some forms of terrorism target those who are *not* innocent, i.e., who are guilty. So the fundamental guiding proposition of this kind of definition, namely, that it is a definition of terrorism in terms of the innocent, has been abandoned.

Moreover, there are other problems. Firstly, with respect to this second species of terrorism (which targets the guilty or non-innocent), one cannot identify an act as an act of terrorism independently of determining whether it is, or is not, morally justified. This is a significant deficiency, both in purely definitional terms and from a political perspective. *Qua* definition, the distinction between an action and its moral justification has been collapsed; now we cannot determine whether or not some action is in fact a terrorist act unless we conduct a full-blown moral assessment of it. So the truth of the claim that some violent act is (or is not) an act of terrorism will now typically depend on – among other considerations – whether it has good or bad consequences.[15]

From a political perspective the definition is also unhelpful. For it has the effect of resolving an important political and moral debate about the justifiability of at least some forms of terrorist action not by substantive moral argument, but by definitional fiat; the possibility that at least some terrorist acts might turn out to be morally permissible is logically excluded from the outset by this definition.

A final point is that the adjusted 'definition' is not as it stands, and perhaps cannot be transformed into, a definition of terrorism. It is not as it stands a definition of terrorism because it requires of itself, but it has not provided, an account of when the relevant kinds of violent acts are morally justified and when they are not. Moreover, it is by no means clear that it can ever meet its own requirements in this regard.

In order to do so, a specification of the relevant kinds of violent acts in question needs to be provided, i.e., a specification of those violent acts with respect to which it is to be asked whether or not they are morally justifiable. It might appear that this could easily be done so by applying the following above-mentioned criteria to violent acts: (1) the violent act is politically motivated; (2) the violence is a means to instil fear or terror; and (3) the violent act receives a high degree of publicity. However, these criteria provide no indication of who the targets of the violent acts are. Recall that the earlier failed definition of terrorism did specify the targets in question, namely, that they were innocents. However, the later revised definition has now retreated to a point that is logically prior to this earlier failed definition, namely, to the notion of a 'person who is a morally justifiable target of violence'. At least the earlier definition provided a specification of this notion: such persons were the innocent, i.e., non-combatants not engaged in acts of injustice or revolutionary activity. However, this latest definition leaves us with the entirely unanswered question: who are the persons that it is morally justified to target? Moreover, it does so in the context of having abandoned as inadequate the earlier specification of this notion of persons it is morally justifiable to target, i.e., the specification in terms of innocents. Therefore, on pain of circularity, the latest definition cannot be retrieved by wheeling back in the notion of innocents to provide the needed specification.

---

[15]   This is not simply so on consequentialist theories of morality, but on any moral account which insists on taking consequences into account, i.e., on any reasonable moral theory. If moral justifiability is understood subjectively, then the same problem will reappear in a different form, i.e., an act will turn out to be (or not to be) a terrorist act depending in part on all of its foreseen consequences (or reasonably foreseeable consequences).

The Definition of Terrorism in Terms of Non-Combatants

In the light of the failure of the above definition of terrorism in terms of innocents, let us consider the following one in terms of non-combatants.[16] The notion of a combatant and, therefore, of a non-combatant might seem to provide the required degree of determinacy; unlike the notion of innocents or of morally legitimate/illegitimate targets. The notion of a combatant both is in itself relatively determinate, and provides a clear sense in which a person is guilty and, therefore, a legitimate target of violence. So on this view, if one is a combatant, then one is using lethal force in the context of some conflict. On the other hand, on this view, if one is not a combatant, then one is innocent; non-combatants do not use lethal force and, therefore, are innocents. Terrorism is, on this account, distinguished from other modes of organized political violence in that it targets non-combatants.

Let us, then, offer the following definition of terrorism. By definition, terrorism is a political or military strategy that:

1   costs in deliberately using violence against *non-combatants*;
2   is a means of terrorizing the members of some social or political group in order to achieve political or military purposes;
3   relies on the violence receiving a high degree of publicity, at least to the extent necessary to engender widespread fear in the target political or social group.

The concept of a non-combatant is different from the concept of being innocent, or of not being morally responsible for attacking or infringing

---

[16] See, for example, C.A.J. Coady, 'Terrorism, just war and supreme emergency', in C.A.J. Coady and M. O'Keefe (eds), *Terrorism and Justice: Moral Argument in a Threatened World*, Melbourne: Melbourne University Press, 2002, p. 9: 'I will define it [terrorism] as follows: the organized use of violence to target non-combatants ("innocents" in a special sense) for political purposes.' He also notes (p. 13) that 'Some civilians, such as political leaders and senior public servants, will be legitimate targets if they are actively directing or promoting unjust violence whether or not they wear uniforms or bear arms.' Coady offers the same definition is his 'Defining terrorism', in Primoratz (ed.), *Terrorism: The Philosophical Issues*, p. 5. Coady appears at times to move beyond a definition in terms of combatants/non-combatants (understood as agents/non-agents in the causal chain of unjust violence) towards a more broad-based definition in terms of innocents. For example, he says, 'The sense in which non-combatants are "innocent" is more that in which they are "non-harming", that is, not engaged in prosecuting the evil that justifies (or is argued to justify) the use of violence to protect or remedy' (ibid., p. 10). This looks now to be pretty much equivalent to Primoratz's definition in terms of innocents.

the rights of others, and so on. As a consequence, non-combatants might, or might not, be innocent in the sense of being morally responsible for acts of violence, injustice or other forms of wrongdoing. Clearly *some* non-combatants are innocent, e.g., young children, and *some* instances of using deadly force against non-combatants, such as bombing restaurants (Hamas) or napalming villages (US forces in the Vietnam War), are acts of terrorism – indeed, morally unacceptable forms of terrorism. However, it does not follow from this that *all* instances of using deadly force against non-combatants are acts of terrorism and/or are morally unacceptable. Nor does it follow that no instance of using deadly force against a combatant is an act of terrorism.

Let us consider the latter possibility first, i.e., the possibility that combatants could themselves be the object of a terrorist attack. Widespread torture of armed insurgents in order to instil fear in a target population is an instance of terrorism, and yet the victims of the torture are combatants. (See Chapter 5 on torture.) In short, *contra* the definition under consideration, it is possible to use some of the methods of terrorism against combatants.[17]

Let us consider another related type of counter-example to the requirement that it is only non-combatants who can be the targets of terrorism. Certain forms of weaponry used against enemy combatants are regarded as morally unacceptable. For example, the use of chemical and biological weapons is often so regarded and, as a consequence, is outlawed by international treaties, e.g., the Chemical Weapons Convention and the Biological Weapons Convention. Here Just War Theory is again relevant. One of the moral principles deployed in the *ius in bello* condition of Just War Theory is to the effect that only a type and extent of force should be used against combatants that is necessary and proportionate in the circumstances. Suppose an authoritarian government is facing an armed insurgency from members of a minority ethnic group seeking self-determination. Suppose further that the government could put down the insurrection relatively easily by using the methods of conventional warfare,

---

[17] It might be argued that in order to count as a combatant, a person has to be able at the relevant time to attack and defend him- or herself by the use of arms (or indirectly having such an ability by virtue of the possession of this ability by an other person who is under his or her control, e.g., in the case of a political leader). Accordingly, prisoners of war, for example, are not combatants in this sense; and nor are those being tortured combatants in this sense. In general, a person being tortured is both defenceless and unable to attack anyone. So, properly speaking, perhaps torture is a violent attack not on combatants, but rather on non-combatants. However, a person does not cease to be a combatant merely because he or she is, for example, disarmed. Thus, other things being equal, prisoners of war are combatants, and so are soldiers who are tortured.

and do so with minimum loss of life. However, in order to instil fear in the civilian population of this ethnic group and thereby break their will to pursue self-determination, the government forces mount a chemical attack against the insurgent group and decimate its members. Moreover, the process of death for those who are affected is a prolonged and excruciatingly painful one. In addition, the small number of combatants who survive are severely and permanently physically and intellectually damaged. Arguably, the authoritarian government has perpetrated a terrorist attack against enemy combatants.

What these examples demonstrate is that the definition of terrorism in terms of non-combatants is deficient by virtue of requiring that only non-combatants can be the targets of terrorism.[18] Accordingly, the definition does not provide a necessary condition for terrorism. Let me now consider whether it provides a sufficient condition. I do so by considering various putative counter-examples involving violence directed at non-combatants.

Prima facie, some non-combatants are guilty in the sense that they are morally responsible for the attacks, rights violations or injustices that some group of putative terrorists are responding to. The leaders of combatants, for example, and those who assist combatants *qua* combatants, such as munitions workers and spies, are guilty in this sense; specifically, they are morally responsible for attacking or waging war against such a group (or contributing to such an attack or war effort).

For the sake of argument, let us assume that such leaders and contributors are a species of combatant, on the grounds that they are jointly morally responsible with the combatants for the killings (and perhaps other serious violent acts) carried out by the combatants themselves.[19] This (standard) assumption carries with it the implication that the key moral notion in play is not that of the bare notion of a combatant *per se*, but that of someone who is morally responsible for a lethal attack, whether or not he or she was the one doing the actual fighting. So the definition of terrorism in terms of non-combatants is now availing itself of the notion of a person who is morally responsible for a lethal attack; it is no longer simply using the narrower and less morally loaded notion of a combatant.[20]

The problem that now confronts the definition of terrorism in terms of non-combatants is that it faces a further extension to the category

---

[18]   Incidentally, these examples are also counter-examples to the definition of terrorism in terms of innocents. It turns out that the guilty, i.e., combatants, can under certain circumstances be the victims of terrorism.

[19]   See Coady, 'Terrorism, just war and supreme emergency'.

[20]   Combatants might be following orders and, as a consequence, they *might* have diminished moral responsibility for their actions.

of legitimate targets. On the revised definition of terrorism in terms of non-combatants, moral responsibility for lethal attacks is sufficient grounds for justifying a lethal response, i.e., for forfeiting one's civilian immunity. If so, then the question that now must be asked is whether or not there are other additional categories of guilty persons who might likewise have forfeited their right to civilian immunity, namely, persons who are morally responsible for serous rights violations or injustices. There are such categories of persons, and in the chapter following this one I will discuss these categories in some detail. Here I will simply content myself with one example. Consider corrupt senior government officials and civil servants who fail to organize the distribution of aid in the form of medicine and food to their starving, disease-afflicted, fellow citizens, but rather sell it to line their own pockets. Suppose the foreseen consequence of this corruption and dereliction of their humanitarian duty is that tens of thousands of the needy die. These officials are not combatants in the required sense; they are not themselves soldiers engaged in an armed attack, nor are they the leaders of such combatants or assisting such combatants *qua* combatants. Accordingly, targeting these public officials would be, on the definition before us, terrorism. But these officials are guilty in the sense that they are morally responsible for ongoing, widespread and serious rights violations. Moreover, using lethal force against some such officials in order to instil fear in their fellow guilty officials, and thereby bring about a cessations to these ongoing, widespread and serious rights violations, may well be, under certain circumstances, morally justifiable. (See Chapter 3 for the details of the argument to this conclusion.)

The question that now arises is whether or not those who respond with lethal force to serious, *non-violent* rights violations are terrorists. I suggest that the advocates of the definition of terrorism in terms of non-combatants face a dilemma in attempting to address this question. There are two salient options for them. They could stand firm and refuse to vary their definition in the face of this kind of example; in doing so they would be insisting that those who respond with lethal force to ongoing, widespread and serious rights violations of this kind are, nevertheless, terrorists. Alternatively, they could concede (rightly or wrongly) that the latter are not terrorists, and seek to adjust their definition. Consider the latter option first.

The definition could be adjusted by excluding as the targets of terrorism those non-combatants who are guilty of serious rights violations. Thus by definition a terrorist is now someone who targets non-combatants, but only non-combatants who are not guilty of serious rights violations. However, in doing so, the definition is no longer a definition that distinguishes terrorists from non-terrorists exclusively on the basis of the combatant/non-combatant distinction. For by the lights of the adjusted definition, although all terrorists target non-combatants, some non-terrorists also target non-combatants, namely, non-combatants who are rights violators. Accordingly, to accept this adjustment to the definition amounts to an abandonment of the definition.

Alternatively, this adjustment to the definition could be resisted and it could be insisted that those who target non-combatants *only* if they are rights violators are, nevertheless, terrorists. So, to revert to our earlier example, the persons who attacked the corrupt officials in order to save the lives of thousands wrongly and unlawfully being deprived by these officials of food and medicine are terrorists. However, this refusal to adjust the definition comes at a price. For we are owed an account of why the difference between bearing moral responsibility for lethal attacks and bearing moral responsibility for serious rights violations (including fatal ones) should make a difference when it comes to defining terrorism. On the view in question, someone who responds with lethal force to lethal attacks is, *ipso facto*, *not* a terrorist. However, someone who responds with legal force to ongoing and widespread, serious rights violations (including fatal ones) is, *ipso facto*, a terrorist. *Ex hypothesei*, there is not, or might not be, any significant moral difference between the two responses: that is, as with lethal attacks, it could be morally justifiable to respond with lethal force to ongoing, widespread and serious rights violations. So the challenge to proponents of the definition of terrorism – the definition in terms of non-combatants – to identify a relevant difference between groups who target only combatants (and who are, therefore, presumably not terrorists) and groups who target some non-combatants (namely, ones who are [non-violent] rights violators) is unmet.[21]

I conclude that the dilemma facing the definition of terrorism in terms of non-combatants is unresolved, if not unresolvable. I now want to turn to a further issue that arises for definitions of terrorism, and that is a source of some of the problems for the two kinds of definition thus far looked at. I am speaking of the problem posed by authoritarian states. Other things being equal, a group which targets the security officials of a liberal-democratic state (or otherwise legitimate nation-state) in peacetime is a terrorist group. Thus the Red Brigades was a terrorist group by virtue of killing Italian police officers (irrespective of its other practices of kidnapping and killing, say, business leaders). Yet a group which targeted security officials of a totalitarian state, even in peacetime, would not thereby be a terrorist group. How so?

---

[21] Naturally, these groups who attack some non-combatants, specifically, non-violent rights violators, might in addition target combatants.

Terrorism, Combatants and Authoritarian States

As we have seen, the definition of terrorism in terms of non-combatants is problematic (as is the definition in terms of innocents). Nevertheless, it is able to accommodate some of the counter-examples raised against the definition of terrorism in terms of innocents. The killing and torture of non-violent political activists by state security agencies, for example, will typically count as terrorism on the definition in terms of non-combatants, since such activists are not combatants.

What of politically motivated, unlawful, peacetime killing of public officials of liberal democracies? Is this terrorism? Given that such public officials are not (in the required military sense) combatants, then, on the definition of terrorism in terms of non-combatants, such killings will be acts of terrorism. This is the correct result: such acts are, indeed, acts of terrorism. However, it is questionable whether or not all such public officials should, properly speaking, be regarded as non-combatants. Doubtless, they are not *military* combatants. But arguably armed police are sometimes properly described as combatants. For example, armed police engaged in a gun battle with a gang of armed robbers are, in a clear sense of the term, combatants, albeit non-military combatants. Likewise, armed police engaged in a gun battle with terrorists are (non-military) combatants.

Evidently, we need to distinguish between military and non-military combatants. Police and other non-military, armed security personnel are, at least in some contexts, combatants, albeit non-military combatants.

This distinction has at least one clear implication for the definition of terrorism in terms of non-combatants. If the notion of a combatant includes non-military combatants (the wide sense of combatant), then politically motivated, unlawful, peacetime killing of, for example, armed police personnel serving in liberal democracies is not terrorism – since these personnel are combatants. But surely such killings are paradigms of terrorism. Consider, for example, groups such as the Red Brigades in Italy in the 1970s, who were somewhat discriminating in their killing, i.e., they targeted, for example, individual political leaders and security personnel, rather than engaging in indiscriminate killing.[22] Indeed, even in the case

---

[22] The Red Brigades also targeted a large number of corporate executive and some individual judges, journalists and professors. However, the point here is twofold. In so far as its members targeted political leaders and security personnel, they were terrorists. Moreover, the members of the Red Brigades were terrorists notwithstanding the fact that they only targeted individuals who were (allegedly) part of the unjust system or who were engaged in counter-terrorism, i.e., they only deployed targeted as opposed to indiscriminate killing (of the kind perpetrated by, say, Al-Qaeda). (See C. Hewitt, *The Effectiveness of Anti-Terrorist Policies*, Lanham, MD: University Press of America, 1984, p. 32.) Obviously, from the fact that killing is targeted in this sense it does not follow that it is morally justifiable.

of terrorist groups such as the IRA and ETA (currently fighting for Basque separatism in liberal-democratic Spain), the overwhelming number of their killings have been targeted rather than indiscriminate, and the majority of their targets have been political leaders and (especially) security personnel.[23] (In this respect, these groups are quite unlike, for example, Al-Qaeda.) Hence, the definition of terrorism in terms of non-combatants, i.e., the definition involving the wide notion of a combatant, faces a counter-example in the form of a specific kind of terrorist attack, namely, targeted killings of combatants, e.g., police, in liberal democracies at peace.[24] What of assassinations of combatants (in the wide sense) in authoritarian states at peace?

Consider a terrorist group operating in a well-ordered, authoritarian nation-state at peace. Assume that this group decides that the government and its security agencies are maintaining and enforcing an unjust society which is unable to be changed by peaceful means. Accordingly, the terrorists decide to engage in assassinations of political leaders currently holding office in portfolios such as defence, as well as of police and other security personnel. However, the terrorist group in question is scrupulous in its policy of avoiding citizens and non-citizens who are not part of the state's security apparatus. The ANC was an exemplar of this kind of policy, at least for most of its history. In earlier times, anarchist groups who assassinated and attempted to assassinate various tsars in nineteenth-century Russia also appear to be of this type. Here there is the well-known case of the Russian terrorist Ivan Kaliayev, who aborted his assassination

---

[23] Ibid., p. 29.

[24] The response of the proponents of the definition of terrorism in terms of non-combatants might be to argue that security personnel and their political leaders in (at least) well-ordered societies at peace are not, properly speaking, combatants. Rather, the notion of a combatant is invariably tied to the context of war. Accordingly, it is simply a misnomer to apply the term 'combatant' to such security personnel and their leaders. However, this restriction on the notion of combatant has the effect of expanding the definitional set of terrorist groups so as to include many non-terrorist groups, e.g., groups who might only be engaged in violent acts of self-defence against state security personnel. Suppose, for example, an authoritarian state uses 'hit squads' comprised of serving police officers against its political enemies, including political leaders who are pursuing only non-violent strategies to achieve political change. Now suppose the latter employ bodyguards for purposes only of self-defence, albeit including deterrence, against these state-run hit squads. There is no war as such and so the security personnel in the hit squads are not combatants. Now assume that the bodyguards shoot members of the hit squads not only to thwart armed attacks in process, but also to instil fear in existing and would-be hit squads so that such attacks are discontinued. On the view before us, such armed bodyguards would be terrorists, for they are using lethal force against non-combatants (the members of the hit squads are not combatants on the view in play here) and doing so in order to instil fear to achieve political ends, i.e., the end of protecting political leaders and, as a consequence, the realization of the political objectives of those leaders.

attempt on Grand Duke Sergei when he realized the prince's family were in the carriage with him.[25]

What, then, are the implications for the definition of terrorism of attacks on the public officials of authoritarian states, as opposed to liberal-democratic states? On the definition of terrorists as necessarily targeting only non-combatants, none of these groups are terrorist organizations, and none of their attacks were acts of terrorism. Or at least this is so on the assumption that such security personnel and their leaders are combatants (even if not always or necessarily *military* combatants).

The definition of terrorism in terms of non-combatants is now inconsistent with certain longstanding and widespread beliefs in relation to what groups are terrorist groups, and what acts are terrorist acts. Indeed, the definition of terrorism as necessarily and only violent acts directed at non-combatants would excise a large part of what has hitherto been the accepted history of terrorism, e.g., assassinations and attempted assassinations of the tsars in nineteenth-century Russia. This is a reason for resisting the proposition that such attacks are not acts of terrorism, albeit not a decisive reason. On the other hand, I suggest that we are less inclined to think of such lethal attacks on combatants in the context of authoritarian states as being acts of terrorism than we would be if the states in question were liberal-democratic states. Hence our uneasiness with the claim that the ANC, in particular, was a terrorist organization during the apartheid years.

We have seen that groups that engage in targeted killing of non-military combatants, e.g., police, for political purposes in well-ordered liberal democracies at peace are perpetrating acts of terrorism. Further, there is some reason to think that some such targeted killings of non-military combatants, e.g., police, in some well-ordered, authoritarian states at peace would also count as terrorism, albeit this is much less certain. I now want to argue that such targeted killings in *some* well-ordered, authoritarian states would definitely *not* count as terrorism.

Consider, for example, a political group attempting to assassinate Hitler and his Nazi henchmen when he was in power prior to the Second World War, or to assassinate Stalin and senior members of his secret police during the period (again) prior to the Second World War. Assume that such a group was seeking to instil fear among the Nazis (or Russian communists) in order to secure their political objectives of bringing about a cessation of the serious rights violations taking place. Would such a group in such a context necessarily be a terrorist group? I suggest that it would not be.

---

[25]   C. Townshend, *Terrorism: A Very Short Introduction*, Oxford: Oxford University Press, 2002, p. 58.

I further suggest that the reason for this is that the political institutional context in Nazi Germany and Stalinist Russia was below the threshold of minimal conformity with the basic moral principles of human decency that govern allowable political institutions in general, and political leaders and security personnel in particular. Specifically, such nation-states are (i) *eo ipso* engaged in ongoing and widespread human rights violations, (ii) (in part as a consequence of (i)) not politically legitimate states, and (iii) (in part as a consequence of (i) and (ii)) states that ought not to be internationally recognized. Some authoritarian states, e.g., totalitarian states, are simply beyond the pale and, therefore, violent attacks on the leadership and security personnel of these states do not count as terrorism, even during peacetime. (Moreover, some non-authoritarian states, e.g., failed states in which large-scale human rights violations are taking place, are also beyond the pale; however, these states are not germane to our purposes here.)

Needless to say, the point at which an authoritarian state is 'beyond the pale' is somewhat indeterminate. Nevertheless, I suggest that the international community needs to address this issue in relation to the issue of terrorism and, for that matter, more generally.

The upshot of this discussion is as follows. Firstly, we need to distinguish between military and non-military combatants, e.g., between soldiers in a war zone and police officers during peacetime, and between liberal-democratic nation-states and authoritarian states. The definition in terms of non-combatants elaborated in the previous section is deficient by virtue of failing to respect either of these distinctions. A more fine-grained version of the definition could accommodate the distinction between military and non-military combatants, but an entirely different definition is called for if the distinction between liberal-democratic and authoritarian states is to be accommodated. As a consequence of failing to respect these two sets of distinctions, the definition in terms of non-combatants faces an unresolved dilemma. If by the use of the term 'combatants' in this definition, it is meant military combatants (but not non-military combatants), i.e., the narrow sense of combatant is in play, then the definition will of necessity wrongly count attacks on police and other non-military personnel in totalitarian states as acts of terrorism. On the other hand, if by the term 'combatants' is meant military *and* non-military combatants (wide sense of combatant), then the definition will of necessity wrongly refrain from counting attacks on police and other non-military personnel in liberal-democratic states as acts of terrorism.

Secondly, we need to acknowledge that authoritarian states exist on a continuum at the extreme end of which are totalitarian states. As we have seen, other things being equal, lethal attacks on the political leadership and security apparatus, i.e., on combatants in the non-military sense, in the context of a well-ordered totalitarian state at peace do not constitute terrorism; and, other things being equal, lethal attacks on non-military combatants in the context of a well-ordered liberal-democratic state at peace do constitute terrorism. However, other things being equal, it is indeterminate whether or not lethal attacks on the political leadership and security apparatus, i.e., on combatants in the non-military sense, in the context of a well-ordered to authoritarian – but non-totalitarian – state at peace constitute terrorism. The above-mentioned nineteenth-century attacks by Russian revolutionaries on the tsars serve to underscore this point.

This concludes our discussion of terrorism and authoritarianism. Earlier we rejected the definition of terrorism in terms of innocents and that in terms of non-combatants. In the light of the identified strengths and weaknesses of these defective definitions of terrorism, and the upshot of our discussion of terrorism and authoritarianism, we now need to turn explicitly to the task of constructing a viable definition of terrorism.

The Definition of Terrorism: An Indirect Strategy

At this stage we are in a position to offer the following incomplete definition of terrorism. Terrorism is a political or military strategy that:

1   consists in deliberately using violence against X and/or deliberately using violence of type M;
2   is a means of terrorizing the members of some social or political group in order to achieve political or military purposes;
3   relies on the violence receiving a high degree of publicity, at least to the extent necessary to engender widespread fear in the target political or social group.

As we have seen, the principal problem lies in specifying X and M. The definitions in terms of innocents and of non-combatants were seen to be unsatisfactory. However, some lessons have been learnt, including from the discussion of terrorism and authoritarianism.

As far as the specification of X is concerned, we have learnt the following two lessons. Firstly, violent attacks on those who are neither military combatants (including leaders of combatants and those who assist combatants *qua* combatants) nor the perpetrators of human rights violations, nor revolutionaries – i.e., those who are innocent (in our above-described sense) – constitute terrorism. Here I am assuming that human rights violations are a particularly egregious moral offence and one distinguished from, for example, injustice. (For further discussion on this issue, see Chapter 3.) Moreover, I am further assuming that the human rights violations in question are on a significant scale; admittedly, there is some indeterminacy in relation to the issue of scale, in particular.

Accordingly, let us provide an initial specification of the membership of X in our overall definition of terrorism by means of the following condition: by definition, X is someone who is not a military combatant, human rights violator or revolutionary.

Secondly, we have learnt that, other things being equal, violent acts directed at political leaders and security personnel in totalitarian nation-states (and other states beyond the pale) are not acts of terrorism. This is because such nation-states (i) are *eo ipso* engaged in ongoing and widespread human rights violations, (ii) are not politically legitimate states, and (iii) ought not to be internationally recognized. Since political leaders and security personnel in totalitarian nation-states (and other states beyond the pale) are engaged in ongoing and widespread human rights violations, they are already accommodated in the definition under the above-mentioned specification of X, i.e., (specifically) they do not belong to the category of X since they are human rights violators.

As far as the specification of M is concerned, we have learnt the following lesson. Some publicity-seeking, highly effective, politically motivated, violent attacks on non-innocents, nevertheless, are acts of terrorism and also human rights violations by virtue of features inherent in them (and, therefore, independent of context). For example, the politically motivated practice in the apartheid years of some ANC supporters (if not ANC members as such) of killing those who were collaborating with the institutions of apartheid by pouring petrol on their bodies and setting them alight was surely terrorism of this kind,[26] as was the widespread torture of Sikh terrorists at the hands of security personnel in the Punjab in India between 1985 and 1992.[27] Moreover, some politically motivated lethal attacks on non-innocents that are grossly disproportionate, ineffective and/or unnecessary – and, therefore, violations of the right to life – are forms of terrorism, e.g., assassinating (morally culpable) political leaders in well-ordered (non-totalitarian) states at peace in order to terrorize the public and/or other leaders. These points concerning the types and/or

---

[26] See entries on 'necklacing' in B. McKendrick and W. Hoffmann (eds), *People and Violence in South Africa*, Cape Town: Oxford University Press, 1990.

[27] It should be noted that the state's terror was itself a response to terror. Tens of thousands lost their lives at the hands of Sikh terrorists during this period. For a detailed discussion of the period, see K. Dhillon, *Police and Politics in India: Colonial Concepts, Democratic Compulsions: Indian Police 1947–2002*, New Delhi: Manohar, 2005, chap. 12.

proportionality, necessity and effectiveness of violence go some way towards providing the needed specification of M in our definition by drawing attention to violent attacks on non-innocents that constitute human rights violations.[28]

Accordingly, let us offer the following specification of M. By definition, M is a type of violent action that constitutes a human rights violation in context. Some such violent actions, such as torture, are human rights violations irrespective of context, i.e., irrespective of whether they are performed during peacetime, under a state of emergency or in a theatre of war, and irrespective of whether they are directed at military combatants, human rights violators, revolutionaries or any other category of persons. On the other hand, some such violent actions might constitute human rights violations in one context but not another, e.g., shooting dead a member of the armed services in peacetime as opposed to in a theatre of war.

We now have a definition of terrorism, including a (rough) specification of the targets of terrorism (specification of X) and the methods of terrorism (specification of M).

At this stage of proceedings, our definition demarcates many, if not most, terrorist actions both from non-violent actions, and from violent actions that are not terrorist actions. Unfortunately, the definition is still incomplete by virtue of leaving a degree of indeterminacy, including in relation to legitimate types of violent attacks (M) and also in relation to legitimate targets of violent attacks (X), e.g., specification of the category of human rights violators. However, this is to be expected if we grant, as it seems we must, that the concept of terrorism is somewhat vague. Moreover, it has the consequence that there is some room for us to be stipulative in relation to types and targets of violent acts, in particular.

Granted that there is this room for stipulation, we need to determine what purposes would be served by this or that stipulative definition of terrorism (or definitional element thereof). I suggest that an important purpose in defining terrorism is to render it a serious crime; a serious crime in terms of both domestic and international law. Here I am assuming that the notion of crime in play is (at least) that of a serious form of moral wrongdoing, objectively considered. (Obviously, crime is also a form of unlawful action.) So murder is a serious crime, but shoplifting typically is not and neither are homosexual acts between consenting adults. Shoplifting is not a sufficiently serious form of moral wrongdoing to count as a serious crime, and homosexuality fails the test of objectivity (albeit some people believe it is a serious form of moral wrongdoing).

---

[28] For purposes of simplification I am categorizing issues concerning the inherent type of violence together with issues concerning proportionality, necessity and effectiveness.

However, we need to keep in mind that there is a distinction between the concept of a serious crime and the concept of a morally justifiable act. Accordingly, there is the conceptual possibility of some action being both a serious crime and morally justifiable. Thus, as I argue in Chapter 6, torture is a serious crime; however, torture might be morally justifiable in some extreme circumstances. The point is that defining terrorism in such a way as to render it a serious crime (or at least an act that ought to be a serious crime) does not settle the question as to whether or not it is morally justifiable (at least in all circumstances). Naturally, since the criminal law tracks morality, the fact that some kind of act, e.g., murder or torture, is a serious crime implies that *in general* – indeed, in all but the most extreme circumstances – it is morally unjustified.

So my suggestion is that we should further demarcate terrorist actions by insisting that they are violent acts that are, or, more precisely, should be, criminalized. Accordingly, as a preliminary, we should trawl through the statute books, human rights charters, etc., of *relevant* jurisdictions and identify the justifiably accepted – and *de facto* more or less universally accepted – set of serious violent crimes against the person, such as murder, torture, grievous bodily harm, rape and kidnapping. (Jurisdictions that are not relevant would include totalitarian states and other nation-states that are beyond the pale.)

This initial *long* list of existing serious violent crimes that are justifiably serious crimes is then cross-tabulated with our set of defining features and additional criteria of terrorist actions to generate a new (shorter) list of violent actions. This shorter list constitutes our initial set of terrorist actions; however, it should be added to if, and when, other violent crimes are justifiably legislated against as violent crimes, and meet the other criteria for being terrorist actions. Accordingly, I recommend that our above definition of terrorism be augmented by a fourth condition, namely, that the violent actions in question be ones that ought to be criminalized.

The final definition of terrorism is, therefore, as follows. Terrorism is a political or military strategy that:

1 consists in deliberately using violence against X and/or deliberately using violence of type M;
2 consists of violent actions that ought to be criminalized;
3 is a means of terrorizing the members of some social or political group in order to achieve political or military purposes;
4 relies on the violence receiving a high degree of publicity, at least to the extent necessary to engender widespread fear in the target political or social group.

NB: In the above definition, X is someone who is not a military combatant, human rights violator or revolutionary, and M is a type of violent action that constitutes a human rights violation in context.

As noted above, my strategy for identifying terrorist actions consists in drawing up an initial, but relatively comprehensive, list of violent crimes that are justifiably violent crimes, and then applying the criteria in the definition to these crimes to yield the desired set of terrorist actions. Let me refer to this as an indirect strategy for defining terrorist acts. This indirect strategy is somewhat conservative in that in practice it would consist in applying a set of criteria to an existing (and evolving) set of (justifiable) serious crimes of violence against the person to generate a list of terrorist acts that are crimes that most people in most jurisdictions will be strongly inclined to accept as such. This conservatism is a virtue in the context of trying to get international agreement as to what constitutes an act of terrorism. And the awareness of this virtue is principally what is motivating the conservative character of the indirect strategy. However, the conservatism of the strategy is also, of course, a vice. It may be that a number of acts that ought to be characterized as terrorist acts will not be so characterized by this strategy because they do not have at their core a violent crime against the person, or because there is cross-jurisdictional dispute as what ought to constitute a violent crime, or because there is dispute in relation to the application of the criteria in my definition to what is agreed justifiably to be a violent crime.

This indirect strategy is not tantamount to the definition in terms of targeting innocents or the definition in terms of non-combatants. For as we saw above, and speaking generally, the definition in terms of innocents is too restrictive. Accordingly, there are forms of terrorism that do not target innocents which, nevertheless, are serious crimes (or ought to be), e.g., torturing revolutionary activists. And, again generally speaking, the definition in terms of non-combatants is too permissive. Accordingly, there are forms of violence directed at certain categories of non-combatants (for the purpose of inducing fear in some target population, etc.) which are not serious crimes (or ought not to be), e.g., shooting administrators engaged in planning and implementing a policy of ethnic cleansing. (See Chapter 2 for more detail on this.)

Nevertheless, in generating this (shortened) list of violent crimes, we are in part endorsing a set of moral principles that underpin the legal definitions of the crimes in question. Thus, murder is a crime precisely because it involves the unjustified, deliberate killing of a non-attacker. Moreover, such moral principles include some of the moral principles invoked by the definitions of terrorism in terms of (respectively) innocents and non-combatants, e.g., that it is morally wrong to attack someone who is both defenceless and unable to attack you.

Our indirect strategy for defining terrorism is not offering a legal – as opposed to moral – definition of terrorism. In the deployment of the indirect strategy a terrorist act is not, thereby, *defined* as a certain kind of unlawful act. Rather, we are simply using the law in order to construct our list, and doing so for two reasons. First, the law has over a long period of time (at least in most relevant jurisdictions) established a set of violent acts as serious crimes. So it constitutes a well-established, time-tested resource. Second, one of the main purposes of our indirect strategy of definition is to try to ensure that terrorist acts are generally regarded, and established in law, as serious *crimes.*[29]

By the lights of our indirect strategy for defining terrorism, roughly speaking, terrorism is a violent crime performed as a means of terrorizing some social or political group in order to achieve political or military purposes. (And we can add that to achieve these purposes it relies on the violence receiving a high degree of publicity.) Moreover, salient forms of terrorism target the innocent and/or non-combatants or, if not, tend to be grossly disproportionate attacks on non-innocents and/or combatants. Further, salient forms of terrorism do not include violent attacks on the political leaders and security personnel of totalitarian states.

So the indirect strategy for defining terrorism does mark off the category of ordinary violent crimes in civil society that are not acts of terrorism from acts of terrorism. Further, by this method for defining terrorism, an ordinary civilian who justifiably kills in self-defence or in defence of the life of another is not engaged in terrorism since, motivations aside, such killing is not murder. So a further strength of the indirect strategy as it stands is that it marks off, as it needs to, many violent actions in civil society that are not crimes from acts of terrorism.

On the other hand, the indirect strategy for defining terrorism, as elaborated thus far, *might* not seem to distinguish between terrorism and legitimate acts of war. Combatants in a conventional war kill and maim other soldiers without their actions being either crimes or justifiable acts of self-defence or defence of the lives of others (as these justifiable acts are understood in civil society); and combatants in a conventional war kill and maim other soldiers in part as a means to terrorize the enemy in the service of the political end of winning the war, but without their

---

[29]   Nor is the definition legal in the related sense that if offers to define what the law ought to be, except in the trivial sense that if attempting to establish a specific set of violent acts as unlawful, we are necessarily trying to determine what the law ought to be in this area.

violent acts being acts of terrorism. However, this is a misunderstanding of the definition; the definition deals with violent acts in the context of war and, specifically, uses the notions of a *military* combatant, of a rights violation *in context* (including the context of a theatre of war) and of a crime that includes war crimes. At any rate, we need now explicitly to attend to terrorist acts conducted in theatres of war.

Here, once again, we can help ourselves to the notion of a crime – or, more precisely, a crime that is justifiably a crime – albeit in this instance violent actions committed in theatres of war that under international criminal law are crimes, i.e., war crimes. War crimes, broadly understood, include: (1) so-called crimes against peace that violate the principles of the *ius ad bellum*, e.g., embarking on a war of aggression; (2) 'war crimes' in the sense of violations of the laws of war in relation to the combatants, e.g., using biological agents against enemy soldiers; and (3) so-called 'crimes against humanity', which are atrocities committed against civilians or non-combatants, e.g., ethnic cleansing. As is the case with ordinary crimes committed in civil society, war crimes are a legal category constructed in large part on the basis of generally accepted moral principles, e.g., the principles of proportionality and necessity.

Assuming that the notion of a war crime is reasonably clear, and a list of such legally defined crimes is available, let us adopt an analogue of the procedure we followed in relation to terrorist acts performed in civil society.

In the context of war, the following are necessary conditions for being an act of terrorism: (i) consisting at its core of a violent attack on person(s), and (ii) being a member of a set of well-established (in international law) war crimes (of violence), including murder, torture, rape (and various other serious violent crimes) – or at least being a member of the set of such war crimes as it ought to be. Having partially defined the sphere of terrorist acts by helping ourselves to an already demarcated category, namely, violent war crimes (or, more precisely, violent war crimes that are justifiably war crimes), we then mark the distinction between terrorist acts and the genus of which they are a species, namely, violent crimes, by recourse to other means, including the above-described defining features, e.g., that they are performed to terrorize some social or political group in the service of a political or military end, and additional criteria, e.g., that they target non-combatants.

Unfortunately, while the latter goes some way in enabling us to mark off acts of terrorism in the context of war both from violence which is not a crime, and from other war crimes that are not terrorism, it does not go far enough, for there is dispute in relation to what ought to count as a war crime. There is, of course, also dispute as to what ought to count as a crime in domestic criminal law in civil society; however, in well-ordered liberal-democratic societies (and most authoritarian states, for that matter), there is a longstanding and well-established list of violent crimes, including murder, rape, assault, kidnapping, and so on. The corresponding list in the case of war crimes is less well established. Nevertheless, there is a fair degree of agreement in relation to war crimes; the list of war crimes under international law is, after all, a list. Moreover, it is a list in large part derived from domestic criminal law, e.g., murder and rape are war crimes. Here the presumption appears to be that a violent act that is a crime in civil society is also a crime in a theatre of war, unless the act is directed at an enemy combatant (and, of course, even if it is directed at enemy combatants it *might* still be a war crime). Accordingly, in wartime, violent acts directed at non-combatants are crimes. This is so notwithstanding that in war, but not in civil society, it is allowed that civilian casualties can be the unintended consequence of attacks on the enemy.

I have suggested an indirect route to the definition of terrorist actions, namely, to begin with a list of well-established violent crimes and then: (1) determine whether these violent crimes are justifiably crimes; (2) add further conditions, including political motivations not present in most violent crimes; and (3) distinguish, as in law, between (in effect) terrorism in civil society and terrorism in wartime. Naturally, this presupposes that the distinction between civil society and wartime can adequately be drawn. It also presupposes that principles are available adequately to demarcate war crimes from other acts of war that are not, and ought not to be, war crimes. Problematic as these distinctions are, the task of drawing them does not appear to be insuperable; for one thing, it is a task in relation to which much progress has already been made.

It is important at this point to note an additional theatre of conflict; additional, that is, to theatres of war and to attacks within civil society (understood as a well-ordered nation-state). The context in question is civil society, but civil society in which the political violence taking place has led to a substantial breakdown of law and order, and typically led to the imposition of a state of emergency, e.g., Northern Ireland in the 1970s. It is also important to distinguish between theatres of war involving armed conflict between nation-states and theatres of war involving armed conflict between a nation-state and a non-state actor, e.g., the armed conflict between Israel and Hezbollah. Internal armed conflict under a state of emergency and external armed conflict with a non-state actor give rise to special problems. I discuss these contexts of armed conflict in detail in Chapter 5.

Conclusion

In this chapter I have argued against definitions of terrorism couched in terms of attacks on innocents and ones in terms of attacks on non-combatants. Building on the strengths and weaknesses of these defective definitions, I have constructed a somewhat different definition. Notably, this definition contains a clause specifying that terrorist actions be actions that ought to be criminalized. I have also suggested a strategy for identifying such actions, namely, consulting existing laws against violent actions and applying the criteria for terrorist actions in my definition to these violent crimes.

One consequence of this indirect strategy for defining terrorism is that identifying terrorism becomes to some extent a legal work in progress. As the definitions and list of, for example, war crimes (as it ought to be) are refined and agreed to, so what counts as an act of terrorism will change and become, it is hoped, more adequate.

Another consequence is that it will always in principle be possible that a putative act of terrorism is morally justifiable; for an act to be unlawful is one thing, for it to be morally unjustifiable is another thing. On the other hand, the criminal law (including international criminal law) in particular tracks morality, or ought to do so. Accordingly, in general, it is less likely that a given act of terrorism is morally justifiable when the legally supported definition of terrorism is well founded (and, correspondingly, it is more likely when the legally supported definition of terrorism is not well founded). This issue is dealt with more fully in the next chapter.

A final point pertains to the political character of terrorism. In general it is a bad idea to criminalize morally justifiable actions, since it is both unfair and likely to bring the law into disrepute. However, politics inevitably involves competing conceptions of what is morally justifiable and what is not. Accordingly, one drawback to defining terrorism simply in terms of what is morally justifiable and what is not is the lack of agreement on this. There is often no agreement on the justice of the ends pursued by terrorists; and even when the ends are accepted as just ones, there is often no agreement on whether or not violence is justified in the service of those ends. Nevertheless, there is a large degree of agreement in relation to the moral desirability of some ends, e.g., eradication of absolute poverty, and in relation to the moral unacceptability of some violent acts, e.g., the bombing of children in marketplaces.

Moreover, the existing and evolving domestic and international criminal law is the concrete embodiment of what moral agreement there has been and is, and what moral agreement there might come to be. Further, criminal law is, at least in principle, enforceable. Accordingly, it makes sense to focus our definitional efforts on trying to develop a possibly narrow, but suitably morally informed and legally supported, list of types of terrorist act; a list that might be enshrined in domestic and international law and, therefore, acceptable to a wide range of, if not all, jurisdictions. (Here, again, I exclude totalitarian and other 'beyond the pale' states.) If this were to be achieved, then there would be a way forward to eradicate at least those forms of terrorism thus identified.

3

Terrorism and Collective Responsibility

As we have seen, the methods of Al-Qaeda, Hamas, Hezbollah and other like groups involve the intentional killing of those who are not military combatants, rights violators or revolutionaries, and are not constrained by the *ius in bello* principles of the proportionate use of force or use of minimally necessary force. Indeed, Al-Qaeda's aim appears to be to maximize the loss of human life amongst 'enemy' populations. In short, the methods of these terrorist groups are an affront to accepted moral principles governing the use of deadly force in conflict situations; these groups are engaged in morally unjustified terrorism.

As far as the terrorism of Al-Qaeda, Hamas, Hezbollah and like groups is concerned, most theorists agree that their methods are completely morally unjustified. However, it remains an open question whether this is so for *all* forms of terrorism. The question that arises now is: under what circumstances, if any, could terrorism be morally justified? Here we need to be scrupulously careful, since the moral justification for terrorism, or lack thereof, turns crucially on the definition of terrorism in play. For example, if terrorism is defined in terms of the killing of (unspecified) innocents, then it is unlikely that any forms of terrorism will turn out to be morally justified. However, this is not the definition that we have proffered. We will return to definitional issues later in the chapter.

In relation to the issue of the moral justification for terrorism, a number of spurious arguments have been put forward. I will briefly consider these before turning to more plausible arguments.

One form of moral justification for terrorism relies on the claim that so-called 'innocent' victims of some terrorist attacks are not in fact innocent, notwithstanding the fact that they might not be military combatants, rights violators or revolutionaries. Specifically, the victims are regarded as guilty by virtue of their *collective moral responsibility* for the injustices the terrorists are seeking to redress. I provide my own account of this notion below. Here I emphasize that if the notion of *collective moral responsibility* is to have any legitimate justificatory role, then it cannot be equated with the *morality of collective identity*.[1] (Narveson[2] and Rosenbaum[3] in effect conflate these two notions.[4])

According to the morality of collective identity, the members of some oppressor or enemy group are guilty purely by virtue of membership of that national, racial, ethnic or religious group. So a white South African who opposed apartheid was, nevertheless, guilty in the eyes of extremist anti-apartheid groups simply by virtue of being white. All Americans are guilty of oppressing Muslims simply by virtue of being American citizens, according to some extremist Al-Qaeda pronouncements.

The morality of collective identity determines the moral guilt of a person not by the actions that he or she as an individual chooses to do or not do, but by virtue of his or her membership of some racial, ethnic or national group.

As such, the morality of collective identity elevates the category of membership of racial, ethnic and national groups above the category of individual human moral agency when it comes to the ascription of moral responsibility; a person is a wrongdoer – and thus liable to lethal attack by way of response – not by virtue of what he or she as an individual has deliberately done, but rather by virtue of (more or less) unchosen aspects of his or her collective identity, e.g., being white or black or Jewish or American.

This collective identity approach to collective moral responsibility is inconsistent with the notions of moral responsibility (individual or collective) that underpin both common morality and criminal justice systems, whether they be contemporary, historical, western or Islamic. It is best regarded as a piece of ideology rather than as a serious intellectual standpoint worthy of analysis and critique.

In addition to this crude collective identity approach to collective moral responsibility, there are various other somewhat more philosophically

---

[1]   On this kind of issue, see P. Gilbert, *New Terror, New Wars*, Edinburgh: Edinburgh University Press, 2003.

[2]   J. Narveson, 'Pacifism and terrorism: why we should condemn both', *International Journal of Applied Philosophy* 17(2), 2003, pp. 157–72.

[3]   A.S. Rosenbaum, 'On terrorism and the just war', *International Journal of Applied Philosophy* 17(2), 2003, p. 6.

[4]   Rosenbaum (ibid., p. 10) mentions an 'older form of terrorism', including the ANC, as a possible exception to his account of modern terrorism, but then fails to see the implications of the existence of such groups for his blanket denouncement of terrorism.

sophisticated collectivist accounts. Such collectivists offer accounts according to which individuals, especially members of national, ethnic and religious groups, can be held responsible for the outcomes of the actions of those groups, even where the individuals in question did not contribute to those outcomes. Thus David Cooper holds that some collective entity can be morally responsible for some outcome, even though no individual member of that entity was even partly morally responsible.[5] Peter French also holds this view.[6] Moreover, these theorists maintain that such collective entities are moral agents, and therefore can be legitimately praised and blamed, rewarded and punished. I have argued against these collectivist conceptions elsewhere.[7]

Here I simply note that in the context of conflict situations, such as war and terrorism, these collectivist theories bring with them a significant problem. Unless we are to assume that collective agents are purely epiphenomenal entities that can be punished or rewarded without any causal effect on their individual members – a view French, for example, explicitly rejects[8] – then the way is clear to harm individuals for wrongs that they did not contribute to, so long as those individuals are members of collective entities that have done wrong. This goes a long way to providing a theoretical justification for Al-Qaeda's terrorist attacks of 9/11. For if we assume that the US government policies in relation to Israel, Saudi Arabia, and so on, are morally unacceptable, then the way is evidently clear to kill US citizens in the name of retaliating against the unacceptable US policies. It is precisely this kind of theoretical justification that an individualist like Narveson is at pains to reject. In this I am at one with him, for the consequences of such collectivist accounts are very unpalatable indeed.

For these and other reasons, these forms of collectivism ought to be rejected. Moreover, there are other theoretical or quasi-theoretical views that are similarly unacceptable. One such view rests on the claim of causal inter-relatedness.[9] If we take harm as including both direct and indirect

---

[5]   D.E. Cooper, 'Collective responsibility', *Philosophy* 43, 1968, pp. 258–68. See also M. Gilbert, 'Collective guilt and collective guilt feelings', *Journal of Ethics* 6(2), 2002, pp. 115–43.
[6]   P.A. French, *Collective and Corporate Responsibility*, New York: Columbia University Press, 1984. For criticisms, see L. May, 'Vicarious agency and corporate responsibility', *Philosophical Studies* 43(1), 1983, pp. 69–82 and S. Miller, *Social Action: A Teleological Account*, Cambridge: Cambridge University Press, 2001, chap. 5.
[7]   Miller, *Social Action*, chaps 5 and 8.
[8]   *Collective and Corporate Responsibility*, p. 110.
[9]   For a detailed treatment of causal inter-relation and its moral significance, see K. Graham, *Practical Reasoning in a Social World: How We Act Together*, Cambridge: Cambridge University Press, 2002, chap. 2.

harm, then, for example, a US citizen might be held to be responsible for the deaths of innocent villagers if the citizen paid taxes that were used to train a US pilot who bombed the Taliban-controlled village in question. Clearly, moral responsibility cannot be ascribed merely on the basis of possibly very indirect, entirely unforeseen, and probably unforeseeable, causal contributions. Moral responsibility implies agency, and agency implies intention, ends, and the like. Permissive causal accounts of moral responsibility are as unpalatable as ones ascribing moral responsibility on the basis of membership of the group.

An alternative conception to these somewhat far-fetched views has been provided by Burleigh Taylor Wilkins.[10] Wilkins is an individualist who nevertheless believes that terrorism can in some instances be morally justified, in part on the basis of group membership.

Roughly speaking, Wilkins's key idea is that the members of a group can be held strictly liable for the policies of the group in an analogous manner to that in which employers can be held liable for the actions of their employees, notwithstanding the fact that the employers did not contribute to these actions of their employees.

I have two fundamental problems with Wilkins's view. Firstly, employers and their employees are functioning in a highly structured and legally regulated organizational setting in which they in effect undertake vicarious and strict liability in relation to a specified range of their employees' actions. This is not analogous simply to being a member of an ethnic or religious or even national group.

Secondly, the actions for which an employer (in effect) agrees to be vicariously strictly liable would not typically include massive rights violations on the part of their employees; what employer would agree to be held liable for these? Moreover, the nature or extent of liability would not typically include giving up one's life.

I conclude that Wilkins has not made out the case for strict liability in the very different context of war and terrorism, and his account is in any case far too permissive.

So much for inadequate conceptions of collective moral responsibility. Our main question is: under what circumstances, if any, could terrorism be morally justified? However, before directly addressing this question, we need to get clearer about the general moral justification for the use of deadly force.

---

[10] B.T. Wilkins, *Terrorism and Collective Responsibility*, London: Routledge, 1992, chap. 7. See also L. May, *The Morality of Groups: Collective Responsibility, Group-Based Harm, and Corporate Rights*, Notre Dame, IN: University of Notre Dame Press, 1987.

Moral Justification for the Use of Deadly Force

In relation to moral rights, two sets of distinctions are salient here. Human rights can be distinguished from institutional rights, and negative rights from positive rights. Human rights, as opposed to institutional rights, are rights possessed by virtue of properties one has *qua* human being.[11] So the right to life is a human right.[12] By contrast, the moral (and legal) right a police officer might have to arrest an offender is an institutional right. Negative rights are rights one has not to be interfered with by others. So the rights not to be killed or not to have one's freedom restricted are negative rights. By contrast, the right to have sufficient food to keep one alive is a positive right; it is a right to assistance from others, if such assistance is required and can be provided.

As is well known, both of these distinctions are problematic in various ways. Indeed, the very notion of a moral right is itself problematic. Nevertheless, for the purposes of this chapter, I am going to assume that there are human rights, and that these rights include at least some of the ones typically referred to as positive rights.

Moreover, I am also assuming the following properties of human rights. Human rights generate concomitant duties for others, e.g., A's right to life generates a duty on the part of B not to kill A. And human rights are justifiably enforceable, e.g., if A has a right not to be killed by B, and if B attempts to kill A, then B can legitimately be prevented from killing A by means of coercive force, including, if necessary, by the use of deadly force. The property of enforceability attaching to human rights reflects their strength, and that of the concomitant duty not to infringe them; infringing human rights is a very serious matter indeed – hence compliance with human rights is, or ought to be, enforced, unlike in the case of many other moral requirements.

While there is an enforceable human right to life, killing another person can only be morally justified in very restricted circumstances. The basic such circumstance is that of self-defence.[13] However, self-defence is not the only justification for taking the life of another person. It is widely

---

[11] For one recent account of human rights that is consistent with the view on offer here, see J. Griffin, 'First steps in an account of human rights', *European Journal of Philosophy* 9(3), 2001, pp. 306–27.

[12] Various attempt has been made to identify and list the set of human rights, notably in the United Nations Declaration of Human Rights of 1948, but also – and from an Islamic perspective – the Cairo Declaration on Human Rights in Islam of 1990. Human rights are by no means simply a western affair.

[13] See my 'Killing in self-defence', *Public Affairs Quarterly* 7(4), 1993, pp. 325–40.

accepted that each of us has the right to kill in defence of the lives of others. I am morally entitled to kill someone attempting to kill my spouse, if this is the only means of prevention.

Indeed, some roles, such as that of police officer or soldier, are such that the occupant of the role might be morally *obliged* to kill in the defence of the lives of others. Here the moral rights and duties constitutive of the role are derived in large part from the moral point or end of the role, e.g., to protect the lives of citizens of the state in question. Note that any such end is itself subject to moral scrutiny and evaluation. If the end in question – or its pursuit in some context – turned out to be morally unacceptable, then the putative rights and duties derived from it may not in fact be *moral* rights and duties, or at least may not be so in that context. So soldiers engaged in a war of conquest on behalf of a psychopathic authoritarian leadership might cease to have a right to kill enemy soldiers, or an obligation to protect their current leaders. Such was the case with Hitler in the Second World War.

Elsewhere I have argued that killing in order to defend one's own life, or the life of another, is morally justified on the grounds that each of us has a right to life and (under certain conditions) the right to life of attackers is suspended (as opposed to being forfeited).[14] We are entitled to defend that right to life by killing an attacker under three conditions.[15] Firstly, the attacker is intentionally trying to kill someone – either oneself or another person – and will succeed if we do not intervene. We are not entitled to shoot dead an attacker whom we know is threatening us only with (say) a replica of a gun. Secondly, we have no way of preserving our own or the other person's life other than by killing the attacker. For example, we are not able to flee to safety. Thirdly, and more problematically, our attacker does not have a decisive, morally justifiable reason for trying to kill. For example, it may be that a legally appointed executioner has a decisive morally justifiable reason for carrying out the death penalty in the case of a serial killer, but that the serial killer does not have a decisive morally justifiable reason for trying to kill the executioner in self-defence, supposing the opportunity arose.

Having outlined an account of killing in self-defence or in defence of the life of others, let me now consider a different, or at least expanded, kind of moral justification for killing, namely, killing in defence of rights other than the right to life.

[14]   Ibid.
[15]   J.J. Thomson offers a more restricted set of conditions for justified killing in self-defence. See her 'Self-defence', *Philosophy & Public Affairs* 20(4), 1991, pp. 283–310. For criticisms see my 'Judith Jarvis Thomson on killing in self-defence', *Australian Journal of Professional and Applied Ethics* 3(2), 2001, pp. 69–75.

In speaking of killing in defence of rights other than the right to life, one would obviously not want to include *all* moral rights, or at least *all violations* of all moral rights. For example, property rights are arguably moral rights, but for (say) a police officer to kill someone to prevent him stealing a handbag would be morally unacceptable. So the question becomes: are there any moral rights, apart from the right to life, the protection of which would justify the use of deadly force? Candidates for such rights might include a right not to be severely physically or psychologically damaged. Perhaps rape, serious child molestation and grievous bodily harm are actions the prevention of which might justify use of deadly force. Candidates would also include the right to various freedoms, including freedom of thought, and freedom of individual and – especially in the context of war – of *collective* action, e.g., national self-government.

What of positive rights? Henry Shue has argued for the existence of what he terms basic moral rights.[16] Such basic moral rights are not restricted to so-called 'negative' rights; rather, they include some so-called 'positive' rights, e.g., the right to subsistence. Moreover, these positive rights include ones that go beyond the right to life. For example, a person has a positive right not to live in a permanent condition of serious malnutrition or debilitating disease, if these conditions are alterable. Accordingly, deadly force might be justified in some circumstances in which someone is refraining from providing for the basic material needs of someone else.[17]

Let us now consider a simple example to test our intuitions for the claim that sometimes the use of deadly force to enforce positive rights is morally justified.

Consider a destitute African person who is dying of HIV/AIDS, and who goes to a pharmaceutical company demanding drugs to enable him to live. Assume further that the pharmaceutical company is a state-subsidized entity, which is subsidized because it has as one of its clearly stated institutional purposes to provide cheap life-preserving drugs to the needy, albeit within the parameters of commercial viability. When the AIDS sufferer is refused the drugs, on the grounds that he must pay for the drugs at a high price – rather than an affordable lower price – he

---

[16]   H. Shue, *Basic Rights: Subsistence, Affluence, and US Foreign Policy*, 2nd edn, Princeton: Princeton University Press, 1996.

[17]   This claim is not be confused with the familiar claim and counter-claim as to whether there is or is not any moral difference between acts and omissions; nor should it be confused with the claim and counter-claim as to whether killing and letting die stand to one another as harming and not aiding in cases in which less than life is at stake.

threatens to kill, one by one, the owner-managers of the company responsible for the high price, unless and until he is provided with the drug at an affordable price. Assume further that although the owner-managers (druggists) know it would be commercially viable to sell the drug at the affordable lower price, they engage in the corrupt practice of selling it at the high price in order to ensure the resulting enormous profits for themselves. Assume, too, that providing this AIDS sufferer with the drugs would not be at the expense of some other (more affluent) AIDS sufferer, and that the druggists know this and know that the AIDS sufferer will die unless he is provided with the drugs (and the druggist is the only practicable source of the drugs). Finally, assume that the only options available to the AIDS sufferer are allowing himself to die or threatening to kill the druggists.

Intuitively, the AIDS sufferer's action seems morally justified, given that this action was the only way to preserve his life, since in this corrupt society there is no legal means of ensuring the company meets its obligations. For he had a positive right to be assisted, and the 'bystander' (or rather, 'bystanders', but to simplify I will use the singular term), i.e., the owner-manager druggist, was refraining from carrying out his institutional and moral duty to respect that right.

The druggist has freely undertaken an institutional role in the state-subsidized company to assist AIDS sufferers, and in effect is paid a salary to do so. He has thereby intentionally put himself under an institutional obligation to assist, and therefore the AIDS sufferer has a reasonable expectation that he will be assisted. Moreover, given the threat to the life of the AIDS sufferer, this institutional obligation is also a weighty moral obligation; so the druggist has put himself under a weighty moral obligation to assist. Indeed, the AIDS sufferer now has a moral right to be assisted. Further, there are no countervailing moral reasons for the druggist not to assist; indeed, his only reason for not doing so is greed. Accordingly, and in the absence of any intervention on the part of anyone else (including the police), the AIDS sufferer is entitled to enforce the druggist's obligation to provide him with the drugs. So the AIDS sufferer is entitled to threaten the life of the druggist in order to cause him to discharge his obligation to assist.

Evidently, this kind of case involving the AIDS sufferer is analogous to those involving negative rights, such as the right not to be killed, or the right not to have one's freedom interfered with. Moreover, the AIDS sufferer's action would be morally justified in some cases in which less than a human life was at stake. This would be so, for example, if the AIDS sufferer could survive without the drugs, but would live a life of intolerable suffering as a consequence of his affliction.

So deadly force can be used, at least in principle, to enforce some positive rights, including presumably rights to subsistence, as well as to enforce negative rights, such as freedom or the right not to be killed.

Here I am assuming the usual principles of proportionate and minimally necessary force; deadly force should be used only as a last resort and loss of life kept to a minimum. So if, for example, the AIDS sufferer could cause the government to intervene on his behalf, or cause the managers to hand over the drug by mere threats, then he should do so.

Moreover, as is the case with negative rights, third parties – at least in principle – have rights, and indeed duties, to use deadly force to ensure that positive rights such as subsistence rights are respected.

Consider a modified version of the above HIV/AIDS scenario. In this modified version the AIDS sufferer is a young African boy dying in his bed, and it is his father who threatens the pharmaceutical managers with deadly force – indeed, he kills one of the owner-managers to get the drugs to save his son. Moreover, the father's action would be morally justified in some cases in which less than life was at stake. This would be so if – as in the previous version of this scenario – the AIDS sufferer could survive without the drugs, but would live a life of intolerable suffering as a consequence of his affliction.

I conclude that under some conditions third parties might be morally entitled to use deadly force to enforce duties to assist.

Civilian Immunity and Human Rights Violations

In this section I want to explore the moral notion of civilian immunity in relation to the category of civilians who are morally responsible for ongoing and widespread serious rights violations. The specific category I want to focus on is the category of non-life-threatening rights violations. In the section following this one, I turn to a category of civilians who are morally culpable, but who are not morally responsible for *actions* that constitute rights violations; their sins are sins of omission rather than sins of commission. It will turn out that these two categories overlap in so far as there are members of civilian groups who are guilty of certain non-life-threatening rights violations by virtue of culpably refraining from assisting the rights bearers in question. However, for ease of exposition, my focus in this section will be on rights violations that are acts, as opposed to omissions.

In a morally justified conventional war, colonial or such-like war of liberation, or internal armed struggle against an oppressive domestic government, enemy *combatants* can be legitimate targets on at least two grounds other than immediate self-defence. Firstly, they might be a sub-set of the *rights violators* in respect of whom the war or armed struggle is being fought. This would be the case in a war of self-defence against an enemy hell-bent on genocide, e.g., the largely Tutsi army fighting against the Hutu army and its militias in Rwanda in 1994.[18]

Secondly, enemy combatants are legitimate targets if they are attempting to *enforce* a policy of rights violations. For example, the government in apartheid South Africa embarked on a policy of removal of so-called 'black spots': that is, moving black people out of designated white areas into impoverished black 'homelands'.[19] This policy was a form of so-called racial or ethnic 'cleansing', and as such was a violation of human rights.[20] However, the role of police and military personnel was one of enforcement of the policy; the policy *in itself* did not necessarily consist of the use of coercive or deadly force. For it is conceivable that such a policy could have been implemented by some means other than coercive force, e.g., by fraud. Similar points could be made in relation to the Israeli government's policy of ethnic cleansing in relation to Palestinians.

Accordingly, civilians – as opposed to military combatants – may be legitimate targets if (but not necessarily only if): (a) they are morally responsible for *the human rights violations*, or threatened rights violations, that justify the waging of an armed struggle; and/or (b) they are morally responsible for the *enforcement* of rights violations.

Such civilians would include politicians, or other non-military leaders, who are responsible for the rights violations, or the enforcement thereof, in the sense that in the context of a chain of command they were the relevant *authority* that directed that the human rights violations be carried out, or that they be enforced.[21] Such civilians would also include persons who, while not necessarily part of any formal chain of command, nevertheless, were responsible for the rights violations (or the enforcement thereof) in that they planned them, and saw to it that other persons performed the rights violations (or the enforcement thereof). Here, the latter are instruments, but not necessarily subordinates, of the former. The former are the principal agents without necessarily being in authority. For example, an ethnic leader might pay an army of mercenaries to engage in ethnic cleansing without being in a relation of authority to the mercenaries.

---

[18]   See F. Keane, *Season of Blood: A Rwandan Journey*, London: Viking, 1995.

[19]   F. Wilson and M. Ramphele, *Uprooting Poverty: The South African Challenge*, Cape Town: University of Cape Town Press, 1988.

[20]   The policy did not necessarily, or in fact, involve large-scale murder of the persons being removed, as happened in, for example, Bosnia in the days of Milošević and his Bosnian Serb allies.

[21]   J.G. Murphy, 'The killing of the innocent', *Monist* 57(4), 1973, pp. 532f.

I take it that civilians who belong to either of the above resulting four categories (authorities or other principal agents of the rights violations, or of the enforcement of the rights violations) are – at least in principle – legitimate targets.

Thus far I have distinguished between rights violations and the enforcement of rights violations. Moreover, earlier I distinguished between positive rights and negative rights, and between life-threatening rights violations and non-life-threatening rights violations.[22] Some violations of negative rights, such as the right to freedom, might not be life-threatening. And some violations of positive rights, such as the right to subsistence, might be life-threatening.

It is easy to see why the use of deadly force in response to life-threatening rights violations might be morally justified. However, the use of deadly force in response to non-life-threatening rights violations is more problematic – especially when such use of deadly force is on a scale properly describable as engaging in war. For it is typically assumed that life is more important than other goods to which people have rights. So it is harder to justify the use of deadly force in relation to non-life-threatening rights violations than it is in relation to the violation of life-threatening rights violations.

Accordingly, I will now address the question of the legitimacy of directing deadly force at a particular class of civilians, namely, persons responsible for non-life-threatening rights violations. So I am not speaking of persons responsible for life-threatening rights violations. Nor am I speaking of persons responsible for *enforcing* non-life-threatening rights violations (or for enforcing life-threatening rights violations).

The use of deadly force against persons responsible for life-threatening rights violations is typically self-defence or defence of the lives of others. (And in the case of life-threatening rights violations that are violations of positive rights, it is self-preservation, or preservation of the lives of others.) But what of the use of deadly force in response to non-life-threatening rights violations?

The use of deadly force in response to those who are *enforcing* non-life-threatening rights violations seems straightforward enough. For such enforcers are themselves using, or are threatening to use, deadly force in response to any attempt on the part of those whose rights are being

<hr>

[22] Elsewhere I have used a somewhat wider notion than that of life-threatening rights violations, namely, rights violations that constitute, or threaten, the destruction of the self, e.g., torturing someone to the point that they lose their mind but remain alive. This wider notion is actually the one I need here, but for purposes of simplification I will talk in terms of life-threatening rights violations.

violated to escape their fate. So the morally unjustified use of deadly force is being met with deadly force. This is not killing in self-defence; rather, it is killing in defence of rights other than the right to life. Nevertheless, it is the use of deadly force against combatants – combatants seeking to enforce non-life-threatening rights violations. And I take it that often in wars of conquest, military combatants fighting on behalf of the aggressor nation-state are seeking to enforce non-life-threatening rights violations, such as violations of the right to freedom, e.g., the right freely to perform various forms of collective political action. Accordingly, if the members of the state whose rights to free collective action are under threat were to cease to resist, then their lives would cease to be at risk.

At any rate, the use of deadly force against such combatants seems justified on the basis of the accumulated moral weight of two considerations: (1) the deadly force is used in order to bring about the cessation of non-life-threatening rights violations, or the removal of the threat thereof, e.g., national self-determination; and (2) the deadly force is used in response to the morally unjustified use of deadly force by the would-be enforcers of these non-life-threatening rights violations.

Moreover, in the light of our earlier discussion, the use of deadly force against civilians who have authority over such combatants enforcing rights violations, or with respect to whom the combatants are instruments, also seems morally justifiable, at least in principle.

However, this does not settle the question of whether it would be morally justifiable to use deadly force against civilians who are responsible for non-life-threatening rights violations, and yet who are not responsible for the enforcement of these rights violations. Consider in this connection public officials who plan and administer a policy of forced removals (racial or ethnic cleansing), but who might not have any role or authority in relation to the enforcement of the policy. Are such officials legitimate targets?

Here it is important to distinguish types of cases. The typical situation involves the existence of some *collective end*,[23] e.g., the removal of people from their homes to an impoverished tract of land, or the occupancy and control of some other nation-state.

Ends such as the removal of people from their homes to an impoverished tract of land, or the occupancy and control of some other nation-state, are collective ends, since their realization requires a large number of different individual persons to perform distinct tasks in the service of a common end; indeed, to occupy a variety of different institutional roles

---

[23]   In my *Social Action*, chap. 2 (*supra* note 6), I offer an account of the notion of a collective end.

in the service of a common end. There are planners, administrators, enforcers (combatants), leaders, and so on, engaged in a collective project, e.g., to dispossess a people, or to win a war of conquest. Given that the collective end in question constitutes a violation of rights (albeit it is non-life-threatening), the participants in this collective project are morally culpable; they are collectively morally responsible for wrongdoing.

As is the case with individual responsibility, we can distinguish three senses of *collective* responsibility. I do so in relation to *joint* actions.

Roughly speaking, two or more individuals perform a joint action if each of them intentionally performs an individual action, but does so with the true belief that in so doing they will jointly realize an end which each of them has, i.e., a collective end in the sense defined above.

Agents who perform a joint action are responsible for that action in the first sense of collective responsibility, namely, *natural* (collective) responsibility. Accordingly, to say that they are collectively responsible for the action is just to say that they performed the joint action. That is, they each had a collective end, each intentionally performed their contributory action, and each did so because each believed the other would perform his or her contributory action, and that therefore the collective end would be realized.

If the occupants of an institutional role (or roles) have an institutionally determined obligation to perform some joint action, then those individuals are collectively responsible for its performance, in our second sense of collectively responsibility. Here there is a *joint* institutional obligation to realize the collective end of the joint action in question. In addition, there is a set of derived *individual* obligations; each of the participating individuals has an individual obligation to perform his or her contributory action. (The derivation of these individual obligations relies on the fact that if each performs his or her contributory action, then it is probable that the collective end will be realized.)

What of the third and target sense of collective responsibility, collective *moral* responsibility? Collective moral responsibility for outcomes which are intended, or otherwise aimed at, is a species of joint responsibility. Accordingly, each agent is individually morally responsible, but conditionally on the others being individually morally responsible; and this interdependence in respect of moral responsibility exists because the action of each is performed in the service of a collective end. This account of one central kind of collective moral responsibility arises naturally out of the account of joint actions. It also parallels the notion of individual moral responsibility.

Thus we can make the following claim about collective moral responsibility: if agents are collectively – naturally or institutionally – responsible for the realization of an outcome, and if the outcome is morally significant, then – other things being equal – the agents are collectively morally responsible for that outcome, and can reasonably attract moral praise or blame, and (possibly) punishment or reward for bringing about the outcome.

Here we need to be more precise about what it is that agents who perform morally significant joint actions are collectively morally responsible for. Other things being equal, each agent who intentionally performs a morally significant *individual* action has *individual* moral responsibility for the action. So in the case of a morally significant joint action, each agent is *individually* morally responsible for performing *his or her contributory* action, and the *other* agents are *not* morally responsible for his or her individual contributory action. But, in addition, the contributing agents are *collectively* morally responsible for the outcome or *collective end* of their various contributory actions. To say that they are collectively morally responsible for bringing about this (collective) end is just to say that they are *jointly* morally responsible for it. So each agent is individually morally responsible for realizing this (collective) end, but conditionally on the others being individually morally responsible for realizing it as well.[24] Actually, the picture is more complicated than this, since each individual (say) military combatant is jointly morally responsible (with others) for a proximate collective end (say, winning a particular battle), which end is a means to the ultimate collective end (say, winning the war as such).

In many cases, enforcement is not only a means to the collective end – to the violation of non-life-threatening rights – it is integral to that end. This is obviously the case in wars of conquest. But it is also the case in our South African forcible-removal example. The policy of the elimination of black spots in apartheid South Africa was a policy that in part consisted of enforcement, i.e., of use of force, or the threat thereof. Therefore, non-enforcers such as public officials who planned and administered this policy are not only morally responsible (jointly with others) for the non-life-threatening rights violations; they are also morally responsible (jointly with the enforcers) for the use of force. To this extent, they are analogous to military planners in respect of a war of conquest. Naturally, the degree of moral responsibility may differ. For example, military combatants who actually use deadly force might have a greater share of the collective responsibility than those who merely assist combatants *qua* combatants, e.g., munitions workers.

---

[24] So I am suggesting that *collective* moral responsibility can be understood in these cases as *joint* moral responsibility. I argue for this in ibid., chap. 8 and in 'Collective responsibility: an individualist account', in P.A. French (ed.), *Midwest Studies in Philosophy: Collective Responsibility* 30, 2006, pp. 176–93.

However, arguably, there are cases in which enforcement is not integral to the collective end that consists of a non-life-threatening rights violation. Consider a variation on our forcible-removal example. In our new scenario, blacks in apartheid South Africa are falsely told that they are being transported to a land of freedom and material well-being, when in fact they are going to an impoverished homeland. Assume further that when some groups of blacks disbelieve these claims, then they are forcibly made to board the transport vehicles; indeed, deadly force is used on a number of occasions. However, enforcement is only used as a supplement to fraud. Now suppose the civilians who planned this policy of removal to homelands by fraud did not envisage or believe that deadly force would be, or was being, used; and nor did the civilians who organized and time-tabled the transport. So in post-apartheid South Africa these civilians claim that whereas they have a share in the collective moral responsibility for violating the rights of the blacks, including their property rights, they are in no way responsible for the use of deadly force that took place from time to time to further this collective end. In short, they acknowledge their guilt in relation to perpetrating non-life-threatening rights violations, but deny that they were guilty of enforcing these violations (and deny, therefore, any guilt in relation to life-threatening rights violations). Their claim seems reasonable.

The upshot of this discussion is that there may well be civilian groups who have a share in the collective moral responsibility for the non-life-threatening rights violations without necessarily being in any appropriately strong sense morally responsible for the enforcement of these rights violations. Such civilians would not have a moral right to immunity in war, as would be case if they were innocent civilians, i.e., civilians who did not perform actions that either consisted of rights violations (or the enforcement thereof) or assisted rights violators *qua* rights violators (or enforcers thereof).

Notwithstanding their lack of a *right* to immunity, these civilians might be expected to enjoy a degree of immunity not possessed by combatants. For the argument in favour of using deadly force against these civilians has less moral weight than it has in the case of others – especially combatants – who are collectively responsible not only for the non-life-threatening rights violations, but also for the enforcement thereof. Accordingly, other things being equal, such civilians might be expected to enjoy civilian immunity in some wars, e.g., ones in which it was not necessary to target both combatants and civilian rights violators who were not enforcers.

In this section I have not considered a whole raft of familiar arguments relevant to the issue of civilian immunity. Let me simply note that there may be other grounds, such as consequentialist or contractarian grounds, for restricting the use of deadly force against civilians.[25] For example, conventions may have been set in place to prohibit the use of deadly force against civilian administrative personnel, and the abandonment of these conventions may bring about a situation which is morally worse, all things considered, than respecting them. Or the policy of violence may lead to counter-violence and a general escalation in violence which is less morally acceptable than the state of affairs in which legitimate targets were left unharmed. Nevertheless, there may be situations in which directing violence at combatants and their leaders alone is not sufficient to terminate the rights violations, and in which widening the set of targets so as to include civilian non-life-threatening rights violators is necessary to terminate the rights violations, and in which such widening is not overridden by consequentialist or contractarian considerations. In such situations these categories of civilians may become legitimate targets, given they lack a moral right to immunity.

Civilian Immunity and Culpable Omissions

Thus far we have mainly been concerned with civilians who are individually and collectively morally responsible for human rights violations implicitly understood as violations of negative rights, e.g., a war of conquest or an active and sustained policy of forcible removal (ethnic or racial cleansing). We have not been concerned, at least explicitly, with positive rights and duties to assist as such. So our focus has not been on culpable omissions. That said, I have already acknowledged that the category of non-life-threatening rights violations includes violations of some positive rights. In this section I will discuss the collective moral responsibility of certain categories of culpable non-attackers.

Earlier on in this chapter I argued that deadly force can in principle be used to enforce some positive rights, as well as to enforce negative rights. These positive rights include rights to goods other than life; they include rights that can be unrealized, even when the right to life is realized.

Moreover, as is the case with negative rights, third parties – at least in principle – have rights, and indeed duties, to use deadly force to ensure that some positive rights are respected.

This point has clear implications for certain civilian members of governments who intentionally refrain from respecting the positive rights,

---

[25]   G.I. Mavrodes, 'Conventions and the morality of war', *Philosophy & Public Affairs* 4(2), 1975, pp. 117–31.

including subsistence rights, of their citizens for governments have a clear institutional responsibility to provide for the minimum material well-being of their citizens; or at least this is so if the governments in question have the capacity to do so. Accordingly, the moral responsibility based on need – and the fact that those in government could assist, if they chose to – is buttressed by this institutional responsibility that they have voluntarily taken on. Consider Saddam Hussein's refusal to distribute much-needed food and medicine to his own citizens, albeit in the context of UN-sponsored sanctions.[26] Citizens in such states may well be entitled to use deadly force against the government officials in question, notwithstanding the fact that these officials are neither combatants nor the leaders of combatants. Perhaps such use of deadly force, including assassination, is to be regarded as terrorism on the grounds that the victims of terrorism are not themselves attackers.[27] If so, then terrorism can be morally justified in some circumstances. However, the civilian victims in this kind of scenario are not innocent; their intentional acts of omission constitute violations of the positive rights of their citizens. I note here that by the lights of the definition provided in the previous chapter, violence directed at rights violators is not necessarily terrorism. I return to this definitional issue below.

Some of these rights or duties to use deadly force to enforce positive rights might be exercised against certain categories of people with diminished responsibility. Consider a variation on our earlier-described HIV/ AIDS example. Suppose that one of the employees of the company is not actually responsible for the company policy not to provide cheap drugs for AIDS sufferers, but is, nevertheless, the person who is refusing to provide the sufferer in question with the drug.[28] Assume also that the AIDS sufferer is not in a position credibly to threaten the company's owner-managers who are responsible for the policy. Although the employee seems to have diminished responsibility for failing to respect the AIDS sufferer's right to the life-preserving drug, nevertheless, the AIDS sufferer might still be held to be entitled to shoot the employee dead, if that was the only means by which he could preserve his own life.

---

[26] S. Mackey, *The Reckoning: Iraq and the Legacy of Saddam Hussein*, London: W.W. Norton, 2002, p. 363. There was moral complexity here in that given Saddam was refusing to dispense food and medicines under the oil for food programme – citing sanctions as his reason – then almost certainly sanctions should not have continued to be applied. But this does not relieve Saddam of culpability.

[27] This depends on the definition of a terrorist.

[28] Assume also that he does not have an adequate reason for refusing to provide the drug, e.g., if he provides the drug he will be fired and unable to get another job, with the consequence that his young children will be brought up in abject poverty.

By analogy, government employees, such as administrators who intentionally refrain from assisting those in need because instructed to do so by their government, might well be legitimate targets of 'terrorists'. Consider our example of blacks in apartheid South Africa who were forcibly removed into desolate homelands, such as Qua Qua, and once there found they could not provide themselves with a basic level of subsistence; malnutrition and disease were rampant. Now suppose South African politicians declare such homelands to be independent states – as in fact happened – and thereby try to absolve themselves and their administrators of their pre-existing institutional responsibility for the minimum material needs of the 'citizens' of these alleged new states. Since the states were not legitimate – and were not in fact internationally recognized as legitimate – these politicians and other officials did not succeed in absolving themselves of their institutional responsibility. Accordingly, the South African government officials who refrained from assisting the relocated people were conceivably legitimate targets, on the assumption that killing these officials was necessary in order to ensure that the subsistence rights of these people would be realized. This might be so, even if the officials in question were not the same officials who planned and implemented the policy of forcible removals. Perhaps by this time the latter officials have retired, and have been replaced by a new cohort of politicians and administrators. If so, these new or succeeding officials would simply have inherited the institutional responsibility to provide for the minimal material needs of the occupants of these alleged new states. (They would also have an institutional responsibility to redress the past injustice of dispossession that was consequent upon the policy of forcible removal; but that is another matter.)

Let us focus on the collective responsibility of the members of a group or community who intentionally refrain from assisting their needy fellows. Here we need some theoretical account of collective responsibility for omissions.

I offer the following account of culpable collective responsibility for omissions; it provides only a rough approximation[29] of a *sufficient* condition for such culpability. Members of some group are collectively responsible for failing to intervene to halt or prevent some serious wrongdoing or wrongful state of affairs if: (1) the wrongdoing took place, or is taking place; (2) the members of the community intentionally refrained from intervening; (3) each or most of the intervening members having as an end the prevention of the wrongdoing probably would have prevented, or would have a reasonable chance of halting, the wrongdoing; (4) each

---

[29] For example, I have not bothered to spell out the conditions for moral responsibility, e.g., that the agents were not under the influence of drugs.

of the members of the community would have intentionally refrained from intervening – and intervening having as an end the prevention or termination of the wrongdoing – even if the others, or most of the others, had intervened with that end in mind; and (5) each of the members of the community had an institutional responsibility – jointly with the others – to intervene. Note that on this account, if an agent would have intervened, but done so only because the others did, i.e., not because he had as an end the prevention or termination of the wrong, then the agent would still be morally responsible, jointly with the others, for failing to intervene (given conditions (1)–(3)).

Now there are additional theoretical complications that arise when the intervention in question has to be performed by representatives of a group or community, rather than by the members of the group or community themselves, or by third parties who are mere bystanders. Thus in representative democracies, the government has to enact policies to intervene; the citizens cannot themselves intervene as a community. Moreover, some organization – authorized by the government – has to implement these policies, has actually to do the intervening. However, it needs to be said that the large voting populations in contemporary democracies cannot be assimilated to organizational structures, such as an army, or to small-scale directly participatory bodies, such as the cabinet in a Westminster-type system of government. Therefore, notions of collective responsibility that might apply to such organizations, or to such small structured groups, do not apply to large populations. Accordingly, the failure of a democratic government to do its duty and engage in humanitarian intervention does not generate a moral justification for the wholesale targeting of the civilian voting population by (say) terrorists, and in the case of a failure of such duty by an authoritarian government, the grounds for this targeting are even weaker.

Nevertheless, in the light of the above definition, it might well be the case that civilian members of governments and their administrations – such as Iraqi politicians and administrators who failed to meet their responsibilities to distribute food and medicine to their own citizens, and South African politicians and administrators who failed adequately to assist destitute blacks in the homelands – are collectively morally responsible for omissions of a kind that might justify the use of deadly force on the part of their citizens to ensure that the rights to assistance in question are realized. In short, members of civilian groups who culpably refrain from assisting those who have a human right to assistance from them might thereby forfeit their right to immunity in the context of a conventional war, war of national liberation or armed struggle against an oppressive government.

Terrorism and Non-Violent Rights Violators

Thus far we have: (a) identified two categories of non-violent rights violators, namely, perpetrators of positive (non-violent) rights violations and perpetrators of culpable omissions; and (b) argued that violence directed at such non-violent rights violators might, under certain conditions, be morally justified. What are the implications of these conclusions for our definition of terrorism and, relatedly, for the claim that some forms of terrorism might be morally justifiable?

In terms of our definition of terrorism, the question that arises is whether or not such violence directed at non-violent rights violators ought to be regarded as a serious crime and – assuming this violence is performed in order to terrorize and in the service of military and political ends – a form of terrorism.

If such violence directed at non-violent rights violators is a form of terrorism, then – assuming that we are correct in claiming that such violence is, under certain circumstances, morally justifiable – there is at least one form of terrorism that is morally justifiable, namely, violence directed at non-violent rights violators. On the other hand, if such violence directed at non-violent rights violators is not a form of terrorism, then *ipso facto* we will not have identified a form of morally justifiable terrorism. Is violence directed at such non-violent rights violations a form of terrorism?

In the light of my definition of terrorism proffered in the previous chapter, the key question now is whether killing non-violent rights violators ought to be criminalized, notwithstanding that it is, under certain circumstances, morally justified. An important consideration against the criminalization of the killing of non-violent rights violators is that in certain circumstances such actions are morally justifiable; in general morally justifiable actions ought not to be criminalized. However, law and morality do not necessarily, and ought not necessarily to, mirror one another at every point. Moreover, there are a number of specific concerns in making it legally permissible to kill non-violent rights violators (even under certain restricted circumstances).

Firstly, it might be argued that non-violent rights violations are typically a lesser evil than their counterpart violent positive rights violations. This is in part because non-violent rights violations are, by definition, not in themselves acts of violence, e.g., refraining from providing medicine is not in itself an act of violence; albeit non-violent rights violations are typically complicit with acts of violence. And it is in part because their perpetrators are typically at some remove from the evil that is ultimately brought about. Thus the administrators who organized the transportation of blacks to the homelands in South Africa were not the ones who bulldozed their houses and forced them at gunpoint onto the trucks that transported them. Again, those government officials who culpably refrain from providing food to the needy are guilty of omissions. But culpably omitting to do what one ought to do with the foreseen, but indirect and non-immediate, bringing about of an evil consequence is typically regarded as a lesser crime than intentionally and directly causing the very same evil outcome.

Secondly, it might be argued that given that non-violent rights violations are typically a lesser evil than violent positive rights violations, killing non-violent rights violators can only be morally justified if killing violent rights violators is not a viable option. It might be argued that there is an analogy here with the case of self-defence; specifically, one ought to choose the lesser evil of, say, wounding one's attacker rather than killing him, supposing this option to be available. However, this is at best a partial analogy, for in the self-defence case it is a question of doing greater or less harm to one and the same perpetrator, whereas this is not so in the case of refraining from targeting one type of perpetrator, namely, non-violent rights violators, in favour of another type of perpetrator, namely, violent rights violators.

There is another more persuasive argument that we can avail ourselves of here, namely, that there is a general presumption in favour of widening rather than narrowing the category of persons with immunity in conflict situations. Given this presumption, and the presumption against any killing unless it is necessary, then the more culpable ought to be killed ahead of the less culpable, and the less culpable ought not to be killed at all unless it is necessary; however, it will not be necessary to kill the less culpable unless the circumstances are such that killing the more culpable is not a viable option.

Let us accept this argument. Is it now justifiable and feasible to extinguish the legal immunity of non-violent rights violators, but do so only in circumstances in which killing combatants is not working as a military strategy? This is extremely doubtful. For it is a highly problematic legal strategy. How can one retain or lose one's legal immunity from being killed simply on the basis of the whether or not some strategy being pursued in respect of other people is or is not succeeding?

The upshot of this discussion is that we are faced with the following two alternative options:

- *Option 1*: Certain categories of non-violent rights violators are not given civilian immunity on the grounds that it is morally justifiable to kill them, if it is necessary. This is consistent with the practice of killing this category of rights violators only if it is not feasible to kill combatants. If this option is the preferred one, then killing non-violent rights violators (under certain conditions) ought to be legally permissible, and hence would *not* constitute terrorism (on our definition of terrorism outlined in Chapter 2).

- *Option 2*: Non-violent rights violators have civilian immunity. This is consistent with it being morally justifiable to kill members of this category of rights violators (if, and only if, it is not feasible to kill combatants). However, on this way of thinking, this is one of those occasions when the law and morality ought to diverge. (However, it may well be that the killers of non-violent rights violations are, nevertheless, afforded an excuse in law; so it is a mitigating circumstance, unlike in the case of killing ordinary civilians.) If this option is the preferred one, then killing non-violent rights violators ought to be a serious crime, and hence could well constitute terrorism (on our definition of terrorism). If so, it may well be morally justified terrorism.

Conclusion

In this chapter I have addressed the question of the moral permissibility/impermissibility of targeting various categories of non-combatants by (alleged) terrorist groups. I have taken it to be self-evidently morally wrong for terrorists to target innocent civilians, such as children. However, there are other civilian groups in respect of which matters are not so clear. Specifically, I have distinguished non-violent rights violators from (military and non-military) combatants (the category of combatants is taken to include the leaders of combatants and those who assist combatants *qua* combatants). Within the former category I distinguished perpetrators of positive (non-violent) rights violations, e.g., those who dispossess a group of its territory by fraud, and perpetrators of culpable omissions, e.g., state officials who refuse to distribute medical supplies to disease-afflicted children, with the consequence that the children die. I have argued that under certain conditions it might be morally justifiable to use lethal force against non-violent rights violators. The implication of this is that *some* forms of terrorism might be morally justified under certain circumstances. (It goes without saying that many, probably most, forms of terrorism, e.g., those perpetrated by Al-Qaeda, are not morally justifiable.)

Moreover, we are faced with the following two alternative options with respect to morally justified forms of (alleged) terrorism:

- *Option 1*: Killing non-violent rights violators (under certain conditions) ought to be made legally permissible, and hence would not constitute terrorism (on our definition of terrorism).
- *Option 2*: Killing non-violent rights violators ought to be made a serious crime, and hence could constitute terrorism (on our definition of terrorism). If so, it may well be morally justified terrorism.

4

Terrorism-as-Crime

Terrorism as I have defined it consists of serious crimes of violence, e.g., murder, torture, grievous bodily harm, rape and kidnapping, albeit crimes of violence committed in order to terrorize a third party and in the service of military or political ends. Accordingly, terrorist acts are both morally unacceptable and unlawful (or, at least, they ought to be unlawful). For example, the attack on the World Trade Center was not only the intentional killing of around 3,000 people, it was the moral and legal offence of *murdering* around 3,000 people.

Moreover, as we saw above, by the lights of my definition (indirect strategy), terrorism is narrower than on some other definitions, such as those couched in terms of killing non-combatants. On the latter type of definition, some of the actions of organizations such as the ANC in apartheid South Africa necessarily would turn out to be acts of terrorism. For example, killing certain categories of non-violent rights violators, such as administrators engaged in implementing a policy of ethnic cleansing, necessarily would be terrorism on this kind of view, since such rights violators are non-combatants. However, on my view, as we saw in Chapter 3, such acts would not necessarily be acts of terrorism and, even if they were, arguably they would be morally justifiable acts of terrorism.

On the other hand, by the lights of my definition, terrorism is wider than on some other definitions, such as those couched in terms of killing the innocent. On the latter type of definition, some of the actions of organizations such as authoritarian governments, e.g., torturing revolutionary activists, would not turn out to be acts of terrorism, yet on my definition they would.

Terrorism-as-Crime

Theoretically, and in practice, some terrorist acts can be regarded as ordinary crimes and subject to domestic criminal law. Accordingly, such terrorists should be investigated, arrested and charged, and tried and punished, in accordance with the principles and processes of the criminal justice system in the same way as an ordinary murderer or other criminal would be. On the other hand, some terrorist acts are perpetrated in the context of wars. Being acts of war, they take place outside the sphere of domestic criminal law. The terrorists operating in theatres of war are *de facto* military combatants, i.e., terrorist-combatants. As such, they can justifiably be shot at, bombed, ambushed and either captured or killed.

Here we need to distinguish between a certain category of what has been termed 'unlawful combatants', and lawful combatants who have, nevertheless, engaged in war crimes, e.g., a US soldier who tortures enemy prisoners. 'Unlawful combatants',[1] or, more precisely for our purposes here, combatants who ought to be regarded as unlawful combatants, include combatant members of terrorist organizations, such as Al-Qaeda. Such combatants, i.e., terrorist-combatants, are by definition unlawful combatants since their individual mode of combat, and the defining mode of combat of the military organization of which they are a subordinate member, is perpetrating terrorist acts, e.g., murdering innocent non-combatants. In the case of terrorist-combatants and terrorist organizations such as Al-Qaeda, their terrorist acts are not an anomaly; it is not simply a case of some individual combatants from time to time breaching the laws of war, i.e., the *ius in bello*, as in the case of some rogue US soldiers who committed atrocities against civilians in the Vietnam War, e.g., Lieutenant Calley in 1968 at My Lai. Rather, the methods of terror are constitutive of Al-Qaeda as an organization and, therefore, the organization and its combatants are, or ought to be, unlawful. As a consequence, terrorist-combatants, once determined to be such by an appropriately constituted judicial body, ought to be subject to a criminal justice process analogous to that to which ordinary criminals are subject. Nevertheless, such terrorist-combatants are military combatants (albeit they are in addition unlawful combatants, indeed war criminals); terrorist-combatants are not *per se* ordinary criminals.

---

[1] The notion of a lawful versus unlawful combatant and cognate notions are deployed and discussed in various contexts. See, for example, the 1949 Geneva Convention concerning the treatment of prisoners-of-war.

Contra the Bush administration and *pace* David Luban[2] and others, I hold that terrorists should not be subjected to a hybrid framework under which they are both ordinary criminals and simultaneously military combatants; certainly, the imposition of a selective hybrid framework by means of which terrorists get the worst of both worlds is morally objectionable.[3] However, in some conflict situations, e.g., internal armed struggles, it is inherently difficult to know which framework to apply; that is, whether to apply the framework of domestic crime or the framework of war.

How are we to adjudicate these competing conceptions of terrorism in such contexts, i.e., terrorism-as-(ordinary)crime versus terrorism-as-war? While it is important to avoid the kind of inconsistency evident in the treatment of prisoners being held at Guantánamo Bay, nonetheless, some terrorist acts ought to be treated simply as crimes committed by criminals who are not also military combatants, and other terrorist acts as acts of war that are also war crimes. To avoid inconsistency a terrorist act that is treated simply as an ordinary crime ought not simultaneously to be treated as a war crime, and vice versa. For example, the Red Brigades' terrorist acts of the kidnapping and murder of Aldo Moro, President of the Christian Democrats, in 1978 in Rome might reasonably be regarded as an ordinary crime.[4] By contrast, the dropping of the atomic bomb on Hiroshima by the US military in the Second World War might reasonably be regarded as a terrorist attack that is also an act of war. The question that now arises is how to separate these two kinds of terrorist act, ordinary crimes and war crimes? I suggest we do so by recourse to two features of terrorist acts, namely, their context and the type of terrorist actor involved.

Terrorist acts take place in a variety of contexts. For my purposes here I will first invoke the following threefold distinction in relation to such contexts, namely: (1) well-ordered (non-totalitarian) nation-states in peacetime and, specifically, well-ordered, liberal-democratic states at peace; (2) theatres of war, i.e., battlefields, in the context of wars between states; and (3) theatres of war in the context of wars involving non-state actors, e.g., a civil war or armed insurgency between a government's security forces and some other armed and organized military force, or a contested foreign occupancy. The attack on the World Trade Center took

---

[2]   D. Luban, 'The war on terrorism and the end of human rights', *Philosophy and Public Affairs Quarterly* 22(3), 2002, pp. 9–14.
[3]   L. May, *War Crimes and Just War*, Cambridge: Cambridge University Press, 2007, chap. 14.
[4]   See D.J. Whittaker (ed.), *The Terrorism Reader*, 2nd edn, London: Routledge, 2003, p. 220.

place in a type (1) context, the Second World War bombing of Dresden took place in a type (2) context, and the terrorist attacks on Iraqi civilians during the current US armed forces occupancy of Iraq are taking place in a type (3) context. Here I note that from the fact that, for example, two states (or for that matter a state and a non-state actor) are at war it does not follow that all or, indeed, any of their respective territories are theatres of war. A theatre of war is a *de facto* battlefield in which military combatants are engaged in combat. In the Second World War the US mainland (as opposed to, for example, Pearl Harbor in Hawaii) was not a theatre of war. I also note that a minimal condition for being the sort of entity capable of waging war is to be an organized armed force. Thus lone individuals and ideological movements that do not possess an armed organized wing cannot engage in wars.

Terrorist acts are performed by a variety of different sorts of actors. For my purposes here I will distinguish two different types of terrorist, namely, *military* combatants (including the leaders of military combatants and those who assist combatants *qua* combatants) and non-combatants, i.e., those who are not military combatants. If we marry these two different categories of terrorist with the three above-mentioned types of context, we end up with six conceptual possibilities, namely, military combatant or non-combatant (roughly speaking, civilian) terrorists functioning in each of the three types of contexts, i.e., well-ordered liberal-democratic states, theatres of war involving state actors, and theatres of war in which one of the protagonists is a non-state actor.

I suggest that, other things being equal, terrorists functioning in type (1) contexts, i.e., well-ordered liberal-democratic states, be regarded as non-combatants and, therefore, as ordinary criminals, irrespective of how they regard themselves. Thus members of the Red Army Faction in Germany or the Red Brigades in Italy engaged in assassinating corporate and political leaders and security personnel in the 1970s should be regarded as non-combatants, i.e., ordinary criminals. This is consistent with their being combatants in a non-military sense as, for example, are armed robbers involved in a gunfight with armed police.

I further suggest that terrorists functioning in type (3) contexts, i.e., theatres of war, be regarded as military combatants, specifically terrorist-combatants and, therefore, as unlawful combatants and war criminals. Thus Al-Qaeda operatives in Afghanistan are unlawful combatants and war criminals. Here it is important to distinguish *unlawful* combatants who are war criminals, e.g., Al-Qaeda operatives in Afghanistan, from *lawful* combatants who are, nevertheless, war criminals. Thus the US airmen who bombed Hiroshima and Nagasaki were lawful combatants functioning in a type (2) context; however, since their acts were acts of terror, they were war criminals. Moreover, the technical and administrative personnel who built the atom bombs and implemented the decision to bomb Hiroshima and Nagasaki, e.g., logistically, should also in this context be regarded as (lawful) combatants, since they assisted the combatants *qua* combatants; moreover, they should be regarded as having perpetrated war crimes.

Notwithstanding the above, the case of terrorists functioning in type (3) contexts, e.g., internecine war, is highly problematic. I address this issue in Chapter 5. In this chapter I will focus on terrorism in type (1) contexts, i.e., in well-ordered liberal-democratic states, and, in particular, on various ethical issues arising out of the response to such terrorism.

As already noted, a terrorist who is not a terrorist-combatant, i.e., who is not a *military* combatant, is a terrorist who is either not a member of a terrorist organization fighting a war, e.g., Timothy McVeigh, or someone who is perpetrating acts of terrorism outside a theatre of war, e.g., a person who is detonating a bomb in a marketplace in the context of a well-ordered liberal democracy at peace.

In accordance with the suggestion made above, I assume in what follows that the conception of terrorism-as-crime is appropriate in the context of a well-ordered liberal-democratic state at peace in which non-combatant citizens of that state are performing acts of terrorism within the territory of that state and directed at that state and its citizens.

If terrorism is to be regarded as an ordinary crime, albeit a very serious crime, then we must first provide an agreed definition – or at least demarcation – of terrorism under which it is a crime. As we saw above, many acts of terrorism consist in familiar crimes, such as murder, rape, kidnapping, and so on. Here we need to recall our definition (indirect strategy) outlined in Chapter 2 for demarcating terrorist acts, a strategy consisting of identifying the class of crimes that consist of violent acts against persons, and deploying the various agreed-upon criteria, e.g., that they are politically motivated actions intended to induce fear in some target population.

There are at least three properties of terrorist actions that are significant from a law enforcement perspective. Firstly, being organized actions, as opposed to, say, a one-off crime committed by an individual acting alone, or even a pattern of crimes committed by an individual acting alone, they are, other things being equal, potentially very destabilizing of law and order in the context of a well-ordered liberal-democratic state. In this respect they are akin to organized crime.

Secondly, they involve not only the violent crime at the core of the terrorist act, e.g., murder, but also the intentional inculcation of fear in a population. By virtue of this fear-inducing feature, terrorist actions are, other things being equal, potentially more destabilizing of law and order in a well-ordered liberal-democratic state than are ordinary crimes. In this respect, terrorist actions in a well-ordered liberal-democratic state are not to be assimilated to those performed by an authoritarian state against its own citizens; the latter may well contribute to the preservation of the authoritarian political order.

Thirdly, being actions in the service of some political or military end that is antithetical to the liberal-democratic state – indeed, being actions that often constitute direct attacks on the state – terrorist actions are, other things being equal, potentially more destabilizing of law and order in a well-ordered liberal-democratic state than are ordinary crimes.

Terrorism-as-Crime and Police Institutions

If terrorism is a species of ordinary crime, then the institution that is primarily responsible for combating terrorism is the institution of the police. By contrast, if terrorism is a species of war, then the institutions that would be primarily responsible for combating terrorism would be military institutions, e.g., the army, the navy and the air force. Here we need some normative theoretical account of the police and how police institutions are to be distinguished from military institutions.

Elsewhere I have argued that the institution of the police can be defined by it use of coercive force in the service of legally enshrined moral rights.[5] Such rights are ones held against fellow citizens and against governments, e.g., the right to life and the rights to freedom of action and thought. On this account, the institution of the police is quite different from other institutions that either are not principally concerned with (legally enshrined) moral rights, or do not necessarily rely on coercion in the service of moral rights.

It might be thought that contemporary military institutions meet this definition of the institution of the police. Moreover, the nature and evolution of military and policing institutions is such that the lines have often been blurred between the two. For example, in the British colonies the police historically had a paramilitary role in relation to what was regarded as a hostile population, e.g., the Royal Irish Constabulary. Indeed, according to Richard Hill:

> Coercion by army and by police have always been distinguished by differences of degree, rather than kind, and through most of the history of policing there was no clear demarcation between the two interwoven strands of

---

[5]   S. Miller and J. Blackler, *Ethical Issues in Policing*, Aldershot: Ashgate, 2005, chap. 1.

control situated towards the coercive extremity of the control continuum. . . . Historically, constables were generally considered to be a reserve military body for mobilisation by the state in potential or actual emergency; conversely soldiers were frequently called upon to conduct duties generally considered to be of a 'policing' nature.[6]

But from this it does not follow that there are not good reasons for a *normative* theory of *contemporary* policing in well-ordered liberal democracies to insist on distinguishing between the fundamental role of the police and that of the military. Such reasons would include the well-documented and highly problematic character of paramilitary police forces, including in relation to the violation by such forces of individual moral rights.

However, the most important reason for insisting on a fundamental distinction between the role of the police and the role of the military in liberal democracies is the inherent danger of military and/or police forces becoming the coercive instrument of governments in relation to the citizenry, i.e., the threat of a police state as existed, for example, in Eastern Europe under communism and currently exists in China and much of the developing world. This danger is averted in liberal democracies by establishing the following division of labour between the military and the police. On the one hand, while the military is a coercive instrument of government, its focus is *external* national defence, not internal policing of the citizenry. On the other hand, while the focus of the police is internal policing of the citizenry, it is not a coercive instrument of government; rather, the police have a *quasi-independent* status as the protectors of the human and other moral rights of the community and as the servants of its laws.

While contemporary military forces may undertake quasi-police roles from time to time, this is not, and has not been, their fundamental purpose; rather, this has avowedly been national self-defence. Moreover, in securing this latter purpose, they operate under the direction of the political leadership of the day; they do not have the quasi-judicial role of the police and do not require the same degree of independence from government as do the police. Let me explain further.

The extent to which an institution – as distinct from an individual member of an institution – ought to have independence from government turns in large part on the function of that institution, and the extent to which it is necessary for that institution to have independence in order properly to carry out its function(s) or end(s). For example, the judiciary needs a

---

[6]   R.S. Hill, *Policing the Colonial Frontier: The Theory and Practice of Coercive Social and Racial Control in New Zealand, 1767–1867,* Wellington: New Zealand Department of Internal Affairs, 1986, part 1, p. 3.

high level of independence from the legislature and the executive if it is prop-erly to carry out its specialized tasks of interpreting and applying the law.

Institutional independence needs to be seen in the context of the so-called 'separation of powers'. Specifically, the executive, the legislature and the judiciary ought to be kept separate; otherwise too much power is concentrated in the hands of a unitary state agency. Those who make laws should not also be the ones who apply those laws. Politicians, for example, need to be subject to laws adjudicated by judges who are institutionally independent of politicians, on pain of undue influence on judicial processes and outcomes.

By parity of reasoning, the police must not simply come to be the instru-ment of government policies. For the priority of the police in a well-ordered liberal democracy is to serve the law, and, on my account, to protect moral rights enshrined in the law. The police states of communist Eastern Europe, Nazi Germany, Iraq under Saddam Hussein, China, and the like, are tes-timony to the importance of a substantial degree of police independence from government in order to ensure that police serve their fundamental purpose of protecting the legally enshrined moral rights of the citizenry; rights both in relation to their fellow citizens and in relation to government.

Police independence is reflected in the 1962 findings of the United Kingdom's Royal Commission on the Police:

> The duties which it is generally agreed in the evidence should be performed by chief constables unhampered by any kind of external control are not capable of precise definition, but they cover broadly what we referred to earlier as 'quasi-judicial' matters; that is, the enforcement of the criminal law in particular cases involving, for example, the pursuit of enquiries and decisions to arrest or prosecute . . .
>
> We entirely accept that it is in the public interest that a chief constable, when dealing with these quasi-judicial matters, should be free from the con-ventional processes of democratic control and influence.[7]

So the notion of the police as simply the instrument of government is unsustainable. On the other hand, determining the precise nature and extent of police independence has turned out to be extremely difficult. I have emphasized the importance of maintaining a degree of police independ-ence from government. However, it is equally important to point to the dangers of high levels of police independence. After all, the police have very substantial coercive powers, and historically the abuse of these

---

[7]   Royal Commission on the Police, Final Report, Cmnd 1728 (chairman Sir Henry Willink), London: HMSO, 1962, paras 87 and 88.

powers has been an ever-present threat. Specifically, police organizations do need to be subjected to (at least) the constraint and influence of their communities via democratically elected bodies, notably the government of the day.

As is the case with the independence of other institutions, there is a need to strike a balance between, on the one hand, the independence of the police and, on the other hand, the need for: (a) community and government control of the police; and (b) police accountability for their methods and actions.

If an institution has substantial independence from other institutions, and if that institution has a very hierarchical structure, then those who occupy the upper echelons will have a relatively high degree of discretionary power. Military commanders, especially in time of war, are a case in point. Police commissioners in times of emergency are a further case in point. For a more extreme example, consider the extraordinary powers possessed by police in authoritarian regimes, such as the former Soviet Union.[8]

Evidently the power of the police needs to be constrained, and there are a number of ways to achieve this. One way is to devolve police authority in a quasi-federated structure, as is the case in the UK, where the police are still to an extent a function of local government; there is no national police force as such.[9] Another way is to delimit the police's sphere of operational autonomy in favour of policies of democratically elected government, including policies in relation to police methods; although, as we have seen, this can be counterproductive. A third, and much favoured, method is to ensure accountability by way of oversight bodies, such as Ombudsmen, Police Boards, and the like.

Thus far we have discussed the institutional independence and accountability of police services *qua* institution. In this section, we turn directly to the consideration of the authority and discretion of individual police officers.[10]

---

[8] See A. Knight, *Beria: Stalin's First Lieutenant*, Princeton: Princeton University Press, 1995.

[9] In fact police are subject to central government via the Home Office, as well as to local government via the Police Authority. However, the authority of local government has been diluted by the 1995 requirement that the Police Authorities have a significant number of members nominated by the Home Secretary. See P. Neyroud and A. Beckley, *Policing, Ethics and Human Rights*, Cullompton, UK: Willan Publishing, 2001, p. 97.

[10] For a useful selection of articles on police discretion, see J. Kleinig (ed.), *Handled with Discretion: Ethical Issues in Police Decision Making*, Lanham, MD: Rowman and Littlefield, 1996. See also K.C. Davis, *Discretionary Justice: A Preliminary Inquiry*, Baton Rouge: Louisiana State University Press, 1969; and E. Delattre, *Character and Cops: Ethics in Policing*, Washington, DC: American Enterprise Institute, 1994, chap. 4.

Police officers need to exercise authority on a daily basis. But the notion of authority is a difficult one. We must distinguish between legal authority and moral authority. A police officer might have legal authority, but in virtue of his lack of credibility in a community, he might have no moral authority. Consider the lack of moral authority of white police officers in a black South African township in the days of apartheid. Authority involves a relation between at least two people. In the case of legal authority, for example, the person *in* authority has a *right to command* the person *over* whom she has authority (to show his driver's licence, say), and, correspondingly, that person has a *duty to obey* such lawful commands.

We also need to distinguish between power and authority. A large man might have power over a smaller one, but it would not follow that he had either legal or moral authority in relation to the small man. In some instances, *de facto* coercive power is a necessary condition for the holding of authority. This is true of police. If, for instance, police did not have the *de facto* power to apprehend criminals because (say) the criminals were too well armed, then not only the effectiveness but also the authority of the police would be undermined. At the same time, it seems unlikely that effective policing could rely purely on the exercise of coercive force. Past a certain point, the exercise of coercive force is actually likely to undermine the authority of police; they come to be seen as a group who will try to have their way irrespective of the wishes and opinions of the community that they are supposedly serving, and ultimately irrespective of what they have been authorized to do. This is a disastrous outcome, in two respects. First, the police will find it difficult to perform their legitimate role, given the dependence of the police on the community for achieving the defining purposes of police work. Second, the police will be engaged in activities that they are not authorized to undertake; they will be abusing their authority.

A further task to be performed here is to clarify the relationship between authority and the related notion of responsibility. In this connection, we must invoke the distinction made in Chapter 3 between two different kinds of responsibility. Sometimes to say that someone is responsible for an action is simply to say that the person had a reason for performing the action, that the person had an intention to perform the action, and that the person actually performed the action. This is the ordinary everyday sense of 'responsible', and we are responsible for most of our actions in this sense.

However, there is a different sense of responsibility. What is meant by the expression 'being responsible for an action' in this second sense is that the person in question occupies a certain institutional role, and that the occupant of that role is the person who has the institutionally or organizationally determined legal and moral right, and duty, to decide what is to be done in relation to certain matters. So, for example, a mechanic in a workshop might be responsible for fixing all problems to do with brakes. Notice that even if the mechanic did not in fact fix any brakes – and therefore was not responsible for fixing brakes in our first sense of being responsible – he can still be said to be responsible for fixing brakes in our second sense.

The notion of authority is a special case of being responsible in our second sense. We saw that the occupant of an institutional or organizational role who has a legal and moral right, and duty, to decide what is to be done in relation to certain matters is responsible for those matters. However, if those matters involve directing the actions of other persons, then the occupant of the role is said to be the person in authority in relation to these people he/she is directing. Thus, a police officer not only has responsibility in the sense in which the mechanic has responsibility, the police officer also has *authority*. For example, police officers have the authority to direct motorists or to arrest an offender.

Historically, policing in the UK and Australia has made use of a distinctive notion of authority, so-called 'original authority'. In relation to the concept of original authority, we need to distinguish compliance with laws from obedience to the directives of men and women, especially one's superiors. Thus, according to the law, an investigating officer must not prosecute a fellow police officer if the latter is self-evidently innocent. On the other hand, he might be ordered to do so by his superior officer. Now individual police officers are held to be responsible to the law as well as their superiors in the police service. However, their first responsibility is to the law. So a police officer should disobey a directive from a superior officer that is clearly unlawful. However, the admittedly controversial doctrine of original authority goes further than this. It implies that there are at least some situations in which police officers have a right to disobey a superior's otherwise *lawful* command, if obeying it would prevent them from discharging their own obligations to the law.[11]

---

[11] Relevant legal cases here are the 'Blackburn cases', principally *R* v. *Metropolitan Police Commissioner; Ex parte Blackburn* [1968] 2 Q. B. 118 (cited in K. Bryett, A. Harrison and J. Shaw, *An Introduction to Policing: The Role and Function of Police in Australia*, vol. 2, Sydney: Butterworths, 1994, p. 43), in which Lord Denning considered the Commissioner of the London Metropolitan Police 'to be answerable to the law and to the law alone' in response to a demand for *mandamus* from a plaintiff seeking to get the courts to require police intervention, and *Fisher* v. *Oldham Corporation* [1930] 2 K.B. 364 (cited in ibid., p. 42), in which the court found the police service was not vicariously liable in virtue of the original authority of the office of constable. Concerning the exercise of original authority in decisions to arrest: in some jurisdictions proceeding by summons has increased significantly and officers do not possess original authority in respect of any part of the summons process. To this extent their original authority has diminished.

According to the doctrine of original authority, there are at least some actions, including the decision to arrest or not arrest (at least in some contexts) or to shoot or not shoot, which are ultimately matters for the decision of the individual officer, and decisions for which he is, or might be, individually legally liable.[12] The contexts in question are ones in which the action of arresting a given person would prevent the police officer from discharging his obligations to the law, and (in this instance) his obligation to keep the peace, in particular. If this is indeed the legal situation, then it reflects a commitment to the ethical notion of professional autonomy. Police are being held to be akin to members of professional groups such as doctors. In the case of a surgeon, for example, it is up to the surgeon – and not the surgeon's employer – to decide whether or not to operate on a patient who might suffer complications as a result.

Consider a situation in which police officers are confronted with passive non-compliance on the part of a criminal known to be dangerous. On the one hand, if they shoot him and he turns out to be unarmed, they might be up on a murder charge. On the other hand, they put their own lives at risk by rushing him and trying to overpower him. After all, there is reason to believe that he might be armed. Faced with this problematic dilemma, it might seem that a third option is preferable, namely, the option to let him go free. Certainly this is an option available to ordinary members of the public when they confront armed and dangerous persons. But matters are somewhat different for the police. They have a moral and a legal duty to apprehend such persons. Failure to try to apprehend an armed and dangerous offender would amount to serious neglect of duty on their part. Indeed, if they simply allowed him to go free, and he went on to (say) murder some innocent person, then this neglect of duty might be held by a court to be criminal negligence.

Moreover, if a senior and superior officer issued an apparently lawful directive to these subordinate officers to shoot the offender, on the grounds that the evidence indicated that he was probably concealing a dangerous weapon and was highly likely to use it, the subordinate police officers might well be acting within their legal rights to refuse to do so. For they might disagree with the senior officer's judgement, and hold that

---

[12] A concept very close to original authority is sometimes referred to as a species of discretionary power, namely, the concept of a discretionary decision that cannot be overridden or reversed by another official. See R. Dworkin, *Taking Rights Seriously*, Cambridge, MA: Harvard University Press, 1977, p. 32. Here we need to distinguish a decision that cannot as a matter of fact be overridden, e.g., the use of deadly force by a lone officer in the field, and a decision that cannot be overridden as a matter of law. Only the latter can be referred to as a species of authority.

they might find themselves liable for wrongful killing if it turned out that the offender was unarmed.

The above-described individual civil and criminal liability of police officers stands in some contrast with military combatants. A civilian would in general sue the military organization itself, rather than the soldier whose actions resulted in harm to the civilian. Moreover, presumably soldiers do not reserve a general institutional right to refuse to shoot to kill when (lawfully) ordered to do so by their commanding officers. In keeping with the absence of such a general right, criminal liability in relation to negligence and many categories of wrongful killing is generally assigned to the military officer who issued the command, rather than his subordinates who were his instrument.

On the other hand, perhaps soldiers do reserve a moral right to refuse to shoot to kill; perhaps this is an inalienable moral right. If so, then the contrast drawn between the police and the military would be much less sharp. It could, however, still be drawn at the institutional level in terms of, for example, the notion of presumption. The presumption might be that an individual soldier would not be the one to decide whether or not he or she would shoot to kill in cases where he or she was directed by a superior to do so (or not to do so); rather, the superior would be the one to decide. In the case of police officers, this would not be the case – there would be no such presumption in favour of a superior officer; rather, the individual police officer about to do the shooting would be the one to decide. The situation is further muddied by the existence of paramilitary police roles, such as police snipers. See below for more on this point.

This notion of individual police officers' responsibility to the law, as opposed to their superior officers, and the concomitant legal liability of individual police officers, is known as 'original' authority in order to differentiate it from mere 'delegated' authority. An office with delegated – as opposed to original – authority is an office whose powers have been delegated by a higher authority. For example, person A might delegate her authority to make payments from her bank account to person B. Perhaps A does this for a brief period while she is overseas, and does it to enable her bills to be paid. Naturally, since B's authority to operate A's bank account is delegated authority only, A is in a position to remove that authority from B or to override B's decisions. Again, consider the role of supervisor in a large organization. It might be that the supervisor of all staff in the Department of Philosophy is the Head of the Department. However, these powers to supervise have been delegated by a higher authority, namely, the Dean of the Faculty. Accordingly, in principle, the decisions of the Head of the Department can be overridden by the Dean.

It is important to note that both the Dean and the Head of Department are subject to the law and to university regulations. Deans cannot override decisions of the Head of Department in a manner that infringes laws or regulations. For example, the Dean could not override a decision by the Head of Department to report a case of assault within the Department to the police. Similarly, the person in whose name the bank account is cannot override the decisions of the person with delegated authority in a manner that infringes laws or regulations. For example, even if it is A's bank account, A cannot override a decision of B's – as A's delegate – not to make a payment to a heroin dealer.

The upshot of this discussion is as follows. Firstly, if terrorism in the context of well-ordered liberal-democratic states ought to be understood as a species of crime, as opposed to being understood as a species of war, then the appropriate institution to combat terrorism in such contexts is the police, not the military. Secondly, police institutions are, or ought to be, fundamentally different in nature and purpose from military institutions. Specifically, the purpose of policing as an institution is to protect the legally enshrined moral rights of the citizenry; police are the servants of the law as such, and not the government *per se*. Thirdly, in serving the law, individual police officers are (in the UK and Australia), or perhaps ought to be, possessed of a kind of authority not possessed by military combatants, namely, original authority.

Naturally, the original authority of police officers is not an absolute moral right, but rather a severely circumscribed legal right (assuming it exists) derived from the institutional purposes of policing. Inevitably, there are some circumstances involving the use of deadly force by police officers in which there might not, and perhaps ought not to be, any legal right on the part of those officers to exercise original authority. Consider police snipers in the context of a gunman shooting at passers-by from a rooftop, e.g., the Martin Bryant episode in Port Arthur, Tasmania, in which Bryant killed 35 people prior to being arrested. Whether and when to shoot is presumptively a matter for the senior police officer in charge of proceedings to determine, not for any individual police sniper. This is consistent with any given police sniper retaining his or her basic human right to be the one to decide whether or not to kill a fellow human being.

On this model of terrorism-as-crime in the context of the well-ordered liberal-democratic state, whereas terrorist acts should be treated as ordinary, albeit very serious, crimes, nonetheless, terrorist acts have additional destabilizing features that might reasonably call for a somewhat different mix of law enforcement tactics and strategies than those deployed against ordinary crime. The question is whether these tactics and strategies reasonably ought to involve an extension of police powers and, in particular, additional constraints – additional, that is, to the ones already in place to protect citizens from one another and from external threats – on the human, civil and political rights that are constitutive of the status of a citizen in a well-ordered liberal-democratic state. It needs to be stressed that these moral and legal rights are quite fundamental to liberal democracy; a polity in which they are not respected is not a liberal democracy. On the other hand, it also needs to be stressed that none of these rights are absolute, and none exist without some constraints, e.g., the right to self-defence is a constraint on the right to life of attackers. Therefore, it is very much a matter of determining whether or not the current threat posed by terrorism morally justifies additional constraints and, if so, which ones. To reiterate, the context in question is that of a well-ordered liberal democracy at peace. Doubtless, matters are somewhat different in theatres of war or under a state of emergency. However, these latter contexts are ones to be addressed in Chapter 5. Here, as elsewhere, I note the importance of not confusing these different contexts and blurring the distinction, for example, between what is an appropriate police power of detention of suspects under a state of emergency, as opposed to normal peacetime conditions.

Some of the fundamental moral and legal rights in question include the right to freedom of speech and thought (infringed by laws against sedition), right to freedom of action (infringed by laws enabling preventive detention and/or prolonged periods of detention without being charged with an offence and brought to trial), right not to self-incriminate (infringed by laws curtailing right to silence), right to privacy (infringed by laws enabling intrusive surveillance), right not to be tortured (infringed by legalized torture warrants) and right to life (infringed by laws enabling the shooting of fleeing suspects).

Since I give detailed consideration in Chapter 6 to the right not to be tortured, I will set it aside here. Let me discuss instead each of the other above-mentioned rights, beginning with the right to freedom of speech and thought and laws against sedition.

Counter-Terrorism and Human Rights in Liberal Democracies at Peace

Freedom of Speech

I take it to be axiomatic that the right to freedom of speech and thought is inconsistent with laws against sedition. Specifically, I assume that it is a fundamental feature of any well-ordered liberal democracy that its citizens have a right to argue for, and disseminate, the view that the political system and/or the government of the day ought to be overthrown by peaceful or, if necessary, by violent means. Arguably, therefore, certain communist parties in, for example, Australia in the 1950s ought not to have been criminalized; in particular, they ought not to have been criminalized if they were simply engaged in advocating revolution, as opposed to being engaged in revolutionary activity, e.g., throwing Molotov cocktails at police officers. This is consistent with criminalizing terrorist organizations such as Al-Qaeda whose members are actually engaged in murderous terrorist attacks, or being trained in terrorist attacks, or financially (or otherwise) supporting those engaged in terrorist attacks. It is also consistent with enacting laws against *inciting* unruly mobs to violence against politicians or police, disseminating information that would *enable* others to overthrow the government, e.g., instructions on how to construct and set off a nuclear device,[13] or a person in authority *ordering* subordinates to engage in violent action against the state, e.g., a military or police officer directing subordinates to engage in acts of terrorism. Consistent with this last point, it might be that the nature of the authority relationship between some fundamentalist Muslim leaders and their followers is such that the latter are subordinates in an appropriate sense, i.e., they will, if directed, engage in terrorist acts. If so, then laws against the issuing of 'directives', e.g., fatwahs, by Muslim leaders might not constitute an infringement of the right to free speech. Moreover, exercising the right to freedom of speech and thought is not equivalent to, indeed it is inconsistent with, indoctrinating children with terrorist and/or jihadist ideology; accordingly, it is morally permissible, indeed morally required, to shut down 'schools' set up for this purpose, e.g., certain madrassas in Pakistan. Doubtless, such policies may also inflame anti-western sentiment and would need to be implemented with due care.

The reason that laws against inciting, enabling or ordering others to engage in terrorist acts do not infringe the human rights to freedom of thought and speech is that inciting, enabling and ordering go beyond merely thinking and expressing one's thoughts to others; inciting, enabling and ordering are modes of *causation*. To cause intentionally or contribute causally to some terrorist act is to be (at least partially) responsible for that act; this is not so in the case of mere reason-based advocacy of terrorism to rational adults capable of making up their own minds. If person

---

[13] Samina Malik was convicted in November 2007 under the Terrorism Act for having 'articles likely to be useful to a person committing or preparing an act of terrorism'. The articles included The Al-Qaeda Manual and The Mujaheedin Poisons Manual (http://news.bbc.co.uk/1/hi/uk/7084801.stm).

A claims that person B ought to perform a terrorist action because it would be a good thing to do, and person B upon reflection makes an independent decision to perform the action, then person B is *fully* responsible for the action. Person A is not responsible for the terrorist action. Rather, person A is responsible for claiming it ought to be done, i.e., expressing the view that it would be a good thing to do; person A is exercising his/her right to freedom of thought and speech.

It is clear that, for example, recently enacted laws against sedition in Australia and the UK are an infringement of the human right to freedom of speech and thought. According to Bronitt, under the UK's Terrorism Act (2006) it is a criminal offence to encourage or glorify terrorism[14] and the new sedition provisions in Australia prohibit, among other things, 'persons urging others to use force or violence against the constitutional system of government'.[15]

Shooting to Kill

The right to life – and closely related rights not to suffer serious physical injury – are at issue when police or other security personnel shoot dead terrorist suspects. Here there are three salient kinds of context. It is self-evident that a suicide-homicide bomber who in the presence of police and civilians is about to detonate a bomb that will kill both police and civilians can justifiably be shot dead by police. The (legal and moral) justifications here are self-defence and the defence of the lives of others; the assumptions are that the threat is imminent, known with a high degree of certainty to be actual, and that there is no method of successful intervention other than that of shooting dead the bomber. Problems arise when the threat is not imminent and/or when known with lower degrees of certainty. Consider, for example, a case in which a terrorist has planted and armed a bomb in a marketplace, but is known to be waiting a few hours for the marketplace to become more crowded prior to actually setting off the bomb by remote control. Here the crime is in process, yet arguably the threat to life is not imminent. Assume that no opportunity had yet arisen to arrest the terrorist, but an opportunity now arose to shoot the terrorist dead; surely it would be morally justifiable to take this opportunity if it was a sufficient condition for saving the lives of innocent people. However, this kind of context is not in principle different from like contexts involving serious crimes other than

---

[14]   S. Bronitt and J. Stellios, 'Sedition, security, and human rights: "unbalanaced" law reform in the war on terror', *Melbourne University Law Review*, forthcoming.
[15]   Ibid.

terrorism, e.g., a crazed sniper-gunman setting forth to his destination in a high-rise building from which he intends to commence shooting at passers-by, or a crazed person who has planted and armed a bomb in his home and is threatening to detonate it and kill not only himself, but also his family.

A second kind of context is one in which police or other security personnel shoot dead a suspected terrorist who is using armed force to resist arrest. A police officer is, or may be, morally and legally entitled – and may be morally and legally obliged – to shoot dead a person if that person is rightly and reasonably suspected of the crimes of serious rights violations (including terrorism), is attempting to avoid arrest, is armed and using those arms to avoid arrest, and if the only way to prevent the suspected offender from escaping is to shoot him/her. Again this kind of context is not in principle different from like contexts involving serious crimes other than terrorism, e.g., an armed robber seeking to avoid arrest by shooting at pursuing police.

The third kind of context is rather more problematic than the first two. A police officer is, or might be, morally and legally entitled – and may be morally obliged – to shoot dead a person if that person (whether known to be armed or not) is rightly and reasonably suspected of a serious crime (including terrorism), is attempting to avoid arrest, and if the only way to prevent the offender escaping is to shoot him/her dead. This is the context for so-called 'cases of fleeing felons'.

Some such cases are ones in which the offender, while reasonably suspected of having in the past committed a serious offence (above and beyond evading arrest), e.g., the murder of his wife, is not in the process of committing a serious offence and is not reasonably believed to be likely to commit a further offence in the future. Accordingly, shooting the offender dead is not morally justified. After all, the offender is only a suspect; he or she has not been tried and found guilty in a court of law. Moreover, the suspect is not reasonably believed to constitute a further danger to anyone. This kind of context is not in principle different from like contexts involving terrorism, e.g., a former terrorist who is suspected some time back of bombing attacks on civilians but who is known to have become disillusioned with the terrorist cause and become inactive.

Other such cases are ones in which the offender is reasonably suspected of having in the past committed a serious offence and reasonably believed to be likely to commit serious offences in the future; however, in the cases in question, it is not necessary to shoot him/her dead in order to effect his/her arrest or prevent his/her future serious offences. Accordingly, shooting the offenders is not morally justified. After all, the offender is only a suspect; he or she has not been tried and found guilty in a court of law. Moreover, it is not necessary to shoot the offender dead. The lethal shooting of suspects when it is not necessary to do so is morally unjustified, whether those shot be suspected of terrorism or of other serious crimes.

A morally problematic category of fleeing felons are those meeting the following conditions:

1   They are reasonably suspected of having committed a serious crime and, as a consequence, are being pursued by police.
2   They are reasonably believed to be highly likely to commit a serious crime in the near future, unless police intervene.
3   There are no non-lethal methods of intervention available to the police.

There are a number of features of such cases that render them morally problematic. On the one hand, there are considerations in favour of not using deadly force against such persons. For one thing, although the persons are suspected of having committed a serious crime, they have not been tried and found guilty of this crime in a court of law. For another thing, although it might be highly likely that they will commit a serious crime in the near future, this is not a matter of certainty. On the other hand, there are considerations in favour of using deadly force; these should be taken cumulatively. They are as follows:

1   The persons in question are justifiably believed to have already committed a very serious crime (one that deadly force could justifiably be used to prevent) and to be highly likely to be about to commit it again.
2   If the police do not intervene, it is highly likely that an innocent person will be murdered or raped or suffer some similarly serious attack.
3   There is no method of intervention other than deadly force.
4   The persons in question are *fleeing*, i.e., they are (unlawfully) seeking to avoid arrest by the police in the context of having the opportunity to give themselves up and, thereby, avoid being killed.

My purpose in drawing attention to such morally problematic cases is not to offer a solution to the dilemma they pose; inevitably, any 'solution' will be a matter for morally informed judgement based on a careful calibration in the particular context in question of the moral weight of specific moral considerations in play (the generality of which I have sketched above) in conjunction with the likely outcomes of selecting one or other of the available options. Rather, I simply note that such cases might include, but are not restricted to, ones in which the serious violent crime in question was terrorism. For example, the above-noted case of a crazed sniper-gunman on his way to a destination from which he intends to shoot at passers-by, and who is in the meantime fleeing pursuing police, is a case in point. Accordingly, when it comes to the moral aspect of such decision-making – including a decision to use deadly force – terrorism does not appear to be different in kind from other serious violent crimes, such as murder or rape; the moral considerations in play are, or can be, the same. For example, and as we saw above, Martin Bryant, the crazed sniper-gunman, murdered thirty-five innocent people in Tasmania, a number that is of the same order of magnitude as the number murdered by terrorists in the July 2005 London bombings.

Of course, terrorism can involve very large-scale killings, e.g., a terrorist attack involving WMDs, or an attack such as that of September 11, 2001 on the World Trade Center in which around 3,000 people were murdered. However, such scenarios involve a kind of context that is very different from that of a well-ordered liberal democracy at peace, if only because the particular city or region under threat is not well ordered, or is about to cease to be well ordered; specifically, such contexts are ones in which there is a need to declare a state of emergency and, thereby, invoke the use of extraordinary powers for police and other security agencies. Such contexts are discussed in the next chapter.

Arguably, such terrorist attacks need to be assimilated to disasters, e.g., the flooding of New Orleans, or to war, e.g., the Israeli–Palestinian conflict. In the case of one-off 'disasters', such as 9/11, there is a need to declare a short-term state of emergency, as there was with the flooding of New Orleans, the Indian Ocean tsunami, a pandemic or any other similar disaster involving substantial loss of life (or the threat thereof). Obviously, it is preferable to declare such states of emergency prior to the disaster, if this is possible – as it might be in the case of a pandemic, or even a military or large-scale terrorist attack (such as the surprise attacks on Pearl Harbor or on the World Trade Center, each of which could – should? – have been known about in advance).

On the other hand, if the terrorist attack is simply one of an ongoing series of such attacks, then there is, or may well be, a *de facto* war in progress. Accordingly, there might need to be the declaration of a state of emergency of a different sort. At any rate, in Chapter 5 I discuss in detail terrorism involving large-scale killings. Here I simply note that such one-off or ongoing terrorist attacks involving large-scale killing ought not to be assimilated to one-off or ongoing terrorist attacks that target individuals or small groups of people. The latter are more akin to ordinary murder, especially killings carried out by crime organizations or killings in the context of gang warfare. There are, of course, thousands of such (non-terrorist) criminal acts of murder in the US, in particular, each year. Italy in the 1970s provides an especially useful perspective from which to view terrorism and organized crime in comparative terms. During the 1970s and 1980s, Italy experienced on average each year dozens of small-scale, terrorist killings by the Red Brigades and other terrorist groups. However, the total casualty list over the twenty-year period was 400 dead and 5,000 injured.[16] At the same time, the mafia was a dominant force in Italian economic, political and judicial life, and carried out dozens of its own killings. Which was the greater threat to the Italian state, the Red Brigades or the mafia? Presumably, the mafia was and continues to be a greater threat.

The upshot of this discussion in relation to the right to life, and closely related rights not to suffer serious physical injury, is that terrorist acts – large-scale killings aside – in the context of a well-ordered liberal-democratic state at peace seem to occupy roughly the same moral territory as rights violations such as murder and rape. Accordingly, it is far from clear that existing police powers to use deadly force ought to be added to in order to deal with terrorists. Indeed, on the contrary, the arguments for the use of deadly force against citizens in well-ordered liberal-democratic states engaged in terrorist acts seem to mirror those governing the use of deadly force against other perpetrators of serious crimes. Here I stress that these arguments pertain to terrorist acts committed by citizens of, and within the borders of, well-ordered liberal-democratic states at peace, and do not pertain to, for example, a large-scale terrorist attack involving a WMD, such as a nuclear device. Matters are somewhat different, as we shall see, if terrorists in question are launching large-scale attacks, or are operating in theatres of war or in the context of failed states.

The right to self-defence is most obviously connected to the right to life. However, that there is something distinctive about self-defence, as opposed to defence of life in general, is indicated by the fact that we have a right to self-defence whereas we do not necessarily have a right to defend others (although they have a right to self-defence and a right not to be killed). Moreover, whereas we may have an obligation to defend the life of someone else, we do not seem to have an obligation to defend our own life. The point is that in relation to self-defence there is a certain asymmetry in our rights and obligations with respect to ourselves, as opposed to our rights and obligations with respect to others. This asymmetry is further evidenced in the right not to self-incriminate.

[16]　Whittaker (ed.), *The Terrorism Reader*, p. 223.

Right Not to Self-Incriminate

The right not to incriminate oneself is closely related to the right to self-defence. The notion appears to be that, no matter how heinous the crime a person may have committed, that person always retains the moral right to protect his or her own life. So a convicted murderer sentenced to death, or a terrorist sentenced to death, is morally entitled to try to prevent his or her executioner from performing the execution, even up to the last moment. On this view, the right to self-defence is inalienable and cannot be suspended. Relatedly – so the argument would go – people, including terrorists, always retain the right not to incriminate themselves. Even people who have committed a heinous crime retain the right not to, in effect, speak against themselves and facilitate their own conviction. (And in the case of jurisdictions retaining capital punishment, they retain the right not to, in effect, bring about, or contribute to bringing about, their own death.)

So the right not to self-incriminate is not suspended when a terrorist suspect is arrested and interrogated by police or other security personnel. This right is conceptually connected to the right to silence; if one has a right to silence and exercises it, then it is difficult, if not impossible, to incriminate oneself. Since the right to silence is derived from the right not to self-incriminate (at least as matters are explained here), then the latter is a more fundamental right than the former, and the former can, at least in principle, be abridged. However, this abridgement of the right to silence would only be acceptable if the right not to self-incriminate was preserved. Thus in a context in which one's immunity from trial and punishment was guaranteed, i.e., one could not be incriminated, either by oneself or anyone else, then the right to silence might be abridged. However, absent such alternative protections of the right not to self-incriminate, the right to silence remains a fundamental one in criminal justice systems that claim to embody and respect fundamental human rights. Hence anti-terrorist legislation that eliminates the right to silence without any countervailing protections of the right not to self-incriminate is in breach of human rights.

Freedom of Action

Let me now turn to infringements of the human right to freedom of action. The relevant infringements of these rights include laws enabling preventive detention of suspects and detention of suspects for prolonged periods without their being charged and tried.

The cornerstone of liberal democracy is individual freedom, and, aside from freedom of thought and speech, the most fundamental freedom, or set of freedoms, is freedom of action. Freedom of action includes freedom of bodily movement, freedom to associate and form relationships with others, freedom to buy and sell, freedom to plan and implement projects, including one's career, and so on. It is self-evident that detention and imprisonment strike at the very heart of individual freedom. For this reason imprisonment ought to be reserved only for serious crimes and in circumstances in which the suspect is guilty beyond reasonable doubt. Moreover, for the same reason, detention for prolonged periods without trial is morally unacceptable.

At this point a tendency has developed to invoke the notion of trade-offs and a balance between individual rights and security considerations; this is especially the case in relation to anti-terrorist legislation.[17]

Here there are two crucial questions. Firstly, whether or not there is in fact a need for a trade-off and, specifically, a trading down of particular individual rights. Arguably, privacy can be traded down somewhat, but not freedom of action. Or perhaps we can increase security by spending more money (and time) on, for example, airport security, surveillance of at-risk installations and border controls without any significant diminution of existing privacy rights or existing rights to freedom. Secondly, in so far as there is a need for balancing and to trade off, what is to be put on the scales, and what is to be traded off against what?

With respect to one side of the scale, what proponents have in mind is perhaps clear enough: individual freedom is on the scales and is to be traded down. However, it is the other side of the scales that is unclear. Notions of national security or community safety are far too general and vague to be helpful here. There is a need for more precise and differentiated notions. Indeed, as far as the notion of community safety is concerned, this presumably largely consists in the human rights to life and other aspects of personal security; so the other side of the scales consists in an individual right after all, namely, the right to personal security. As is often the case, balancing rights to freedom and rights to personal security – if this is what has to be done – is a complex matter; sometimes the latter will trump the former, e.g., searching luggage for bombs at airport security points, and there are contexts in which the former will trump the latter, e.g., British soldiers going to war against Hitler's Nazi forces.

However, it is by no means clear that there is a need for a trade-off between fundamental rights to individual freedom and rights to personal security in well-ordered liberal-democratic states at peace. For one thing,

---

[17] See, for example, what Philip Ruddock, the former Australian Attorney General, has to say about this. He is quoted in S. Bottomley and S. Bronitt, *Law in Context*, 3rd edn, Sydney: Federation Press, 2006, p. 412.

security actually consists in large part in the provision of the conditions for the exercise of individual freedom. National security and law and order in liberal-democratic polities, as I have argued elsewhere,[18] largely consist in, or are heavily dependent on, respect for human and other moral rights, especially rights to personal security and property rights. Without respect for personal security and respect for property rights, there is no law and order in a liberal democracy and, therefore, the exercise of individual liberty is difficult, if not impossible.

For another thing, the trade-off can be, and ought to be, a trade-off between the rights of offenders and suspected offenders, on the one hand, and the rights of innocent people, on the other. It is not as if what are to be traded down are the rights to, say, life and liberty of innocent civilians. I take it that the proposition is not that police and other security personnel ought to be empowered to shoot to kill, or indefinitely detain, *innocent* people in order to protect the rights of other innocent people. Unfortunately, some recent anti-terrorist legislation trades down the rights of people known to be innocent. Consider, for example, the right to silence. As noted in Chapter 1, in Australia, new anti-terrorist legislation (ASIO Bill [No. 2]) permits ASIO (Australian Security Intelligence Organization) to detain and question persons who are not even suspects, if it is believed these innocents could provide relevant information.[19]

However, the main problem concerns the rights of suspects. Suspects are, by definition, not identical to those who have been tried and found guilty of a crime. So, unlike those who have been tried and found guilty, suspects continue to be presumed to be innocent and, as a consequence, cannot be, or ought not be, detained for lengthy periods, or otherwise subjected to restrictions or harms. Rather, suspects who are arrested must be either charged and brought to a speedy trial, or released following on from a brief period of interrogation. Moreover, suspects who are subjected to detention and interrogation ought to be afforded appropriate rights to protection, e.g., the right to an attorney.

This is not to say that there might not be a need to calibrate, for example, periods of detention without trial in the context of changing circumstances, including the current threat of terrorism in the US, UK and elsewhere. Thus it may be that terrorist suspects ought to be able to be detained for weeks rather than days in the context of the need to extract evidence from encrypted communications on seized computers. Currently in the UK there is a controversy in relation to whether or not

---

[18]   Miller and Blackler, *Ethical Issues in Policing*, chap. 1.
[19]   A. Lynch and G. Williams, *What Price Security? Taking Stock of Australia's Anti-Terror Laws*, Sydney: University of New South Wales Press, 2006, pp. 33–4.

to extend the period of detention without charge for terror suspects from 28 days to 42 days.[20] But such calibration must not be assimilated to a circumstance in which a terrorist suspect can be detained indefinitely without trial (including by the device of ongoing renewal of a detention order), as is currently the case with non-British citizens in the UK. In the UK there is currently provision for indefinite detention of suspects without bringing them to trial if they do not have British citizenship and expelling them is judged to present a real risk of their being tortured.[21]

A procedure that is closely related to detention without trial is the so-called 'control orders' introduced in the UK under the 2005 terrorism legislation. These control orders enable terrorist suspects to be restricted in various ways, including in respect of travel (domestic and/or foreign), and communications, e.g., use of the Internet, and/or by the requirement to report regularly to the police. As is the case with detention without trial, control orders are an infringement of central aspects of the human right to freedom; and, again as in the case of detained terrorist suspects, those under control orders should either be prosecuted or be allowed to enjoy their human right to freedom.

Preventive detention is yet another counter-terrorist measure that infringes individual freedom. India, in particular, is well known for the use of its laws enabling this procedure. Preventive detention is morally problematic in that, at least in principle, it does not necessarily pertain to those suspected of a past or present crime – let alone tried and convicted of a crime – but to those suspected of being likely to commit a *future* crime; that is, persons are to be detained, notwithstanding the fact that the crime for which they are being detained has not been committed and is not in the process of being committed. Here it is important to distinguish between: (a) someone suspected of having already committed a crime – this first crime is in the present – as a precursor to committing a second crime in the future, e.g., conspiring in the present to commit a murder in the future; and (b) someone who is not suspected of any present (or past) crime, but only of being likely to commit a future crime, e.g., someone who is not suspected of any past or present crime, such as the crime of conspiracy to murder, but who is, nevertheless, believed to be likely to commit a murder in the future. At least in principle,

[20] http://news.bbc.co.uk/1/hi/uk_politics/7130072.stm.

[21] Sections 21 to 32 of the Anti-Terrorism, Crime and Security Emergency Bill 2001 now allow detention without trial where the option of deportation is not available. Article 3 of the European Convention on Human Rights, to which the UK is a signatory, forbids torture and inhuman treatment. See D. Haubrich, 'September 11, anti-terror laws and civil liberties: Britain, France and Germany compared', *Government and Opposition* 38(1), 2003, p. 15.

preventive detention might pertain only to a person in the situation
described in (b), and not to a person in the situation described in (a).
As such, preventive detention infringes the basic moral principle that a
person should not be detained, or otherwise penalized, for a crime that
he or she is known not to have committed or to be in the process of
committing. Accordingly, preventive detention cannot be morally justified
under normal circumstances, and ought not to be a standing police power.

Notwithstanding the above, preventive detention for limited periods
might be morally justified in some emergency situations. For example, in
the context of ongoing, large-scale, caste-based and communal violence
of the sort experienced in Bihar and Gujarat in India in recent years,
preventive detention for limited periods of persons highly likely to incite
massed crowds to violence might be morally justified. However, this is a
moral justification for preventive detention of select individuals for a limited period and only in the context of a well-founded, and lawfully decreed,
state of emergency. By contrast, preventive detention is not justified in
well-ordered liberal-democratic settings in which there is no emergency,
e.g., most parts of most contemporary liberal-democratic states. Moreover,
preventive detention under a state of emergency should be subject to
stringent accountability processes, including judicial oversight.

Earlier I raised the issue of trading down of the rights of, especially,
terrorist suspects. One illicit way in which the scales on the right-hand
side (the security side) are being given increased weight with a consequent trading down of the rights of suspects is by the broadening of
the scope of anti-terrorist legislation so as to embrace not simply actual
specific acts of terrorism or actual membership of terrorist organizations,
but also *threatened* acts of terrorism and the consequences of actual acts
of terrorism in terms of the *fear* that they might produce. In some jurisdictions,[22] terrorism includes the (possibly indirect and distant) *threat* of
bombings and like actions, and therefore brings with it actions which have
the potential to cause harm, e.g., undertaking terrorist training; moreover, some anti-terrorism laws also focus on the motivation to intimidate
and therefore bring into play the intentional causing of the *fear* of harm,
as opposed to harm itself. There are other ways of widening of laws
against terrorism, e.g., associating with a terrorist, and new crimes (or
resuscitation of ones in disuse), e.g., sedition (discussed above). Here, as
elsewhere, there is a need to analyse each of these elements on a piece-
meal basis. Undergoing terrorist training, for example, manifests a high
degree of culpability and, in the context of an increasing terrorist threat,
warrants severe penalties. On the other hand, whether or not an action
intentionally or otherwise caused fear is arguably so indeterminate a

[22]   Bottomley and Bronitt, *Law in Context*, p. 402.

matter as to lead to abuse in the application of any laws enacted to eliminate or reduce such fear-causing actions.

Privacy

Many people feel seriously diminished by the disclosure of personal information, even when it is accurate and they are not damaged professionally or socially. Small wonder that more than sixty years ago a prominent Boston lawyer who became one of our greatest jurists, Louis D. Brandeis, characterized the rights of privacy as 'the most comprehensive of rights and the one most valued by civilized men'. The thought was echoed by the late, great William O. Douglas, who said, 'The right to be left alone is the beginning of all freedom.'[23] Brandeis et al. are surely correct in holding that privacy is an important moral value.[24]

Privacy is not simply a desirable *de facto* condition, it is a moral right to something that a person might or might not in fact possess. Specifically, privacy is a moral right a person has in relation to other persons with respect to: (a) the possession of information about him/herself by other persons; or (b) the observation/perceiving of him/herself – including tactile interference, such as body searches – by other persons. The range of matters regarded as private in this basic sense embraces much of what could be referred to as a person's 'inner self'. This inner self comprises a person's unexpressed thoughts, feelings, bodily sensations and imaginings. But it may also comprise elements or aspects of a person's body: roughly speaking, those elements or aspects that are not normally perceptually accessible to others in public spaces.

Certain facts pertaining to a person's various public roles and practices, including one's voting decisions, are regarded as private.[25] These kinds of facts are apparently regarded as private in part in virtue of the potential, should they be disclosed, of undermining the capacity of the person to function autonomously in these public roles, or to compete fairly in these practices. If others know how a person votes, the person's right freely to support a particular candidate might be undermined. If business competitors have access to a person's business plans, then they will gain an unfair advantage over the person. If a would-be employer knows a job applicant's sexual preferences, then the employer might unfairly

---

[23] A. Miller, *Miller's Court*, New York: Houghton Mifflin, 1982.

[24] Earlier versions of the material in this section appeared in S. Miller and J. Blackler, 'Privacy, confidentiality and security in policing', in *Ethical Issues in Policing*, chap. 4; S. Miller, 'Privacy and the Internet', *Australian Computer Journal* 29(1), 1997, pp. 12–16; and S. Miller, *Issues in Police Ethics*, Wagga Wagga, Australia: Keon Publications, 1996.

[25] See S.I. Benn, *A Theory of Freedom*, Cambridge: Cambridge University Press, 1988, p. 289.

discriminate against the job applicant by not hiring that person because of his or her sexual preferences.

The sphere of an individual's privacy can be widened to include other individuals who stand in a professional relationship to the first individual. Here part of the sphere of an individual's privacy, e.g., the bodily states of a sick person, is widened to include another person, e.g., the person's doctor, and the result is a *confidential* relationship. An analogous point can be made in relation to lawyers and their clients, and in relation to police and the victims of crimes who are also witnesses to those crimes. Again, law enforcement agencies must retain confidential information in relation to the activities of criminal organizations if they are successfully to investigate those organizations.

The notion that privacy is an absolute right that cannot be overridden under any circumstances is unsustainable. The rights to privacy of some individuals, and the right to confidentiality of members of some organizations, will in some cases be overridden by the rights of other individuals and other members of organizations to be protected by the law enforcement agencies from rights violations, including murder, rape, and terrorist attack. Moreover, in the context of an ongoing terrorist threat, a *de facto* diminution in privacy as a consequence of an increase in the circumstances in which privacy rights are overridden, or at the very least of an increase in the level of intelligence/evidence gathering within those rights, is likely to be justifiable.[26] This is in part because the right to privacy is, speaking generally, less morally weighty than most other moral rights, such as the various rights to freedom. It is one thing to monitor a person's communications or financial transactions, quite another to lock that person up. But it is also because in the context of a well-ordered liberal democracy at peace yet facing a terrorist threat, the terrorism-as-crime framework is applicable, and under the terrorism-as-crime framework the emphasis is on increasing the intelligence/evidence gathering activities of security agencies and perhaps also selective and limited widening of the intelligence/evidence gathering powers of police – almost inevitably at the expense of privacy – so as to facilitate the prosecution of terrorist offenders and reduce the effectiveness of their operations by, for example, denying them financial resources. By contrast, under a terrorism-as-war framework, the emphasis is on capturing or killing terrorists, i.e., the human rights at issue are the right to life and the right to freedom. This is not to deny the applicability of the terrorism-as-war framework in certain contexts. (See the next chapter.) However, it is to

---

[26] I provide a more detailed account of privacy and confidentiality rights in S. Miller, *Investigative Ethics*, Oxford: Blackwell, forthcoming.

insist that one of those contexts is *not* a well-ordered liberal democracy at peace. Accordingly, in the context of a well-ordered liberal democracy at peace it is politically dangerous and morally unacceptable to infringe citizens' rights to life, e.g., by shoot-on-sight provisions, and rights to freedom, e.g., by detention without trial; that is, it is politically danger-ous and morally unacceptable to apply the terrorism-as-war framework to well-ordered liberal democracies at peace.

In relation to accessing of data and/or intercepting of communications by law enforcement agencies, trade-offs might need to be made between the rights of citizens – including suspects – to privacy and confidentiality, on the one hand, and the rights of actual and potential victims to pro-tection from serious crime, such as terrorism, on the other. Specifically, the right to privacy and confidentiality might need to be traded down in order to protect the right to life of those threatened by terrorists. Thus, limited use of data-mining might be justified, e.g., cross-tabulating a data-base of suspected terrorists – it being a crime to be a member of the ter-rorist organization in question – against a data-base of the registered hotel guests in a specific location and time period. However, definite limits need to be placed on any such trading down, e.g., reasonable suspicion in rela-tion to serious crime, and appropriate accountability mechanisms put in place, e.g., destruction of data only justifiably acquired for a specific invest-igation, a requirement for judicial warrants. Moreover, here as elsewhere, creative solutions to the threat of terrorism might minimize the threat to privacy while maximizing protection against terrorists. For example, footage from video surveillance cameras operating continuously in public areas might be subjected only to limited access by a restricted group of investigators and subsequent to the performance of some criminal act.[27] Additionally, continuous monitoring of such surveillance cameras might be by way of an automated process that 'detected' only certain pre-determined and programmed-in suspects (e.g., on the basis of their photographs) and – having detected them – alerted security staff to their presence.

Clearly, the state of technology at a given point in time to some extent determines the possibility of minimizing the threat to privacy while max-imizing protection against terrorism and other crimes. However, as is frequently pointed out, technology can also simply provide the means to maximize infringements of privacy without any concomitant, or morally justifying, increase in protections against terrorism. Moreover, technology can also provide the means to maximize privacy and reduce the possibil-ities of successfully combating terrorism and other crimes. For example,

---

[27] Jeroen van den Hoven provides this kind of example. See J. van den Hoven, 'Computer ethics and moral methodology', *Metaphilosophy* 28(3), 1997, pp. 234–49.

the current availability to the general public of very secure computer systems and of high-level encryption products makes accessing of data and/or intercepting of communications on the Internet by law enforcement agencies extremely difficult and expensive.

Given such an array of technological possibilities, it is important to determine an appropriate set of principles by means of which to give direction to the use of surveillance and communication interception technology. These principles include the following ones,[28] first developed in relation to the interception of communications by telephone and infringed in recent years by the National Security Agency in the US:[29]

1 Because such accessing and/or intercepting are by definition an infringement of the right to privacy, the presumption must be against their use. This presumption can be overridden by other weighty moral considerations – especially the need to protect other moral rights – or by exceptional circumstances, such as might obtain in wartime or under a state of emergency. But the presumption cannot be overridden by a blanket appeal to the common good or to the general need for security.

2 The benefits of such accessing and/or intercepting must offset the likely costs, including the costs in terms of the erosion in public trust.

3 The accessing and/or interception in question must be in relation to serious crimes, e.g., terrorism.

4 There must be at least a reasonable suspicion[30] that the person whose privacy is to be infringed has committed, or intends to commit, a serious crime – or is implicated in a serious crime – and that the resulting information is likely substantially to further the investigation under way in relation to that crime.

5 There must be no feasible alternative method of gathering the information that does not involve an infringement of privacy.

6 The law enforcement officials must be subject to stringent accountability requirements, including the issuing of warrants in circumstances in which the justification provided is independently adjudicated.

7 Those whose privacy has been infringed must be informed that it has been infringed at the earliest time consistent with not compromising the investigation, or connected investigations.

---

[28] An earlier version of the material in this section appeared in Miller, 'Privacy and the Internet' and in Miller and Blackler, *Ethical Issues in Policing*, chap. 4.

[29] First disclosed in *New York Times* in December 2005.

[30] The more intrusive and sustained the infringement of the right to privacy, the higher the standard of evidence that ought to be required in relation to demonstrating 'reasonable suspicion', e.g. probable cause, or perhaps (even higher) good and decisive reasons.

An increasingly important issue in relation to privacy is the integration and sharing of different sets of information available to different government – including law enforcement – agencies. This is morally problematic in that, as we have seen, there is a presumption against the gathering of information on citizens by government officials, including law enforcement personnel. This presumption can be overridden in relation to specific kinds of information required for specific legitimate purposes, such as tax gathering or the investigation of someone reasonably suspected of engaging in serious criminal activity, such as terrorism. But information gathered for one purpose should not be made available for another purpose, unless a specific case can be made out for doing so and appropriate accountability processes are in place.

Nor is this simply a problem for isolated individuals whose rights might be infringed; the problem is potentially a societal one. One of the purposes of privacy law is to deny, as far as possible, the formation of linkages between statutory bodies, and thereby to prevent such linkages enabling the coming into being of a 'Big Brother' system of invasive inquiry and social control of the kind that existed in Eastern Europe under communism.[31] Accordingly, organizational 'Chinese walls' are supposed to separate the investigators employed by one of the several different organs of government from the investigators employed by another of these organs. Limited contact across the statutory barriers might only be made – or denied – at the highest level, and for good reason; and done so in a parsimoniously sanctioned and limited manner following stringent protocols.

As noted above, an investigation into a serious crime, including a terrorist attack, necessarily involves adherence to the principle of confidentiality on pain of compromising said investigation. The moral underpinning of the principle of confidentiality in such cases consists in the moral obligations to victims and potential victims. However, once the investigation is completed, there is no longer this basis for confidentiality. Indeed, respect for the rights of those accused of the crime and the requirement of investigator accountability dictate that secrecy gives way to transparency.

So far so good. However, matters are more complicated when what is under investigation is not simply an individual one-off crime, but a criminal organization or, in this case, terrorist organization which has mounted a series of attacks and continues to do so; necessarily the investigation is large, complex and ongoing. Here, as before, we are concerned with an investigation, or set of connected investigations, into a terrorist organization operating within the confines of a liberal-democratic state.

---

[31] See, for instance, S. Cohen, *Visions of Social Control: Crime, Punishment and Classification*, Cambridge: Polity Press, 1985.

Here the nature and scale of the activities of the terrorist organization are important. Notwithstanding some notable 'successes' on the British mainland, e.g., the 1996 bombing of London's prestigious business centre at Canary Wharf, the IRA at no time threatened the existence of the UK state as such. On the other hand, the political status quo in Northern Ireland was certainly threatened by the terrorism and counter-terrorism involving the IRA, the loyalist paramilitary forces, and the British and Northern Ireland security forces. Arguably, therefore, Northern Ireland in the last thirty years of the twentieth century was, in effect, experiencing an extent and degree of insecurity analogous to a state of war and warranting, as a consequence, the imposition of an ongoing state of emergency.

However, notwithstanding the rhetoric of the 'war against terrorism', neither the US nor the UK is experiencing this level of internal insecurity. Accordingly, the nature of the ongoing investigations in relation to terrorist groups and activities in the US and the UK is arguably at this stage more analogous to ongoing investigations into organized crime networks, than full-blown counter-terrorist campaigns of the kind engaged in by the British army and the Royal Ulster Constabulary in Northern Ireland.

That said, the investigations into terrorist attacks and networks in the US and the UK are large-scale, complex and ongoing. Accordingly, it cannot reasonably be expected that there be full disclosure of the sort following on a completed investigation of a one-off discrete crime. For example, lists of suspects and police informants, the *modus operandi* of security personnel and planned raids need to be kept confidential on pain of compromising counter-terrorist operations.

Here it is important to distinguish operations from policy. Notwithstanding the need for operational autonomy and associated secrecy, it would be unacceptable for police and other security personnel to use tactics and possess powers that are not transparent to, and consistent with, liberal-democratic government. Hence the unacceptability of the warrantless domestic wire-taps conducted by the National Security Agency and secretly authorized by President Bush in contravention of the Foreign Intelligence Surveillance Act.[32] Moreover, there is a need for ongoing oversight of security operations, and such oversight cannot wait for the 'end of the war on terrorism' – a war without a determinate end, as is the 'war on crime'.

Here it is worth describing some of the dangers attendant upon state secrecy.[33] Firstly, excessive secrecy can undermine operational effectiveness.

---

[32] First reported in the *New York Times*, 16 December 2005.
[33] Sissela Bok makes these points in her *Secrets: Concealment and Revelation*, Oxford: Oxford University Press, 1982, chap. 23.

Evidently, this is what happened in the case of the 1980 helicopter incursion by the US into Iran to rescue unlawfully held US citizens. The mission failed in large part because the secrecy requirements were such that the various helicopter crews were unable to coordinate their activities.[34]

Secondly, high levels of secrecy can mask incompetence. Evidently – and this is thought be many to be a generous interpretation – incompetence is at least in part what happened in relation to the WMDs falsely thought to be possessed by Saddam Hussein. Saddam Hussein's believed possession of these weapons was the primary justification for invading Iraq. In retrospect it is clear that the evidence possessed by the US and UK security agencies did not justify a belief in the existence of these WMDs.

Thirdly, high levels of secrecy can mask not simply incompetence but also corruption, illegality and gross immorality, including human rights abuses. This is obvious in the case of authoritarian regimes, but it is also a problem for liberal democracies. Consider the Pentagon Papers. These gave a detailed account of US involvement in the war in Vietnam. Daniel Ellsberg, a public servant, leaked the papers to the *New York Times* in 1971. The papers detailed the incompetence, illegality and immorality of US foreign policy in Vietnam over many years. Ellsberg breached the principle of administrative confidentiality. On the other hand, the revelations he made possible demonstrated the dangers of state secrecy and the need for accountability. If recent disclosures of the apparently unlawful, but in any case definitely warrantless, wire-tapping by the National Security Agency in the US illustrate state secrecy and an absence of executive accountability – as they certainly do – then recent disclosures of torture at Abu Ghraib in Iraq illustrate the inherent dangers of state secrecy and an absence of accountability.

Conclusion

The principal focus of this chapter has been the infringement of human rights, e.g., freedom of speech, freedom of action, right to privacy, within a well-ordered liberal-democratic state at peace as part of a counter-terrorism strategy. I have argued that the morally legitimate actions of a liberal-democratic state are significantly constrained by the human rights of its individual citizens, specifically, the various rights to freedom. Accordingly, there are a range of in-principle limits to counter-terrorism strategies adopted to protect the lives of citizens; it is not simply a matter of weighing up, or trading off, the right to life of some citizens against the rights to freedom of others in the abstract. To put matters somewhat crudely,

---

[34] Ibid., p. 195.

there are significant in-principle limits on what a liberal-democratic state is entitled to do, even in order to protect the lives of its citizenry.

An important distinction in play here is that between a one-off action that is morally justified, all things considered, and a law, or lawful institutional practice, that is morally justified in the setting of a liberal-democratic state. A particular, one-off action performed in a specific context might be morally justified, all things considered, without the action in question either being lawful, or being an action of a type that ought to be lawful, in a liberal democracy. In general, the law, especially the criminal law, tracks – and ought to track – morality; however, this is not necessarily or invariably the case. I make use of this distinction in a number of the chapters in this book, including Chapter 6 on torture.

In the context of a well-ordered liberal democracy at peace yet facing a terrorist threat, the terrorism-as-crime framework is applicable. Under the terrorism-as-crime framework the emphasis is on widening the intelligence/evidence gathering powers of police – almost inevitably at the expense of privacy, albeit these infringements ought to be in a context of clearly defined legal limits and accountability – so as to facilitate the prosecution of terrorist offenders. By contrast, under a terrorism-as-war framework the emphasis is on capturing or killing terrorists, i.e., the human rights at issue are the right to life and the right to freedom. This is not to deny the applicability of the terrorism-as-war framework in certain contexts. (See the next chapter.) However, it is to insist that one of those contexts is *not* a well-ordered liberal democracy at peace. Accordingly, in the context of a well-ordered liberal democracy at peace it is politically dangerous and morally unacceptable to infringe citizens' rights to life, e.g., by shoot-on-sight provisions, and rights to freedom, e.g., by detention without trial; that is, it is politically dangerous and morally unacceptable to apply the terrorism-as-war framework to well-ordered liberal democracies at peace. Confusing the different contexts of a well-ordered liberal democracy at peace, a liberal democracy under a state of emergency, and a theatre of war leads to a dangerous blurring of the distinctions, for example, between what is an appropriate police power of detention of suspects under a state of emergency, as opposed to normal peacetime conditions.

5

Terrorism, War and States of Emergency

In Chapter 2 I offered a definition of terrorism that involved an indirect strategy for demarcating terrorist actions from other violent acts, namely, one that involves a list of well-established violent crimes (that are justifiable as crimes) that: (1) meet various conditions for being acts of terrorism, including political motivations not present in most violent crimes; and (2) distinguish, as in law, between terrorism in civil society and terrorism in war. This strategy yields two sets of violent crimes describable as acts of terrorism, namely, terrorism-as-crime (ordinary violent crimes that are also acts of terrorism) and terrorism-as-war-crimes (war crimes that are also acts of terrorism).

I take it that the terrorism-as-crime model – as opposed to the terrorism-as-war model – is the preferred and, therefore, default, framework when a liberal-democratic state is suffering lethal attacks from a terrorist organization. More precisely, the terrorism-as-war framework should be applied only under the following general conditions:[1]

1 The terrorism-as-crime framework cannot adequately contain serious and ongoing terrorist attacks.
2 The application of the terrorism-as-war framework is likely to be able adequately to contain the terrorist attacks.
3 The application of the terrorism-as-war framework is proportionate to the terrorist threat.
4 The terrorism-as-war framework is applied only to an extent, e.g., with respect to a specific theatre of war but not necessarily to all areas that have suffered, or might suffer, a terrorist attack, and over a period of time that is necessary.

---

[1] These conditions mirror many of the conditions in the *ius ad bellum* of Just War Theory.

5 All things considered, the application of the terrorism-as-war framework will have good consequences in terms of security, and better
   overall consequences, e.g., in terms of lives lost, freedoms curtailed,
   economic impact, institutional damage, than the available alternatives.

Accordingly, it is only when the liberal-democratic state cannot adequately contain the terrorist activity of a specific terrorist organization that
the terrorism-as-war model might need to be applied, e.g., in a theatre of
war involving ongoing, large-scale terrorist attacks and military counter-
strikes by government security forces. The Israeli–Hezbollah conflict is
arguably a case in point. Moreover, even if the terrorism-as-war model
is to be applied in a given theatre of war, it would not follow that it
should be applied outside that theatre of war. Thus, even if it is desirable
and necessary to apply the terrorism-as-war model to the armed conflict
between Al-Qaeda combatants and US forces in Afghanistan seeking to
destroy Al-Qaeda military bases and personnel, it would not follow that
it was desirable or necessary to apply it to Al-Qaeda operatives functioning
in the US homeland.

This way of proceeding presupposes that the distinction between civil
societies at peace and theatres of war can adequately be drawn. The
concept of war is, of course, somewhat vague; the point at which a violent attack, or set or attacks, on one militarized organization by another
militarized organization constitutes a war is indeterminate. Moreover, the
concept of war is especially vague in its application to armed conflict between
nation-states and non-state actors. Nevertheless, I am obviously assuming
that a liberal-democratic nation-state can engage in wars with non-state
actors, e.g., a civil war, a revolutionary war or a war against an armed,
organized, belligerent, external, non-state entity. I take it that Israel, for
example, is engaged in a war with the terrorist organizations Hamas and
Hezbollah. I also take it that the US is at war with the Taliban and Al-
Qaeda in Afghanistan.[2] On the other hand, as noted above, from the fact
that two states (or a state and a non-state actor) are at war, it does not
follow that all or any of their respective territories are theatres of war,
i.e., are *de facto* battlefields.

I further take it that notwithstanding President George Bush's (rhetor-
ical?) pronouncements, the US is not literally at war with terrorism *per se*,
for terrorism *per se* is not an organization; nor is a terrorist ideological

---

[2] It goes without saying that in claiming that such and such liberal democratic state is
waging an internal or an external war, I am not *eo ipso* claiming that the war is morally
justified. Liberal democratic states can and have engaged in wars that, for example, fail to
comply with the conditions of Just War Theory; the ongoing Iraq War is a case in point.

movement necessarily an organization. Moreover, as we have seen above, there are some terrorist groups, e.g., the Oklahoma City bombers, that are not the sort of entities that are able to conduct a war. Moreover, there are many terrorist groups – whatever their military capacity might be – that are simply not engaged in a war with the US. It is obviously false that the US is at war with all the dozens of disparate terrorist groups all over the world, Islamic and otherwise, and at war also with numerous nation-states that engage in terrorism, e.g., North Korea and Zimbabwe. Indeed, arguably, to the extent that the US anti-terrorist campaign widens its focus – and is seen or believed to be widening its focus – to include terrorist groups other than Al-Qaeda, President Bush will reduce the effectiveness of the US counter-terrorism measures against Al-Qaeda; this is not simply a matter of spreading military and other resources more thinly and fighting on multiple fronts, but also of tending to drive various (especially Islamic) terrorist groups to enter into mutual support arrangements with Al-Qaeda that they might otherwise not have entered into. A better strategy might be an explicitly stated, narrow, perhaps even exclusive, focus on Al-Qaeda.

Moreover, President Bush's claim to be at war with terrorism conveniently masks the fact that even liberal democracies do not have an entirely clean record when it comes to terrorism. Consider, for example: the bombing of civilian areas in Lebanon conducted by Israel in recent times (in response to Hezbollah terror bombings of civilian areas in northern Israel); the bombing of civilian areas of Dresden and other German cities by Britain during the Second World War; and the dropping of atomic bombs on Hiroshima and Nagasaki by the US at the close of the Second World War. The US has also supported terrorist groups such as the Contras in Nicaragua. More recently, there have been accusations of US support for anti-Castro terrorists such as Luis Posada Carriles. Posada is a former CIA operative who is accused of involvement in the 1976 bombing of a Cuban airliner that killed seventy-three people and has admitted being involved in a series of bombings of Cuban hotels and nightspots in 1997.

I assume that wars waged by liberal-democratic states can be either external or internal wars. India, for example, is fighting an internal war in Kashmir against a variety of terrorist and separatist groups. In this conflict India is deploying hundreds of thousands of military and police personnel,[3] and tens of thousands of civilians, soldiers, police, insurgents and terrorists have lost their lives.[4]

---

[3] See S. Sen, *Law Enforcement and Cross Border Terrorism*, New Delhi: Concept Publishing, 2005, p. 65.
[4] See K. Dhillon, *Police and Politics in India: Colonial Concepts, Democratic Compulsions: Indian Police 1947–2002*, New Delhi: Manohar, 2005, chap. 13.

In this chapter I consider a number of problems posed by terrorism for the duality of the terrorism-as-crime framework and the terrorism-as-war framework that I outlined in Chapters 2 and 4, in particular. Here it is also important to bring to mind the following threefold distinction between contexts: (1) well-ordered liberal democracies at peace; (2) liberal democracies under a state of emergency; and (3) theatres of war (whether in the context of a war between states or a war between a state and a non-state actor).

Terrorist Attacks, Disasters and States of Emergency

The first problem concerns large-scale, one-off, lethal terrorist attacks by non-state actors against, and within the territorial jurisdiction of, a well-ordered liberal-democratic state during peacetime, e.g., the September 11, 2001 attack on the World Trade Center in New York and the Pentagon in Washington in which around 3,000 people were murdered.[5] Such a large-scale attack ought to be distinguished from ongoing, small-scale, lethal terrorist attacks of the kind perpetrated by, for example, the Red Brigades in Italy in the 1970s. For none of the latter terrorist attacks taken by itself constituted a disaster as such; rather, each individual terrorist attack could be assimilated to, say, the murder of a public official by the mafia, e.g., the bombing of Judge Falcone in Italy in 1984. The point here is that such small-scale killings can be readily accommodated within the terrorism-as-crime model outlined in Chapter 4. However, large-scale terrorist attacks, including (potentially) chemical, biological, radiological and/or nuclear (CBRN) terrorist attacks, are in some respects more akin to disasters, such as the Indian Ocean tsunami in 2004 (in which approximately two hundred thousand lost their lives) or the flooding of New Orleans in 2005, than they are to ordinary small-scale murders. Admittedly, a key difference between disasters and large-scale terrorist attacks is that the latter are intentionally (and culpably) brought about by criminals. But this is also the case for some disasters, such as bushfires in Australia started by arsonists. Such bushfires regularly destroy hundreds

---

[5]   By the use of the term 'peacetime' here I mean two things. Firstly, the terrorist attack is not an element of an ongoing war, i.e., each suicide-bombing attack in post-Saddam Hussein Iraq is an element of an internal war. Secondly, the state in question is not engaged in any all-out war that threatens its existence to the point that it is essentially on a war-footing. Thus the US was engaged in all-out war in this sense during the Second World War, but not if it is merely deploying an armed force in Afghanistan or Iraq. I will refer to the latter kind of wars as *limited* wars.

of thousands of hectares of forest-land, hundreds of homes and, at times, lead to loss of human life. The point is that a large-scale bushfire is a disaster independently of whether or not it was started by an arsonist or by a lightning strike. Similarly, the attack on the World Trade Center would have been a disaster if the pilots of the two planes had had heart seizures and, as a consequence, accidentally crashed their planes into the building, causing the same loss of life as the terrorist attack did. That the event was in point of fact intentionally (and culpably) brought about by terrorists did not make it any less of a disaster.[6] At any rate, the question is: how should a well-ordered liberal-democratic state respond to such a large-scale, one-off terrorist attack by a non-state actor during peacetime?

My suggestion here is that such attacks should be treated, firstly, as disasters, and, as such, they call for the imposition of a legally circum-scribed, geographically limited state of emergency during the period of the disaster and its immediate aftermath, but not beyond, and certainly not for a prolonged period. I suggest, secondly, that if the terrorist actions in question are perpetrated outside a theatre of war, then they should be treated as crimes, i.e., the most appropriate framework to apply is the terrorism-as-crime framework – as opposed to the terrorism-as-war framework.

My reason for preferring the imposition of a state of emergency and the application of the terrorism-as-crime framework to one-off, large-scale terrorist attacks is as follows. Such a terrorist attack is clearly a crime; the further questions are, firstly, whether it is also an act of war and, secondly, whether the terrorist attack has been undertaken in what was, or what now is, a theatre of war. Here I am not disputing that the 9/11 attack by Al-Qaeda on the World Trade Center is assimilable to an act of war, given the nature, goals and military capability of Al-Qaeda as an organization. Nor am I disputing the legitimacy of the US military operations against Al-Qaeda in Afghanistan; Afghanistan is a theatre of war, and US forces are justifiably engaged in a military campaign to capture and kill Al-Qaeda terrorist-combatants. Whether or not a one-off, large-scale terrorist attack should be treated as an act of war depends in part on the nature, goals and lethal capability of the person or persons who mounted the attack. (More on this below.) However, I am disputing that by virtue of the 9/11 attack, New York became a theatre of war. So my specific

---

[6] The fact that such a disaster was brought about by terrorists and was, therefore, not an accident does of course make a difference, e.g., in the response to it. The criminals have to be investigated and brought to justice. The question that now arises is whether or not the response was appropriate and proportionate, in respect of its character both *qua* disaster and *qua* criminal action.

point here is that a single terrorist attack by a non-state actor – even a large-scale attack – does not of itself constitute a war and, therefore, should not necessarily be regarded as having been undertaken in what was, or now is, a theatre of war. Even if Timothy McVeigh's bombing in Oklahoma City had killed 3,000 people, it would not have meant that the US was at war or that Oklahoma City had become a theatre of war. Accordingly, such one-off, large-scale terrorist attacks do not in themselves warrant the application of the terrorism-as-war framework (and, therefore, the terrorism-as-war-crime model); the terrorism-as-crime framework will suffice. Naturally, if the domestically based terrorist group mounted a series of such large-scale terrorist attacks, then the liberal-democratic state in question could no longer be said to be well ordered; under these circumstances the government and its security forces would be in a *de facto* state of internal war not of their own making but against some of their own citizens. Indeed, even if the terrorist attacks were not large-scale, but, rather, widespread and ongoing, then the government could well be in a *de facto* state of internal war. The ongoing terrorism in Kashmir is an example of such an internal armed struggle, if not an all-out internal war.[7] The special problems posed by internal armed struggles involving terrorist groups are discussed in the next section.

Let us now consider the possibility that the one-off, large-scale terrorist attack is perpetrated by a non-state actor based in some state outside the jurisdiction of the liberal-democratic nation-state under attack. Here there are two salient possibilities. Firstly, the state in which the terrorist group is based is itself well ordered, and is willing and able successfully to apply the terrorism-as-crime framework (under its domestic law or derivatively under international law) to the terrorist attack. If so, then there is no need to apply the terrorism-as-war framework; the terrorism-as-crime framework will suffice.

Secondly, and alternatively, let us assume that the state in which the terrorist group is based is itself not well ordered, and/or is unwilling or unable successfully to apply the terrorism-as-crime framework. In these circumstances the liberal-democratic state that had suffered the one-off, large-scale terrorist attack could reasonably regard itself as the victim of an act of war by an external aggressor – albeit a non-state actor – and respond accordingly. The point here is that the non-state actor is not only a belligerent actor, it is a belligerent actor that is operating outside the authority and control of any state actor. An example of an external war

---

[7] At least some of the terrorist groups operating in Kashmir are trained, financed and otherwise assisted by Pakistan. See Dhillon, *Police and Politics in India*. To this extent the conflict in Kashmir is an 'impure' case of an internal war.

between a liberal-democratic nation-state and a non-state actor is the recent conflict between Israel and Hezbollah. The terrorist attacks against Israel perpetrated by Hezbollah, e.g., rocket attacks on Israeli settlements, and Israel's response in bombing parts of Lebanon (including civilian areas) constitute such a war. However, this is not an example of a response to a single large-scale terrorist attack. On the other hand, the US attack on Al-Qaeda bases in Afghanistan following September 11, 2001 is such an example.

In so far as Al-Qaeda is based in Afghanistan and supported by the Taliban in Afghanistan and various groups in Pakistan (or is otherwise beyond the control of the Afghanistan government), and in so far as the terrorist threat to the US citizenry posed by Al-Qaeda operatives and training facilities based in Afghanistan is ongoing post-9/11, then the US is presumably entitled to wage a (limited[8]) *external* war on Al-Qaeda in Afghanistan to remove the threat. In so doing, US forces are military combatants confronting Al-Qaeda terrorist-combatants, i.e., the terrorism-as-war framework applies to the conflict in Afghanistan. Accordingly, the US forces seek to capture or kill Al-Qaeda terrorist-combatants.

Here I note that international law apparently does not recognize, or at least should not recognize, terrorist-combatants as lawful combatants. As discussed in Chapter 4, unlawful combatants, or, more precisely, combatants who ought to be regarded as unlawful combatants, include combatant members of terrorist organizations, such as Al-Qaeda. Such terrorist-combatants are, by definition, unlawful combatants since their individual mode of combat, and the defining mode of combat of the military organization of which they are a member, is perpetrating terrorist acts, e.g., murdering innocent non-combatants, and thereby breaching the laws of war, i.e. the *ius in bello*.

If captured, Al-Qaeda combatants ought to have the status of prisoners-of-war until such time as they are determined to be terrorists by a properly constituted judicial body; after all, this judicial body might, for example, determine that a given captured combatant is a member of the Taliban and not necessarily a terrorist. As prisoners-of-war, they can be subject to detention until such time as the US–Al-Qaeda–Taliban war in Afghanistan comes to an end; they also have various rights not accorded to criminals, e.g., they must be released on cessation of hostilities. On the other hand, if individual combatants in Afghanistan are determined to be members of Al-Qaeda and, therefore, unlawful combatants, then they will need to be tried for committing some specific terrorist act(s), i.e., for committing a particular species of war crime, e.g., by killing innocent

---

[8] See note 5, *supra*.

civilians. As such, they are not merely prisoners-of-war, but suspected war criminals to be prosecuted accordingly. In short, if the US wants to claim that a given combatant detained in Afghanistan is a terrorist, i.e., has infringed one or more (morally justified) anti-terrorist laws, then the US should instigate the appropriate judicial process of prosecution.

The fact that there is an external war of the kind in question does not mean: (a) that one large-scale terrorist attack by a non-state actor of itself constitutes a war; (b) that even if the large-scale terrorist attack constitutes an act of war, the installation, city or region attacked is, thereby, a theatre of war; and (c) that the US (including the US government) need consider itself to be anything other than a well-ordered, liberal-democratic nation-state that has suffered a one-off large-scale terrorist attack, i.e., in effect a 'disaster' (with the consequent need to take reasonable precautions against a repeat disaster). Specifically, the US does not have an internal war on its hands, nor is it engaged in an all-out external war of a kind that would require it to go on a war-footing, e.g., it is not confronting an enemy that threatens its existence. Moreover, the fact that it might be at war with Al-Qaeda as an organization does not mean that US homeland-territory itself is a theatre of war. Accordingly, other things being equal, US residents suspected of being members of Al-Qaeda terrorist cells within the US, and of plotting to murder US citizens by bombing buildings, should not be regarded as military combatants (terrorist-combatants) functioning in a theatre of war. Rather, the terrorism-as-crime model should be applied. Similarly, the terrorism-as-crime framework model should be applied in the UK to terrorists such as those who perpetrated the 2005 London bombings; the UK is not a theatre of war and, in any case, the UK terrorists were not members of the core Al-Qaeda organization, but, rather, home-grown UK terrorists influenced by Al-Qaeda ideology and terrorist methodology (and, as such, at most members of the Al-Qaeda 'movement').

On the other hand, the terrorism-as-war framework (and associated terrorism-as-war-crime model) might justifiably be applied given the various above-mentioned conditions are met, notably that the terrorism-as-crime framework is unable to be applied due, for example, to the inability or unwillingness of relevant external state actors, e.g., Afghanistan and Pakistan, successfully to apply it.[9] Thus, to reiterate, the terrorism-as-war framework might justifiably be applied to Al-Qaeda operatives engaged

---

[9]   This does not necessarily have the implication that the Al-Qaeda operatives responsible for the attack on the World Trade Center and captured in the US are combatants and, therefore, war criminals (as opposed to ordinary criminals). Certainly they should be tried as criminals (whether as war criminals or as ordinary criminals) and, if found guilty, sentenced to lengthy prison terms.

in combat with US military forces in Afghanistan; after all, unlike the US homeland itself, it is a theatre of war in which US forces are principally and (arguably) justifiably focused on capturing or killing Al-Qaeda combatants. Nevertheless, it should be stressed that the *default* framework to be applied to one-off large-scale terrorist attacks is the terrorism-as-crime framework.

One-off large-scale terrorist attacks on well-ordered liberal-democratic states do pose problems that ordinary violent crime, and even ongoing but sporadic small-scale terrorist attacks, do not. Certainly, the scale of criminality, e.g., the number of lives lost, is greater in the case of such a terrorist attack than it is for most other violent crimes. If so, then this will affect the moral weightings attached to different police responses to such a terrorist act in progress (or at least in prospect); the risks attached to non-intervention, in particular, are correspondingly greater. Hence the option of declaring a state of emergency and giving police and other security agencies extraordinary powers (for the limited period of the emergency).

However, as already noted, there are significant dangers attached to confusing the distinction between a state of emergency and a well-ordered liberal-democratic state that is facing an ongoing terrorist threat but is not under a state of emergency. Moreover, as we have seen, states of emergency involving terrorist attacks are not necessarily theatres of war, although they can be. (See next section.) Confusions between these three contexts, i.e. well-ordered liberal-democratic states at peace, states of emergency and theatres of war, can lead to a dangerous blurring of the distinction between the police powers that are appropriate to (say) states of emergency, but not to contexts in which there is no state of emergency. Such police powers include the use of deadly force.

In London in July 2005, a day after a failed bomb attack, police shot dead a terrorist suspect who turned out to be an innocent, defenceless Brazilian electrician, Jean Charles de Menezes, going about his day-to-day business. This incident serves to highlight the dangers attendant upon any increase in the powers of police to use deadly force, whether under a state of emergency or not. (For a discussion of police use of deadly force in well-ordered liberal-democratic societies, see Chapter 4.)

The general point here is that whatever calibration is called for in relation to police procedures for the use of deadly force against suspected terrorists (as opposed to other armed and dangerous suspects), police procedures for the use of deadly force in well-ordered liberal-democratic societies ought not be assimilated to the rules of engagement for combatants involved in high-intensity combat situations (theatres of war), e.g., the former, unlike the latter, ought not to have a shoot-on-sight procedure. Moreover, any increase in police powers to use deadly force outside theatres of war, even under a state of emergency, is fraught with problems. (For more on this issue see below.)

Arguably, large-scale terrorist attacks perpetrated in peacetime are more likely than other criminal acts perpetrated in peacetime to give rise to one-off acute moral dilemmas of a kind confronted in wartime, but almost never in peacetime. Consider, for example, the notional possibility that the US Air Force might have been called upon to shoot down a US domestic aeroplane in order to prevent it crashing into the World Trade Center.

Here the alleged dilemma is whether intentionally to refrain from protecting the lives of the innocent many (those in the building and its surrounds) or intentionally to kill the innocent few passengers (relatively speaking) to protect the lives of the innocent many (and given the passengers were almost certain to be killed in any case). This particular example seems to me not to be a dilemma for Presidents, senior security personnel and other government officials *qua* government officials. Governments, including liberal-democratic governments, are not, and cannot be, legitimately authorized to (in effect) execute some of their own citizens in order to save the lives of other people (whether they be their own citizens or not) – or indeed for any other 'larger' purpose. The reason for this is simply that the moral legitimacy of governments – liberal-democratic governments in particular – derives in large part from, and crucially depends on, respecting the human rights of autonomous human persons considered individually, and not simply in aggregate. Put simply, individual citizens in liberal-democratic societies have not relinquished their right to life to governments, and the only conditions under which it is permissible for governments intentionally to take the lives of their citizens are ones in which the rights to life of the citizens in question have been suspended by virtue of their own rights violations, e.g., these citizens are themselves unjustifiably attacking other citizens.[10]

Even if the government officials of liberal democracies – and perhaps of any morally legitimate system of government – are not, and could not be, justifiably authorized to take the lives of their own innocent citizens intentionally, scenarios like the one just described give rise to acute moral dilemmas for any human agent who has the opportunity to intervene; generally, such human agents will be, in fact, senior political, military or police personnel. These and other like dilemmas have given rise to ongoing and detailed philosophical debates between consequentialists, e.g., utilitarians, and deontologists, e.g., Immanuel Kant.

---

[10]   There may be one other condition in which the right to life of innocent citizens have been suspended, for it is conceivable that innocent citizens consent to their lives being taken in order to save the lives of a much larger number of fellow citizens.

I do not have space to review these debates in detail here. Nevertheless, I note that it is far from self-evident that any human being has the moral right or moral duty deliberately to kill one or more innocent human beings in order to save the lives of other innocent human beings. For, arguably, the only morally acceptable justification for one human being deliberately killing another is that the second is an attacker, a rights violator or is otherwise not innocent. In short, only one's own moral fault can justify the suspension or overriding or discounting of one's right to life.

Most people would agree that unjustifiably trying to kill someone constitutes sufficient grounds for the suspension or overriding of one's right to life; more generally, moral fault in some sense diminishes one's moral rights. However, the question is whether or not there could be a different kind of justification, namely, one based on aggregating the value of individual lives. Thus, so the argument might go, I am justified in killing one innocent person in order to save 100, because 100 lives are a hundred times more valuable than one life.

One historically important line of philosophical reasoning here is provided by Immanuel Kant. In company with common-sense morality, Kant believed that a human being is intrinsically – as opposed to instrumentally – morally valuable, and of greater value than non-human animals and inanimate objects. However, Kant also held the view that the moral value of human beings is such that one human being is not equivalent in moral value to, and therefore not replaceable without loss of value by, another human being, as is the case with, say, a piece of jewellery that has a price of $100 and, therefore, can be exchanged without lose of monetary value for a $100 note.[11] Accordingly, the moral value that attaches to one human being is, numerically speaking, incommensurable with the moral value that attaches to another human being; the moral value of one human being is neither numerically equivalent to the moral value of another human being, nor is it numerically greater or smaller. Accordingly, it is not true that 100 human beings are 100 times as valuable as one human being.

The upshot of this discussion is that deliberately killing a few innocents in order to save the lives of many innocents is inherently morally problematic; it necessarily involves doing what is morally wrong, given the incommensurable and 'undiminished' moral value that attaches to the life of an innocent person. For deliberately killing one or more innocent persons is morally wrong, irrespective of whether it was done in order to save the life of one or more innocent persons. On the other hand, deliberately refraining from saving the life of one or more innocent persons is also morally wrong, irrespective of whether it was done in order to avoid

---

[11] I. Kant, *Groundwork of the Metaphysics of Morals* (any edition).

the morally wrong action of deliberately killing some other innocent person or persons.

At this point it will no doubt be pointed out that, other things being equal, it is morally worse deliberately to kill someone than it is deliberately to refrain from saving them. This is so. Moreover, this moral difference between doing and allowing provides a rational decision procedure in cases where the choice to be made is between the same number of innocent lives. Other things being equal, if one must choose between deliberately killing one innocent person in order to allow a second to live, and simply allowing the second innocent person to die and (as a consequence) the first to live, one should choose the latter option.

On the other hand, the moral difference between doing and allowing does not provide an entirely satisfactory solution to the kinds of moral dilemma under consideration here. For although not killing and not saving anyone is in these types of circumstances is – other things being equal – the morally preferable option, it is still morally wrong to refrain from saving an innocent human being; one has done evil, albeit a lesser evil.

Invoking the doing/allowing distinction does not settle the question as to whether the number of lives to be taken or saved is a morally relevant consideration. What if one's choice is between deliberately refraining from saving one innocent person and deliberately refraining from saving 100 innocent persons? Or, even harder, what if one's choice is between deliberately killing one person and deliberately killing 100 innocent persons? That is, one cannot choose deliberately not to kill anyone.

It is self-evident – at least to most of us – that the numbers of human beings to be taken or saved is a moral consideration. However, what I have said thus far is not necessarily inconsistent with this. The incommensurability thesis should not be confused with the thesis that the moral value of one human being is equivalent to the sum of the moral value of all other human beings; nor should it be confused with the thesis that each human being has absolute moral value (whatever Kant might have thought on this issue). Rather, I simply need to make the point that the numbers do make *some* moral difference; since the loss of one morally valuable entity is a bad thing, then, presumably, the loss of two is a worse thing. However, this does not commit me to any simple process of numerical quantification, such as that advocated in classical utilitarianism, in the resolution of the kind of moral problem before us; it is not as if all we have to do is start counting and let the numbers arrived at do the rest.

So let us now return to the aeroplane scenario. The upshot of our discussion is that it is by no means clear that a government official, or anyone else, would be morally justified in deliberately killing the smaller cohort of innocent aeroplane passengers in order to save the lives of the larger cohort of innocent occupants of the building. Firstly, as we saw above, such a decision is not one a government official *qua* government official could justifiably be authorized to make. Secondly, other things being equal, it is morally preferable to avoid deliberately killing an innocent person than it is deliberately to refrain from saving an innocent person, i.e., other things being equal, it is morally preferable to allow the plane to crash into the building and kill the occupants than it is deliberately to kill the passengers in the plane oneself. Thirdly, although other things are not equal, given the smaller number of aeroplane passengers and the fact that the numbers count for something, this is not decisive. For the number of aeroplane passengers relative to the number of occupants of the building does not enable us – consistent with the dictates of morality, i.e., with the principle of the incommensurability of the moral value of a human being – to quantify numerically the moral value of a live cohort of aeroplane passengers relative to the moral value of a live cohort of occupants of the building.

There may, of course, be other, softer options in a scenario like this one, such as impeding the further progress of the domestic aeroplane by disabling one of its engines and, thereby, causing it to make a crash landing. Under these circumstances the terrorists might seek to ensure that the plane did not land safely, but, rather, crashed, killing all on board.[12] However, this would be an outcome deliberately caused by the terrorists. Crucially, even if the option of disabling the plane's engine had this outcome, it would not involve the deliberate killing of the passengers in the domestic plane by the authorities, albeit it might involve putting the passengers' lives at risk.

Here I am implicitly invoking the intended/foreseen consequences distinction. Whether one deliberately intended an outcome, as opposed to merely foreseeing it, can make a moral difference. It is surely morally preferable to refrain from shooting dead an innocent person, even though one knows that if one does so refrain, the innocent person will be shot dead by someone else. Indeed, to choose the first option would be murder; not so, to choose the second.

That said, I take it that if one did not intend but did foresee, or ought to have foreseen, a harmful outcome of one's action, then this makes a moral difference: other things being equal, an action with a foreseen (or foreseeable) harmful outcome is morally worse than the same action with an unforeseen (or unforeseeable) but identical harmful outcome.

Moreover, I also take it that unintended, unforeseen and unforeseeable harm caused by one's actions is, other things being equal, morally worse

---

12 Matthew Peterson alerted me to this possibility.

than identical harm not caused by anyone's actions; indeed, arguably, the latter kind of harm is not even susceptible of *moral* evaluation.

In short, whether a harmful outcome was intended or not can make a moral difference; and one greater than whether or not this outcome was foreseen (or foreseeable). However, internal states, such as intentions and beliefs, are not the only kind of thing to make a moral difference; whether or not a harm was *caused* by a human action also does. Indeed, the primary object of moral evaluation is a (deliberately) intended outcome that was caused by that very intention: which is to say, a morally significant human action.

Notwithstanding the above, in some cases this conceptual distinction between intended and foreseen consequences makes no moral difference, since it cannot be applied in the circumstances in question. Consider the well-worn philosopher's example of a man who smashes the fly on a second man's head with a sledgehammer, and then insists that cracking the poor fellow's skull was not intended, but merely a foreseen consequence of his action of 'swatting' the fly. This is implausible, not because there is no general distinction between intentions and foreseen consequences, or because when the distinction applies then it is morally irrelevant. Rather, what the 'fly-swatter' claims is implausible because in this particular case the distinction does not have application: it is a case of *intending* to crack the man's skull, and not merely foreseeing it as an outcome. A real-life terrorist scenario in which the intended/foreseen consequences distinction does not have application is the killing of the Hamas official Salah Shahada carried out by the Israeli military in Gaza in 2002 and involving bombing (using a one-ton bomb) his house, killing thirteen other Palestinians, including children. As with the 'fly-swatter', it would be implausible for the Israelis to claim that they did not intend to kill anyone in the house other than Salah Shahada, but rather only that they foresaw that they would do so.

Notwithstanding the non-dilemmatic character of a scenario in which a government must execute one cohort of its innocent citizens if it is to save another cohort of its innocent citizens, there are disaster scenarios which do pose acute moral dilemmas for governments. Consider, for example, the above-mentioned dilemma in which the government has to decide whether to disable a terrorist-controlled domestic plane in flight and, thereby, put at risk the lives of the passengers. Assuming that there is sufficient time for them to be contacted, the decision-maker in such scenarios ought not to be the police, nor ought it to be the military. Rather, such decisions are a matter for governments, either (and preferably) by way of a pre-existing law or at least a prior policy decision with community support (assuming the kind of scenario in question has been anticipated) or on the basis of a one-off, on-the-spot, morally informed judgement. In this respect such decisions are not different in principle from other one-off decisions made in relation to acute moral dilemmas arising from peacetime disasters. Some such decisions (made under a state of emergency) pertain to criminal actions, e.g., a government's decision to order police to shoot looters in the context of a flood disaster. Other decisions do not pertain to any criminal actions, e.g., a government's decision to order police to cordon off an area of a city to prevent the further spread of a pandemic, i.e., to enforce a large-scale quarantine, with the consequence that those who are not infected but who live within the area cordoned off will very likely become infected and die. Crucially, none of the above decisions involve governments or their security personnel deliberately killing innocent citizens.

The general points to be extracted here are fivefold. Firstly, states of emergency should not be assimilated to theatres of war; although some areas declared to be under a state of emergency, e.g., some regions under martial law, are theatres of war, many are not. Specifically, some contexts involving a one-off large-scale terrorist attack, e.g., the Al-Qaeda attack on the World Trade Center, warrant the declaration of a state of emergency but are, nevertheless, not theatres of war.

Secondly, disastrous occurrences in liberal-democratic states in peacetime, including large-scale one-off terrorist attacks, do not justify an increase in the *standing* powers (as opposed to the *emergency* powers granted for the limited period of the disastrous occurrence) of governments to order the use of, or security personnel to use, deadly force against offenders, terrorists or otherwise; and even disasters do not justify the granting to governments and/or security personnel of a legal power deliberately to kill innocent citizens.

Thirdly, any imposition of a state of emergency must be comprehensively legally circumscribed in respect of: (a) the geographical area in which it is in force and the time period; (b) the conditions under which it can be imposed (and the conditions under which it must be terminated); (c) the precise powers granted to government and security agencies during the state of emergency. Moreover, the imposition of states of emergency, and the granting and use of emergency powers, must be subject to judicial oversight.

Fourthly, notwithstanding the granting of emergency powers, the default framework to be applied domestically by well-ordered liberal-democratic states to large-scale one-off terrorist attacks is the terrorism-as-crime – not the terrorism-as-war – framework. For the terrorist attack and the security response to it do not constitute an internal war within the liberal-democratic state. (This is consistent with the application of the terrorism-as-war framework in the case of externally based terrorist groups to which the terrorism-as-crime framework has not been successfully applied by relevant external states.)

Fifthly, unlike in war, decisions in peacetime – including under a state of emergency – that will potentially result in large-scale loss of life are to be made (wherever possible) by the government, and not by the police (or military) leadership.

Terrorism, Internal Armed Struggles and Theatres of War

Let us now focus on an additional theatre of terrorist attacks, namely (mainly liberal-democratic) societies in which the political violence taking place has led to a substantial breakdown of law and order, i.e., the state is not well ordered. Examples of this kind of context would include Northern Ireland in the 1970s, parts of South Africa at various times under apartheid rule (e.g., the so-called Independent States and some townships within the 'official' South African state), and, at the present time, the West Bank and Gaza Strip in the Middle East, and Indian-controlled Kashmir.

In these kinds of contexts, martial law or a state of emergency is typically declared. However, such contexts are not necessarily theatres of war in the normal sense. For one thing, the protagonists are not nation-states. For another thing, the combatants are not members of armies engaged in conventional warfare. Nor are they contexts in which essentially well-ordered liberal-democratic nation-states at peace are suffering a degree of political violence. I take it that the present-day mainland UK is an instance of the latter kind of context: the UK is a well-ordered liberal-democratic nation-state at peace, but one which has recently suffered political violence, i.e., the London terrorist bombings in 2005 in which approximately fifty people lost their lives. Moreover, I take it that many (but by no means all) states within the contemporary nation-state of India that have experienced political violence, nevertheless, constitute well-ordered liberal-democratic societies at peace, e.g., the state of Maharashtra, notwithstanding the Mumbai bombings in 2006.

There are two salient conceptualizations of liberal-democratic nation-states undergoing a substantial breakdown of law and order as a consequence of political violence and operating under emergency rule. The first is that the state is facing an extraordinary crime problem. An example of an indisputably extraordinary crime problem – albeit not one that arose initially from political violence – is that posed by Pablo Escobar in

Colombia in the 1980s.[13] Escobar was a major drug dealer whose crime organization was able to threaten the Colombian state as such. Accordingly, there were grounds for declaring a state of emergency, and increasing judicial and police powers for a limited period to deal with the criminal threat to the state. (There is further discussion of Escobar below.) Perhaps Northern Ireland in the 1970s should be assimilated to this model: IRA operatives should have been held to be criminals (not combatants in a war) and the IRA itself a criminal organization, albeit one that was threatening the state as such in Northern Ireland. (I don't mean to dispute the proposition that the IRA's ultimate motivation was a political one, unlike Escobar.) On this conception, terrorist acts performed in a polity in which a state of emergency has been imposed can, nevertheless, be regarded as ordinary crimes and, as such, be subjected to domestic criminal law, i.e., the terrorism-as-crime framework prevails.

On this model of terrorism-as-crime, terrorists should be investigated, arrested and charged, and tried and punished in accordance with the principles and processes of the criminal justice system in the same way as an ordinary murderer or other criminal would be. On the terrorism-as-crime conception, terrorists, like ordinary criminals, should enjoy the rights afforded to suspects and offenders, e.g., the right not to be assaulted or killed, the right not to be arrested without reasonable suspicion, the presumption of innocence, habeas corpus, and the right to a fair trial. On the other hand, on this conception, the terrorist, if convicted, loses any immunity from punishment, e.g., he could serve a life sentence for his actions, notwithstanding the abandonment early on in his period of servitude of his terrorist organization's policy of violence.

This first conceptualization assumes that the state – including its government and legal system – has political and moral legitimacy in the eyes of its subjects, including its subjects in the region or sub-national unit in which there is a security problem. Relatedly, it assumes that the state is ultimately able to assert its authority in the region or sub-national unit in question. If both of these conditions obtain, then the state is arguably the lawful authority and, presumably, the application of the terrorism-as-crime model is appropriate.

Perhaps the Israeli–Palestinian conflict is one in which the second, but not the first, condition obtains: the Israeli state is able to exercise control over the Palestinians within Israel itself, as well as within the West Bank and (formerly) Gaza, but it does not have political or moral legitimacy in

---

[13]   See, for example, M. Bowden, *Killing Pablo: The Hunt for the World's Greatest Outlaw*, London: Atlantic Books, 2001.

the eyes of the Palestinians whom it controls (let alone among the ones it does not).

At any rate, a second salient conceptualization is one in which the state is facing a civil war or at least is in the midst of internecine warfare. Perhaps the ANC's armed struggle in apartheid South Africa eventually reached the status of a low-level civil war, given the ongoing ungovernability of many of the townships in the context of domestic and international financial and other pressures, including sanctions.

Internecine warfare, including actual or potential civil wars, provides grounds for the government to put its armed forces on a war-footing, albeit in relation to an internal, armed group that is threatening the authority of the state. Legally speaking, it might do so within provisions for emergency rule or martial law. However, the substantive point here is not a legalistic one; rather, it pertains to *de facto* control. The government has lost, or is in danger of losing, control over the contested area. Moreover, to the extent that it has or can retrieve control, it is essentially relying on military force. Perhaps Kashmir should be assimilated to this model. That is, perhaps Lashkar-e-Toiba operatives in Kashmir should be held to be terrorist-combatants (and, therefore, unlawful combatants, but not ordinary criminals) and the organization itself a military force engaged in a war (albeit a terrorist organization and, as such, an unlawful organization). On this conception, and notwithstanding the legal situation under emergency rule or martial law, certain terrorist acts, namely, ones perpetrated by terrorist-combatants in theatres of war, should probably be regarded as acts of war, indeed as war crimes, and therefore as acts that take place outside the sphere of ordinary domestic criminal law. The reason for this is that the context is a *de facto* theatre of war.

In relation to armed internal struggles, we can make use of the threefold distinction adumbrated above, namely, that between terrorist-combatants, lawful combatants guilty of war crimes, and non-combatant terrorists. In *de facto* theatres of war in internal armed struggles involving terrorist non-state actors, the terrorist operatives are terrorist-combatants and, therefore, unlawful combatants.

Let us now turn to a consideration of counter-terrorism measures on the part of states confronting internal armed struggles by non-state actors. In so doing we need to keep in mind the distinction between terrorist-combatants and terrorist-non-combatants. In order to focus our discussion, I consider one salient counter-terrorist measure, namely, the ambush. My assumption here is that a person performing acts of terrorism can, at least in principle, be regarded either as an ordinary civilian perpetrating a crime (terrorist-non-combatant), or as a terrorist-combatant perpetrating a war crime, but not as both simultaneously.

In wartime, killing the enemy in the context of an ambush is legally and morally acceptable. Now consider the ambushing and killing of IRA operatives in Northern Ireland. During the 1969–94 period, the police of the Royal Ulster Constabulary and Britain's armed forces, including the Special Air Service (SAS) and the 14th Intelligence Company, conducted anti-Provisional IRA ambushes. Having located an arms cache, security forces would stake out and attempt to arrest terrorist suspects who came to collect the weapons, knowing that in doing so they would provoke a fire-fight in which the suspects would be killed; in short, a military-style operation was being conducted. The alternative strategy of confiscating the weapons, or rendering them inoperable and arresting the unarmed suspects, would normally be required of police operating under civilian rule. In short, the Northern Ireland context of the time was one in which offenders and security forces were engaged in a form of urban guerrilla warfare, notwithstanding the British government's insistence that the IRA was essentially a criminal organization, and the fact that members of the SAS could be convicted of murder for such acts.

Similarly, ambushes, or so-called 'fake encounters', are a feature of anti-terrorist operations conducted in Indian-controlled Kashmir and parts of India by the Indian security forces, including police.

The question here is whether or not police and other security personnel ought to treat a group of terrorists as if they are a criminal gang committing their crimes in peacetime, or as military combatants (albeit terrorist-combatants) fighting a war.

Here we need to get clear on the difference between theatres of war and conditions of peace in well-ordered liberal democracies. In the latter the presumption is that one is among one's fellow citizens and that, therefore, one's right to life will be respected; this is so whether one is an ordinary citizen, a police officer or, for that matter, a member of the armed services. Naturally, this presumption can be offset by, for example, the escape of a dangerous, armed offender or the existence of a terrorist cell. However, the point is that there is a presumption to be offset. However, in theatres of war the presumption is the reverse: one's life is presumed to be under threat. In the case of combatants, it is kill or be killed. And even in the case of non-combatant civilians there is a presumption of insecurity in theatres of war. On the one hand, the lives of non-combatants are at risk as a consequence of being caught in the crossfire between combatants. On the other hand, in theatres of war there is no effective, organized security agency, such as the police, to guarantee their safety; rather, citizens must seek to preserve their own lives as best they can.

This distinction between theatres of war and well-ordered liberal democracies in peacetime is mirrored in the difference between the role of military combatants and that of police officers. The role of police is to apprehend suspected criminals in order that they can be tried by the courts and, if found guilty, punished. Accordingly, police – as we argued above – are only entitled to use deadly force in limited conditions and as a last resort, e.g., in self-defence or in defence of the lives of others. Police are not legally or morally entitled to ambush and kill criminals, as would be the case if they were fighting enemy soldiers on the battlefield. Even if the only moral and legal justification for waging war is self-defence, a particular military unit conducting a specific military operation does not necessarily have to meet the criterion of acting in its own self-defence with respect to the particular group of enemy combatants being engaged in that operation at that time. This is in part because the presumption in war is the reverse of that in a well-ordered liberal-democratic state at peace.

The difficulty that arises at this point is that Lashkar-e-Toiba, Naxalities, the IRA (in, say, the 1970s) and like groups are, in effect, operating as soldiers fighting a war; indeed, they regard themselves as such. Accordingly, they have the practice of ambushing, bombing, shooting at and other-wise killing police in the manner of soldiers fighting a war against enemy soldiers. In light of this, it might be unrealistic to expect police to respond to Lashkar-e-Toiba, Naxalites or IRA terrorists in the manner that they would respond to ordinary armed criminals; further, it might be difficult to enforce any policy that required police to so respond. Indeed, the prac-tice that is likely to emerge among police is one of treating terrorists as enemy combatants being confronted in a theatre of war. Moreover – and notwithstanding the legal situation – this practice appears to have a readily available moral justification, namely, self-defence: for all intents and purposes the police are confronting organized enemy soldiers hell-bent on trying to kill them.

In summation, then, we have a contradictory situation. On the one hand, the terrorists in question are, let us assume, legally speaking, ordinary crim-inals; the state has chosen to designate them as such because it regards itself as the lawful authority applying the terrorism-as-crime framework to criminals. Accordingly, the terrorists must be investigated, arrested, tried and, if found guilty, punished; they should not simply be ambushed and killed or shot on sight. On the other, the terrorists are acting as enemy combatants and, therefore, the practice of ambushing and killing them has an available moral justification, i.e., self-defence.

How are we to adjudicate such cases? As we have seen, in the context of a *well-ordered* liberal-democratic state at peace, such as the contem-porary US, the presence of a terrorist group, such as the group that per-petrated the Oklahoma bombing, does not warrant treating the terrorists in question as military combatants engaged in a war. The state as such is not under threat; it is not a context of war by any stretch of the imagination, irrespective of what the Oklahoma bombers themselves believed. Rather it is best understood as an act of criminality in the context of a well-ordered liberal-democratic state which is not at war with any group of its citizens. Accordingly, the terrorism-as-ordinary-crime framework should be applied to the terrorist attack – and to the terrorists themselves. Needless to say, this framework allows for the shooting to kill of dangerous, armed persons, e.g., by police snipers. However, the offenders should be afforded the full protection of the domestic criminal law: they cannot, for example, be shot on sight or ambushed in the manner of combatants engaged in war. Unfortunately, this is not the kind of case under consideration; the kind of case under consideration is internecine warfare.

On the other hand, when Hezbollah fired rockets from its bases in Lebanon into Israel in 2006, these were presumably acts of war, albeit ones perpetrated by a non-state actor. Israel and Hezbollah were at war. Again, unfortunately, this is not the kind of case under consideration; this is not a case of internecine warfare.

I suggest that in relation to cases of internecine warfare, the terrorism-as-war-crime framework should be applied in some cases, but not others, and done so in light of the above-mentioned set of conditions, e.g., necessity, likelihood of success, proportionality, likelihood of good consequences.

Let us first consider otherwise well-ordered liberal-democratic states which, nevertheless, contain a territorial region which is, by virtue of the terrorist activity of some political group, not well ordered, i.e., the domestic criminal justice system is unable adequately to contain the terrorist activities.

One solution might be to impose emergency rule or martial law in the disputed territory, e.g., Indian-controlled Kashmir has at various time been under one or other of these legal impositions.

On pain of ceasing to be a liberal democracy, a liberal-democratic government can impose martial law only for a definite and limited period, and only once the security situation has seriously deteriorated, i.e., the domestic criminal justice system is unable to provide security to the citizenry. In this context members of terrorist groups can be designated as military combatants (albeit terrorist-combatants) rather than ordinary criminals. Nevertheless, combatants can be tried and punished for war crimes, including terrorism. Accordingly, this is tantamount to the application of the terrorism-as-war-crime model, notwithstanding the difference between an unlawful combatant committing a war crime and a lawful combatant committing a war crime. For example, in Assam in India, martial law was declared in January 2007. Following on the slaughter of dozens of Hindi-speaking migrant workers by a separatist terrorist organization, the United Liberation Front of Asom (ULFA), a curfew was imposed by authorities and shoot-on-sight orders were issued to security personnel. There have been similar attacks in the past, e.g., in 2000 ULFA militants killed 100 migrants.

A closely related alternative to martial law is the imposition of a state of emergency in which the military remain, nevertheless, under the authority of the civil authorities, including the police. This was the situation during the IRA's armed struggle in Northern Ireland in the 1970s. This solution stops short of the application of the terrorism-as-war-crime model; it remains an application of the terrorism-as-crime model. It is essentially an extension of the state of emergency concept discussed above in relation to well-ordered liberal-democratic states at peace confronting one-off disasters. As is the case with the imposition of states of emergencies in the context of disasters, it involves significant restrictions on civil and other rights of a kind that is inconsistent with liberal democracy; hence the imposition of emergency powers should be only for a definite and limited period, and should be comprehensively legally circumscribed.

There appear to be a number of other kinds of scenario in which the terrorism-as-war-crime model might be thought to have application, depending on a variety of considerations, some of which I will now canvass. Is the terrorist group a state or a non-state entity? Or, more likely in the contemporary world: is the terrorist group being sponsored by a nation-state, e.g., armed by a state or used as a proxy by the state? If it is a state actor, or is being sponsored by a state, then the terrorist attacks may well constitute acts of war on the part of one state against another; if not, the question remains an open one. Libya sponsored various terrorist groups in the 1970s and 1980s, and US President Reagan chose to regard the actions of these groups as acts of war perpetrated by Libya. Indeed, in 1986 the US launched an air strike against selected targets in Libya. In the 1980s the US sponsored the terrorist group the Contras in Nicaragua; arguably this was an act of war perpetrated by the US against the Sandinista government of Nicaragua.

Let us now consider cases in which the terrorist group in question is not a state actor and is not being sponsored by a state. Accordingly, the terrorism-as-war-crime model cannot be applied simply by virtue of the terrorist attack in question being (in effect) an act of war perpetrated by one state against another. (Here it is important to remember that there can be wars between a state and a non-state actor, e.g., revolutionary wars.)

Let me now consider international terrorism. Is the terrorist group mounting ongoing terrorist attacks against a well-ordered liberal-democratic state at peace, but doing so outside the territorial jurisdiction of this state? (Above we discussed the case of terrorist attacks within the territory of the state, e.g., Al-Qaeda's attack on the World Trade Center.) For example, the terrorist group might be shooting US tourists on holiday in Egypt or attacking merchant ships in international waters. If so, then the terrorism in question is international terrorism and, as such, might or might not constitute an act of war. Whether or not it could reasonably be regarded as act of war – as opposed to a mere act of ordinary criminality – would turn in large part on the efficacy of the relevant domestic and/or international criminal justice system: e.g., does this system (or systems) have the capacity (including, politically speaking) successfully to investigate, apprehend and prosecute the members of this terrorist group for their acts of terror? If not, and if these terrorist acts involve significant loss of life, and are widespread and ongoing, then they may constitute a threat to the capacity of the liberal-democratic state to function as a member of the international community, e.g., the state is no longer able to guarantee protection to its citizens when they engage in international tourism, trade, and so on. Accordingly, the terrorist organization in question might reasonably be deemed to be engaged in an external war with the liberal-democratic state in question. Certainly, one state actor perpetrating this kind and extent of politically motivated violent interference with the international transactions of another state actor would reasonably be regarded as engaged in a form of warfare.

Many acts of international terrorism by non-state actors do not meet the latter conditions, i.e., they are not instances of serious, widespread and ongoing violent interference with the international transactions of a liberal-democratic state actor. However, such acts might still reasonably be regarded as acts of war if taken in conjunction with terrorist attacks mounted by the terrorist group in question within the territorial jurisdiction of the liberal-democratic state itself. For example, the murder of Israeli athletes by the PLO at the Munich Olympics reasonably might be regarded as an act of war on the part of the PLO, if the PLO (at the time) was subjecting Israelis to widespread and ongoing terrorist attacks within Israel itself.

Targeted Killings

What of targeted killing of terrorists? Assassination of one's political enemies in the context of a well-ordered liberal-democratic state is murder and, given the potentially destabilizing effects, a very serious political crime. Accordingly, it cannot be, and is not, tolerated; it is both unlawful and morally unjustifiable. However, assassination in the context of a war is a very different matter. As suggested above, the assassination of Hitler during the course of the Second World War would have been morally justifiable, even if not legally allowed. For one thing, military and political leaders who direct the combatants under their command to commit atrocities, e.g., genocide, are morally responsible for these actions of their subordinates; pacifism aside, these leaders do not have a moral right not to be killed, any more than the combatants they command have any such right. For another thing, pragmatic arguments based on, for example, the untoward outcomes of 'leaderless' defeated nations do not necessarily apply, and certainly not in the case of totalitarian regimes such as that of Nazi Germany or the Soviet Union under Stalin.[14]

What of targeted killing by, or of, non-state actors in the context of non-conventional wars between liberal-democratic states and terrorist groups? Targeted killings by non-state actors would include IRA killings of extremist Protestant leaders in Northern Ireland in the 1970s and Lashkar-e-Toiba assassinations of security personnel in Kashmir since the early 1990s. However, my focus here is on targeted killings by liberal-democratic states of non-state actors. These include the targeted killings of Hezbollah and Hamas leaders by Israeli forces during, for example, the period of the recent rocket attacks by those terrorist groups on Israeli cities. I am assuming that such targeted killings take place in a theatre of war, albeit war against a non-state actor or, at the very least, in a setting in which there is no effective enforcement of the law in relation to terrorists perpetrating ongoing serious terrorist attacks against the liberal-democratic state in question. Perhaps the firing of a rocket by a US unmanned aircraft in Yemen in 2002 that killed six Al-Qaeda operatives is an instance of the latter kind of case.[15] I am further assuming that any such targeted assassinations are limited by reasonable criteria strictly applied, e.g., a well-confirmed, high-ranking terrorist-combatant, and subject to accountability mechanisms, including judicial oversight.

Yael Stein has argued that the Israeli government policy of targeted killings ('assassinations', as she calls them) is unlawful and morally unjustifiable.[16] I will set aside the question of their legality, and focus only on the question of the possibility that targeted killing of terrorist-combatants is

---

[14] On the other hand, the argument might apply that it would make no difference because the leader will be replaced by someone equally as bad. It would probably not apply in the case of Hitler, but might in the case of Stalin, since Beria might well have taken over (depending on when Stalin was to have been assassinated). On this kind of issue, see D. Lackey, 'Assassination, responsibility and retribution', in H. Zellner (ed.), *Assassination*, Morristown, NJ: Schenkman: 1974.

[15] *Washington Post*, 5 November 2002.

[16] Y. Stein, 'By any name illegal and immoral', *Ethics & International Affairs* 17(1), 2003, pp. 127–37.

morally justifiable. However, I note that the fact – if it is a fact – that international law admits only of combatants and civilians, and defines combatants in such a way that they must bear arms openly, provides very weak grounds for refraining from regarding terrorists as combatants in contexts of internecine war, such as the Israeli–Palestinian conflict. Surely, persons who are trained in military techniques, are armed, and are engaged in killing combatants (as well as civilians) for military and political purposes are, for all intents and purposes, combatants, notwithstanding the fact that they do not wear uniforms and do not bear arms openly. At any rate, let me turn to Stein's moral arguments.

In responding to Steven David,[17] Stein argues that Israeli targeted killings do not comply with the Just War principles of necessity, proportionality and discrimination. (The principle of discrimination forbids the killing of non-combatants.) She gives as an example the above-mentioned killing of the Hamas official Salah Shahada carried out in Gaza in 2002 and involving bombing his house, killing thirteen other Palestinians, including children. Her point in relation to this specific example is well made: such actions constitute, or should constitute, war crimes.[18] However, using a one-ton bomb on a house containing innocents is hardly a necessary feature of targeted assassinations. Consider, for example, firing a rocket into a car occupied only by a terrorist leader and his terrorist companions.

Stein's second argument invokes the necessity (as she sees it) to deploy the law in relation to the application of principles of justice. That is, punishing (killing?) terrorists might be morally justified, but only if they have been found guilty according to a court of law.[19] However, there are many instances of morally justifiable killing, e.g., in self-defence, that do not require, indeed cannot require, prior adjudication by a court of law. Accordingly, if it is known with certainty that a person is a terrorist and the terrorist cannot be apprehended, tried and punished, then it may well be that – other things being equal – it is morally permissible to kill the terrorist in order to save the lives of the terrorist's future victims (although not necessarily to punish the terrorist). More generally, Stein's

---

[17] S.R. David, 'If not combatants, certainly not civilians', *Ethics & International Affairs* 17(1), 2002, pp. 138–40.

[18] See also Kimmerling, who suggests that the victims of Israeli targeted killings are not necessarily terrorists, but, rather, political leaders killed as a means of provocation. B. Kimmerling, *Politicide: Ariel Sharon's War against the Palestinians*, London: Verso, 2003, p. 162.

[19] Haig Khatchadourian makes a similar point in his 'Counter-terrorism: torture and assassinations', in G. Meggle (ed.), *Ethics of Terrorism and Counter-Terrorism*, Frankfurt: Ontos Verlag, 2005. See also his 'Is political assassination ever morally justified?', in Zellner (ed.), *Assassination*.

argument does not apply to terrorist-combatants. Thus if a given area is a *de facto* theatre of war (and/or perhaps is operating under martial law), then justifiably there might be rules of engagement permitting the shooting on sight of persons reasonably and rightly taken to be terrorist-combatants. Targeted killing of persons outside *de facto* theatres of war is a different matter. However, it might be justified, if the persons in question were members of an organization that was perpetrating serious and ongoing terrorist attacks, the persons themselves were perpetrating serious and ongoing terrorist attacks, and it was not possible to bring either the organization or these individuals to justice, i.e., the terrorism-as-crime framework was unable to be applied.[20]

Stein is on stronger ground when she points out the problems of ineffectiveness, e.g., targeted killing of some terrorists might not reduce terrorist attacks since others take their place, and of error, e.g., the wrong person might be targeted and killed. However, these are not *in-principle* problems with targeted killings; they do not demonstrate that targeted killing is always or necessarily morally unjustified.

I conclude that targeted killing of terrorist-combatants might be morally justifiable in certain circumstances. I now want to turn to an important residual question that arises in relation to targeted killings of terrorist-combatants.

Other things being equal, targeted killing of terrorist-combatants is morally preferable to non-targeted killing of terrorist-combatants for the simple reason that it avoids – or at least it is more likely to avoid – civilian casualties, i.e., it targets the guilty and avoids killing the innocent. However, Asa Kasher and Amos Yadlin have put forward an argument that, if sound, would reduce the moral benefits of targeted (as opposed to non-targeted) killing of terrorist-combatants.

Kasher and Yadlin argue that:

> Military acts and activities carried out in discharging the duty of the state to defend its citizens against terror acts or activities while at the same time protecting human dignity, should be carried out according to the following priorities which reflect the order of duties the state has toward certain groups:
>
> (d.1) Minimum injury to the lives of members of the state who are not combatants during combat; . . .
>
> (d.3) Minimum injury to the lives of the combatants of the state in the course of their combat operations;

---

[20] Naturally, there are additional conditions that would have to be met if such targeted killings were to be justified. Such conditions would include the following: there was minimal or no risk to innocent bystanders; and targeted killing of these individuals would have good consequences (all things considered).

(d.4)   Minimum injury to the lives of other persons (outside the state) who are not involved in terror, when they are not under the effective control of the state; . . .

(d.6)   Injury as required to the liberties or lives of other persons (outside the state) who are directly involved in terror acts or activities.[21]

My concern here is only with Kasher and Yadlin's prioritization of (d.3) over (d.4). (Hence I have omitted a couple of categories that are irrelevant to this issue.) The group identified by (d.3) are the military combatants targeting the terrorist-combatants, e.g., Israeli soldiers targeting Hamas terrorists. The group identified by (d.4) are non-combatant innocents who are not members of (or otherwise under the effective control of) the state whose military combatants are targeting the terrorist-combatants, e.g,. innocent Palestinians who happen to be in the vicinity of the terrorist-combatants.

In effect, this view of Kasher and Yadlin puts the moral value of the lives of innocent, non-combatant Palestinians at a discount, both *vis-à-vis* Israeli innocent non-combatants and *vis-à-vis* Israeli military combatants. What is Kasher and Yadlin's argument for this prioritization? Essentially their claim is that the state has moral duty to protect the rights of its own citizens – including its citizens who are military combatants – and it does not have this duty to non-citizens. This special duty, argue Kasher and Yadlin, is compatible with the general moral obligation on the part of the state to respect the human dignity of all.

Bashar Haydar claims that there is a flaw in Kasher and Yadlin's argument at this point.[22] From the proposition that the state ought to give more weight to the interests of its citizens – and, specifically, the proposition that it has a special moral duty to prevent harm to its citizens – it does not follow that the state is morally permitted to cause harm to non-citizens for the sake of preventing harm to its citizens. This is correct; it does not follow. However, the question remains whether, nevertheless, the special moral duty to prevent harm to its citizens overrides the duty not to harm non-citizens. Haydar disputes this, claiming that the moral permissibility of giving more weight to special ties (in this case the ties between a state and its own citizens) when it comes to helping or preventing injury does not apply when it comes to harming or causing injury. So the state might have a duty to rescue its own citizens

[21]   A. Kasher and A. Yadlin, 'Military ethics of fighting terror: an Israeli perspective', *Journal of Military Ethics* 4(1), 2005, pp. 14–15.

[22]   B. Haydar, 'The ethics of fighting terror and the priority of citizens', *Journal of Military Ethics* 4(1), 2005, pp. 52–9.

that it does not have to the citizens of other states, e.g., the US has a duty to rescue US citizens taken hostage by Hezbollah, but China, for example, has no such duty to the US citizens. However, from this it would not follow that that the US Special Forces personnel are morally entitled to throw grenades at gunmen positioned on the balcony of a Hezbollah safe-house as a prelude to rescuing US hostages being held in the basement, if the exploding grenades would likely also kill Chinese tourists standing on the adjoining balcony of a hotel.

I find Haydar's argument on this point persuasive. I am not, for example, convinced that that the distinction between refraining from assisting those who one has a duty to assist is morally equivalent to killing them.[23] However, I want to press a somewhat different point.[24]

As already mentioned, an important respect in which Kasher and Yadlin's view is distinctive pertains to their putting of the lives of *non-combatant* (entirely innocent) non-citizens at a discount *vis-à-vis* the lives of *military combatant* citizens. I want to argue against this claim.

Let us grant that military combatants have a special duty to protect the lives of their fellow citizens and that they do not have this duty in respect of non-citizens (or, at least, in respect of persons who are not under the effective control of the state). Moreover, let us assume that there is an important difference between military combatants and non-combatants in relation to this duty. Specifically, military combatants have a duty to put themselves in harm's way – indeed, to risk their own lives – in order to protect the lives of their non-combatant fellow citizens. Obviously, non-combatant non-citizens (of the state in question) do not have either of these duties. For example, non-combatant (innocent) Palestinians living outside Israeli-controlled areas in the Middle East do not have a moral duty to protect the lives of Israeli non-combatants; much less do they have a duty to put themselves in harm's way (indeed, risk their lives) in order to protect Israeli non-combatants.

Now consider the following two options confronting Israeli soldiers. They can intentionally fire a rocket into a building known to house Hamas terrorist-combatants and, thereby, intentionally put the lives of non-combatant (innocent) Palestinians, including children who attend an adjoining kindergarten, in harm's way, i.e., there is a reasonable chance that some of these innocent Palestinian children will be killed. Alternatively,

---

[23]   Kasher and Yadlin, 'Military ethics of fighting terror', p. 20.

[24]   No doubt the distinction collapses in certain extreme cases. But in this respect it is no different from many morally significant distinctions. The distinction, for example, between intentions and foreseen consequences is morally significant. However, in some extreme cases it collapses. I take it that dropping a one-ton bomb on a house in which one *knows* there to be children is in effect intentionally to kill those children. See the earlier example.

they can send in a group of soldiers to storm the building and kill the Hamas terrorist-combatants by using small arms at close range. The latter option puts the Israeli soldiers in harm's way, since there is a reasonable chance that some of them will be killed by the terrorist-combatants. On the other hand, the lives of the innocent children will not be put at risk. Kasher and Yadlin are committed to the first option, i.e., the option of intentionally putting the lives of innocent children in harm's way in order to avoid putting Israeli soldiers in harm's way.

This conclusion is strongly counter-intuitive. Let me explain why. The Israeli soldiers have a moral duty to put themselves in harm's way in order to protect the lives of non-combatant Israelis. The Palestinian children have no such moral duty. However, the Israeli soldiers are, in effect, intentionally bringing it about that the Palestinian children (unintentionally) discharge part of the Israeli soldiers' duty for them, i.e., the part that involves putting themselves in harm's way.

It might be argued against this that the Israeli soldiers' duty to put themselves in harm's way (in order to protect fellow Israeli citizens) is a duty that must be discharged *only if it is necessary to do so*; in this case it is not necessary to put themselves in harm's way, since the Palestinian children are available (unintentionally) to discharge this role for them. However, the necessity in play here is relativized to the role (and attendant duties) of the Israeli soldiers. It would not be necessary for the Israeli soldiers to put themselves in harm's way if either one of two salient conditions obtain. The first condition is that it is not necessary for any person (other than the terrorist-combatants) to be to be put in harm's way in order for Israeli soldiers to protect the lives of the Israeli citizens. This condition does not obtain: either the Palestinian children or the Israeli soldiers themselves will have to be put in harm's way. The second condition is that someone else (other than the Israeli soldiers) has the duty to protect the Israeli citizens by putting him- or herself in harm's way, or, at least, someone else is able and willing (has consented) to discharge the soldiers' duty for them. As we have seen, the Palestinian children have no duty to protect Israeli citizens, much less any duty to put themselves in harm's way to do so; moreover, the Palestinian children did not consent to be put in harm's way, thereby relieving the Israeli soldiers of their own duty.

Targeted Killings and the Problem of Dirty Hands

Targeted killings in most circumstances, e.g., assassination of one's political opponents, are morally unjustifiable and unlawful. However, as we have argued above, targeted killings of political and military leaders of terrorist groups in theatres of war might be morally justifiable, and at times, e.g., in present-day Israel, lawful. I now want to consider the possibility that targeted killing might be morally justifiable (or at least morally excusable), but not (and ought not to be) lawful. This kind of claim is sometimes made in the context of a discussion of the so-called 'problem of dirty hands'.

Here it is important first to note some conceptual differences between the concept of dirty hands and the concept of noble cause corruption. The idea of dirty hands is that political leaders, and perhaps the members of some other occupations such as soldiers and police officers, necessarily perform actions that infringe central or important principles of common morality, and that this is because of some inherent feature of these occupations. Such dirty actions include lying, betrayal and especially the use of violence, e.g., targeted killings.

The first point to be made here is that by my lights it is far from clear that such acts are necessarily acts of corruption, and hence necessarily acts of noble cause corruption. In particular, it is not clear that all such acts undermine to any degree institutional processes, roles or ends. (This is compatible with such acts having a corrupting effect on the moral character of the persons who perform them, albeit not on those traits of their moral character necessary for the discharging of their institutional role responsibilities as, say, politicians, police or soldiers.)

The second and related point is that some putatively dirty actions are indeed definitive of political roles, as they are of police and military roles. For example, elsewhere I have argued that a defining feature of police work is its use of harmful and normally immoral methods, such as deceit and violence, in the service of the protection of (among other things) human rights.[25] Clearly, a similar definition is required for the role of soldier. And since political leaders necessarily exercise power and – among other things – lead and direct police and soldiers, they, too, will participate in dirty actions in this sense. However, such use of deceit, violence, and so on, can be, and typically is, morally justified in terms of the publicly sanctioned, legally enshrined ethical principles underlying police and military use of harmful and normally immoral methods, including the use of deadly force. In short, some putatively dirty actions are publicly endorsed, morally legitimate, defining practices of what I, and most people, take to be morally legitimate institutions, namely, government, and police and military institutions. I take it that the advocates of dirty

---

[25] S. Miller and J. Blackler, *Ethical Issues in Policing*, Aldershot: Ashgate, 2005, chap. 1.

hands intend to draw our attention to a phenomenon above and beyond such publicly endorsed, legally enshrined and morally legitimate practices. But what is this alleged phenomenon?[26]

According to Walzer, politicians necessarily get their hands dirty, and in his influential article on the topic he offers two examples.[27] The first is of a politician who in order to get re-elected must make a crooked deal and award contracts to a ward boss. The second is of a political leader who must order the torture of a high-ranking terrorist if he is to discover the whereabouts of bombs planted by the latter and set to go off, killing innocent people. I take it that these examples consist of scenarios in which politicians are not acting in accordance with publicly endorsed, legally enshrined, morally legitimate practices; indeed, they are infringing moral and legal requirements.

The first example presupposes a corrupt political environment of a kind that in a liberal democracy ought to be opposed and extinguished rather than complied with. Moreover, it is far from clear why the politician's re-election is an overriding moral imperative. The second example is hardly an example of what politicians in liberal democracies routinely face; indeed, it is evident that even in the context of the 'war against terrorism' such cases only arise very occasionally, if at all. I conclude that Walzer's examples go nowhere close to demonstrating the necessity for politicians to dirty their hands in the sense of infringing central or important moral principles. At best, the second illustrates the requirement to infringe moral principles for the sake of the greater good in some highly unusual emergencies.

There might in fact be *some* political contexts in which central or important moral principles do need to be infringed on a *routine* basis, albeit for a limited time period. Such contexts might include ones in which fundamental political institutions had themselves collapsed or were under threat of collapse. Consider the following case study concerning the Colombian drug baron Pablo Escobar.[28]

---

[26] Max Weber seems to want to avoid the whole problem by defining political leadership purely in terms of one of its distinctive means, namely, the exercise of physical force. (M. Weber, 'Politics as a vocation', in H. Gerth and C. Wright Mills (eds), *From Max Weber: Essays in Sociology*, London: Routledge, 1991, pp. 77–8.) This seems to me to be an unjustifiably narrow and negative view of political leadership and politics more generally.

[27] M. Walzer, 'Political action: the problem of dirty hands', *Philosophy and Public Affairs* 2(2), 1973, pp. 164–7.

[28] This case study is taken from S. Miller, P. Roberts and E. Spence, *Corruption and Anti-Corruption*, Saddle River, NJ: Prentice Hall, 1995, pp. 27f.

Case Study: Pablo Escobar

After one of the biggest manhunts in recent history, Pablo Escobar, the notorious drug baron from Colombia, was cornered and shot dead on the roof of his hideout in his home town, Medellin, on 2 December 1993. There is some evidence to suggest that the precision shot to the head that killed him was delivered from close range after Escobar's escape was thwarted by a debilitating initial shot to the leg.[29] In short, he was very possibly executed. He was a man who from the time of his rise to power in the early 1980s had terrorized a whole nation. The hunt that lasted over four years and cost the United States and Colombian governments hundreds of millions of dollars and several thousand lives, involved members of the Colombian Search Bloc, a special police unit set up to capture Escobar, and special intelligence and anti-terrorist units from the US, including elite units of the CIA, Centra Spike, Delta Force, as well as the DEA, the FBI and the Bureau of Alcohol, Tobacco and Firearms. This was not merely a hunt for the capture of a criminal – albeit an international criminal who headed the largest cocaine cartel in Colombia, accounting for up to 80 per cent of the multi-billion dollar export of Colombian cocaine to the US – but all-out war. Indeed, the Colombian state, with the technical, military and intelligence support of the US, was fighting this war for the sake of its very own survival.

The means to combat Escobar included the 'dirty means' of an unofficial alliance of the Colombian special police unit, Search Bloc, with a vigilante group or 'civilian militia', Los Pepes (People Persecuted by Pablo Escobar), which comprised known drug criminals from other drug cartels and some disaffected ex-associates of Escobar. In their willingness to use the same unlawful and violent means to destroy Escobar as those used by Escobar himself against his enemies, Los Pepes wreaked havoc against Escobar's operations, killing many of his associates and members of his family and destroying many of his estates.

During his criminal reign, Colombia became a war zone of daily kidnappings, car bombs that killed and maimed indiscriminately, murders often preceded by torture, and bribery of the police, politicians and the judiciary. Though prevented by other politicians

[29]   See Bowden, *Killing Pablo*.

from taking up his office in Parliament as an elected member of Congress, Escobar nevertheless had the Colombian government bribed and bombed into acceding to his demands of banning the extradition treaty with the US that would have seen him tried and imprisoned in America for drug trafficking. His method of dealing with the authorities, or anyone else who dared challenge him, came to be known as *plata o plomo* (silver or lead). If he couldn't bribe those who opposed him, he had them killed.

By the time of Escobar's death, hundreds of people had been killed, including many innocent civilians, foreign citizens, police officers, judges, lawyers, government ministers, presidential candidates and newspaper editors. In the first two months of 1991 there was an average of twenty murders a day in Colombia.[30] Assassinations included those of the Justice Minister Rodrigo Lara, more than thirty judges killed after Lara's assassination, the Editor of *El Espectador* – for speaking out against Escobar and his drug trafficking operations – Luis Galan (the Liberal Party candidate for the presidency), and at least 457 police officers during the period of the manhunt for Escobar (1989–93). During the latter period Escobar was offering 5 million pesos to each young man in Medellin for killing a cop. When he realized that he could not defeat the manhunt against him – and in keeping with his *modus operandi* of *plata o plomo* – he offered $6 million to Colonel Hugo Martinez, the leader of Search Bloc, to abandon the operation. Martinez flatly refused the bribe. As Mark Bowden pointedly remarked, 'sometimes the fate of a nation can hinge on the integrity of one man'.[31]

The first point to be made here is that even if such dirty methods are morally justified, it is in the context of an argument to the effect that their use was necessary in order to re-establish political and other institutions in which the use of such dirty methods would presumably not be permitted. Accordingly, such scenarios do not demonstrate that the use of dirty methods is a necessary feature of political leadership, and certainly not in the context of a well-ordered liberal democracy at peace.

The above situation is one of emergency; however, it is *institutional* emergency that is in question, e.g., it is not a one-off terrorist attack that threatens lives but not institutions. So even if one wanted to support all or some of the methods used by the Colombian authorities, one would

---

[30] Ibid., p. 127.
[31] Ibid., p. 91.

not be entitled to generalize to other states of emergency in which the there is no threat to institutions *per se*. Moreover, there are reasons to think that many of the above-described dirty methods, e.g., execution and use of criminals to combat criminals – or at least the extent of their usage – were in fact counter-productive. For example, use of other criminal groups against Escobar tended to empower those groups. Further, such methods, although dirty, are not as dirty as can be. In particular, methods such as execution of drug lords are directed at morally culpable persons, as opposed to innocent persons. I take it that at the dirty end of the spectrum of dirty methods that might be used in politics are those methods that involve the intentional harming of innocent persons.

Conclusion

In this chapter I have addressed a variety of moral issues that arise for a liberal-democratic state operating under a state of emergency and/or engaged in armed conflict with a terrorist non-state actor. A liberal democracy might justifiably be operating under a state of emergency because it is confronting a one-off disaster, e.g., the 9/11 attack on the World Trade Center, and/or because of a serious, ongoing, internal armed struggle, e.g., the Israeli state's armed confrontation with various Palestinian terrorist groups. Any such state of emergency must be comprehensively legally circumscribed, both in relation to the precise powers granted to the government and its security agencies, and in relation to the termination of those powers and their judicial oversight while in use.

Even under a state of emergency, fundamental moral principles concerning human rights need to be respected. Thus it is not morally permissible for a government to possess the legal power (say) intentionally to kill one cohort of its (innocent) citizens in the service of some (alleged) larger purpose, such as (say) the protection of a second, but larger, cohort of its (innocent) citizens. Some theorists have argued that a government ought to have the legal power to order the mid-air destruction of an aircraft under the control of terrorists, but whose passengers are innocent civilians, if the government deemed this necessary to prevent the aircraft crashing into a large building and killing a much larger number of innocent civilians. Such scenarios raise the related questions of the moral permissibility of legalizing: (a) the unintended (but foreseen) killing of persons known to be innocent; and (b) the intentional killing of persons known to be innocent. I have argued that the legalization of (a), but not (b), is (under certain circumstances) morally acceptable.

It might be morally justifiable for liberal-democratic states to apply a terrorism-as-war model (as opposed to a terrorism-as-crime model) to armed conflicts with terrorist non-state actors, e.g., in *de facto* theatres of war. This might involve a shoot-on-sight policy in relation to known terrorists; moreover, it might be morally justifiable to deploy the practice of targeted killings (assassinations) of individual terrorists. The terrorism-as-war framework should be applied only under the following general conditions:

1 The terrorism-as-crime framework cannot adequately contain serious and ongoing terrorist attacks.
2 The application of the terrorism-as-war framework is likely to be able adequately to contain the terrorist attacks.
3 The application of the terrorism-as-war framework is proportionate to the terrorist threat.
4 The terrorism-as-war framework is applied only to an extent – e.g., with respect to a specific theatre of war but not necessarily to all areas that have suffered, or might suffer, a terrorist attack – and over a period of time, that is necessary.
5 All things considered, the application of the terrorism-as-war framework will have good consequences security-wise and better overall consequences than the competing options.

Notwithstanding the possible moral acceptability of such counter-terrorism measures in theatres of war involving terrorist non-state actors, fundamental moral principles concerning human rights must be respected. In particular, it is not morally permissible for a government to discount the lives of innocent non-citizens in favour of protecting the lives of its own non-combatant, let alone combatant, citizens (as has been argued by some theorists in relation to the Israeli counter-terrorism strategy).

6

Torture

Recent disclosures of torture in US army detention centres in Abu Ghraib in Iraq and Guantánamo Bay in Cuba, as well as attempts by the Bush administration in the US to legalize what appear to be various forms of torture ('torture lite'), have focused international attention on the use of torture in the context of the 'war against terrorism', i.e., on torture as an instrument of counter-terrorism. In this chapter I offer a detailed ethical analysis of torture and consider the proposition that the use of torture might be morally justified as a method of counter-terrorism, in particular.

The chapter is in four parts. In the first part the question addressed is, what is torture? In the second part, what is wrong with torture? In the third part, is torture ever morally justifiable? And in the fourth and last part, should torture ever be legalized or otherwise institutionalized?[1]

In relation to the definition of torture, two of the most sustained contemporary philosophical accounts on offer are those of Michael Davis and David Sussman.[2] Sussman also offers the most up to date and detailed account of what is wrong with torture. This contemporary debate concerning the justifiability of torture tends to conflate the issue of justifying torture in possibly one-off emergencies, and justifying the legalization of torture in states confronting an ongoing terrorist threat. The debate principally concerns the torture of terrorists and is dominated by two groups. There are those who argue in the affirmative and point to so-called

---

[1] An earlier version of especially the last three sections appeared in S. Miller, 'Is torture ever morally justified?', *International Journal of Applied Philosophy* 19(2), 2005, pp. 179–92.

[2] M. Davis, 'The moral justifiability of torture and other cruel, inhuman, or degrading treatment', *International Journal of Applied Philosophy* 19(2), 2005, pp. 161–78; and D. Sussman, 'What's wrong with torture?', *Philosophy & Public Affairs* 33(1), 2005, pp. 1–33.

'ticking bomb' scenarios to support their case. These include Fritz Allhoff.[3] Then there are those who argue in the negative and point to the depravities, injustices and damage to liberal institutions consequent upon the legalization and institutionalization of torture. These include David Luban and Jeremy Waldron.[4] A qualified version of the affirmative answer is offered by Alan Dershowitz, who argues for torture warrants in extreme emergencies.[5] A qualified version of the negative answer is offered by Michael Davis, who argues that in practice, if not in abstract theory, there is no justification for torture.[6] A third perspective combines elements of both of these two groups, namely, that torture can in some extreme emergencies be morally justified, but that torture ought never to be legalized or institutionalized. This position has been argued for by Tibor Machan.[7]

Before proceeding to the question, or questions, of the moral justifiability of torture, we need some understanding of what torture is. We also need some account of what is morally wrong with torture.

Definition of Torture

Torture includes such practices as searing with hot irons, burning at the stake, electric shock treatment to the genitals, cutting out parts of the body (e.g., tongue, entrails or genitals), severe beatings, suspending by the legs with arms tied behind back, applying thumbscrews, inserting a needle under the fingernails, drilling through an unanaesthetized tooth, making a person crouch for hours in the 'Z' position, waterboarding (continuously immersing the head in water or dousing until close to drowning), and denying food, water or sleep for days or weeks on end.[8]

[3]   F. Allhoff, 'Terrorism and torture', *International Journal of Applied Philosophy* 17(1), 2003, pp. 105–18.

[4]   D. Luban, 'Liberalism and the unpleasant question of torture', *University of Virginia Law Review* 91(6), 2005, pp. 1425–61; and J. Waldron, 'Torture and positive law: jurisprudence for the White House', *Columbia Law Review* 105(6), 2005, pp. 1681–750.

[5]   A.M. Dershowitz, *Why Terrorism Works: Understanding the Threat, Responding to the Challenge*, Melbourne: Scribe Publications, 2003, chap. 4.

[6]   Davis, 'The moral justifiability of torture and other cruel, inhuman, or degrading treatment'. See also H. Shue, 'Torture', *Philosophy & Public Affairs* 7(2), 1978, pp. 124–43. Shue seems to be arguing, implicitly at least, that in practice torture is never justifiable. However, he does countenance the possibility of an extreme emergency – a ticking bomb scenario – in which torture would be morally justifiable.

[7]   T.R. Machan, 'Exploring extreme violence (torture)', *Journal of Social Philosophy* 21(1), 1990, pp. 92–7.

[8]   For an account of torture by a victim of torture, see J.E. Mendez, 'Torture in Latin America', in K. Roth and M. Worden (eds), *Torture: Does It Make Us Safer? Is It Ever OK?* New York: New Press, 2005.

All of these practices presuppose that the torturer has control over the victim's body, e.g., the victim is strapped to a chair.

Most of these practices, but not all of them, involve the infliction of extreme physical pain. For example, sleep deprivation does not necessarily involve the infliction of extreme *physical pain*. However, all of these practices involve the infliction of extreme *physical suffering*, e.g., exhaustion in the case of sleep deprivation. Indeed, all of them involve the *intentional* infliction of extreme physical suffering on some *non-consenting* and *defenceless* person. If A *accidentally* sears B with hot irons, A has not tortured B; intention is a necessary condition for torture. Further, if A intentionally sears B with hot irons and B consented to this action, then B has not been tortured. Indeed, even if B did not consent, but B could have physically prevented A from searing him, then B has not been tortured. That is, in order for it to be an instance of torture, B has to be defenceless.[9]

Is the intentional infliction of extreme *mental* suffering on a non-consenting, defenceless person necessarily torture? Michael Davis thinks not.[10] I tend to agree. Assume that B's friend, A, is tortured by C for one hour only, e.g., A is undergoing electric shock treatment, but that B himself is untouched. Assume that B is locked for ths one-hour period in a hotel room in another country and live sounds and images of the torture are intentionally transmitted to him in his room by the torturer (C) in such a way that he cannot avoid hearing the sounds and can only avoid seeing the images by closing his eyes after initially seeing them. However, A is being tortured for the purpose of causing B to disclose certain information to C. B is undergoing extreme mental suffering. Nevertheless, B is not himself being tortured by C. To see this, reflect on the following revised version of the scenario. Assume that A is not in fact being tortured; rather, C is only pretending to torture A. However, during the one-hour period of this pretence, B believes that A is being tortured (and C intends that B have this belief and undergo mental suffering as a consequence of having it); so B's mental suffering is as in the original scenario. In this revised version of the scenario, contrary to B's contemporaneous belief, C is definitely not torturing A. Moreover, subsequently B comes to know that C did not torture A. In that case surely C is not torturing B either.[11] To be sure, C intentionally caused

---

[9]   Suppose a woman agrees to be savagely beaten for a specific time period in exchange for money, but she can choose to abort the beating if she wants; however, if she aborts the beating, she does not get the money. On the definition put forward here, this is an ordeal that the woman has freely chosen to put herself through, but it is not torture. See the discussion of ordeals at the end of this section.

[10] Davis, 'The moral justifiability of torture and other cruel, inhuman, or degrading treatment'.

[11] A real-life example of this general kind was provided to the author by an Indian police officer.

B unavoidably to undergo severe mental suffering (for one hour) by inducing in B a false belief. But a pretence of torture does not constitute torture, even if this pretence is designed to induce extreme mental suffering and succeeds for a short time in doing so.

On the other hand, it might be argued that *some* instances of the intentional infliction of extreme mental suffering on non-consenting, defenceless persons are cases of torture, albeit some instances (such as the above one) are not. Consider, for example, a mock execution or a situation in which a victim with an extreme rat phobia lies naked on the ground with his arms and legs tied to stakes while dozens of rats are placed all over his body and face. The difference between the mock execution and the phobia scenario, on the one hand, and the above case of the person being made to believe that his friend is being tortured, on the other hand, is that in the latter case the mental suffering is at one remove; it is suffering caused by someone else's (believed) suffering. However, such suffering at one remove is in general less palpable, and more able to be resisted and subjected to rational control; after all, it is not *my* body that is being electrocuted, *my* life that is being threatened, or *my* uncontrollable extreme fear of rats that is being experienced. An exception to this general rule might be cases involving the torture of persons with whom the sufferer at one remove has an extremely close relationship and a very strong felt duty of care, e.g., a child and her parent. At any rate, if, as appears to be the case, there are some cases of mental torture, then the above definition will need to be extended, albeit in a manner that does not admit *all* cases of the infliction of extreme mental suffering as being instances of torture.

In various national and international laws, e.g., the Convention against Torture and Other Cruel, Inhuman and Degrading Treatment or Punishment,[12] a distinction is made between torture and inhumane treatment, albeit torture is a species of inhumane treatment. Such a distinction needs to be made. For one thing, some treatment, e.g., flogging, might be inhumane without being sufficiently extreme to count as torture. For another thing, some inhumane treatment does not involve physical suffering to any great extent, and is therefore not torture, properly speaking (albeit, the treatment in question may be as morally bad as, or even morally worse than, torture). Some forms of the infliction of mental suffering are a case in point, as are some forms of morally degrading treatment, e.g., causing a prisoner to pretend to have sex with an animal.

---

[12] Convention against Torture and Other Cruel, Inhuman and Degrading Treatment or Punishment, New York: United Nations, 1984.

So torture is the intentional infliction of extreme physical suffering on some non-consenting, defenceless person. Is this an adequate definition of torture? Perhaps not.

It is *logically* possible that torture could be undertaken simply because the torturer enjoys making other sentient beings endure extreme physical suffering, i.e., quite independently of whether or not the victim suffers a loss of autonomy. Consider children who enjoy tearing the wings off flies. Nevertheless, in the case of the torture of human beings, it is *in practice* impossible to inflict extreme physical suffering of the kind endured by the victims of torture without at the same time *intentionally* curtailing the victim's exercise of his autonomy during the torturing process. At the very least the torturer is intentionally exercising control over the victim's body and his attendant physical sensations, e.g., extreme pain. Indeed, in an important sense the victim's body and attendant physical sensations cease to be his own instrument, but rather have become the instrument of the torturer. Moreover, by virtue of his control over the victim's body and physical sensations, the torturer is able heavily to influence other aspects of the victim's mental life, including his stream of consciousness; after all, the victim can now think of little else but his extreme suffering and the torturer. In short, torturers who torture human beings do so with the (realized) *intention* of substantially curtailing the autonomy of their victims.

So torture is: (a) the intentional infliction of extreme physical suffering on some non-consenting, defenceless person; and (b) the intentional, substantial curtailment of the exercise of the person's autonomy (achieved by means of (a)). Is this now an adequate definition of torture? Perhaps not.

Here we need to consider the purpose or point of torture.

The above-mentioned UN convention identifies four reasons for torture, namely: (1) to obtain a confession; (2) to obtain information; (3) to punish; (4) to coerce the sufferer or others to act in certain ways. Certainly, these are all possible purposes of torture.[13]

It seems that *in general* torture is undertaken for the purpose of breaking the victim's will.[14] If true, this distinguishes torture for the sake of breaking the victim's will from the other four purposes mentioned above. For with respect to each one of these four purposes, it is not the case that *in general* torture is undertaken for that purpose: e.g., in most contemporary societies torture is not generally undertaken for the purpose of punishing the victim.

---

[13]   See Davis, 'The moral justifiability of torture and other cruel, inhuman, or degrading treatment'. Davis identifies two other purposes, namely, to destroy opponents without killing them and to please the torturer.

[14]   See ibid., and Sussman, 'What's wrong with torture?', for a similar view.

One consideration in favour of the proposition that breaking the victim's will is a purpose central to the practice of torture is that achieving the purpose of breaking the victim's will is very often a necessary condition for the achievement of the other four identified purposes. In the case of interrogatory torture of an enemy spy, for example, in order to obtain the desired information the torturer must first break the will of the victim. And when torture – as opposed to, for example, flogging as a form of corporal punishment – is used as a form of punishment, it typically has as a proximate, and in part constitutive, purpose to break the victim's will. Hence torture as punishment does not consist – as do other forms of punishment – of a determinate set of specific, pre-determined and publicly known acts administered over a definite and limited time period.

A second consideration is as follows. We have seen that torture involves substantially curtailing the victim's autonomy. However, to curtail substantially someone's autonomy is not necessarily to break his or her will. Consider the torture victim who holds out and refuses to confess or provide the information sought by the torturer. Nevertheless, a proximate logical endpoint of the process of curtailing the exercise of a person's autonomy is the breaking of his or her will, at least for a time and in relation to certain matters.

These two considerations taken together render it plausible that in general torture has as a purpose to break the victim's will.

Accordingly, we arrive at the following definition. Torture is: (a) the intentional infliction of extreme physical suffering on some non-consenting, defenceless person; (b) the intentional, substantial curtailment of the exercise of the person's autonomy (achieved by means of (a)); (c) *in general*, undertaken for the purpose of breaking the victim's will.

Note that breaking a person's will is short of entirely destroying or subsuming his or her autonomy. Sussman implausibly holds the latter to be definitive of torture:

> The victim of torture finds within herself a surrogate of the torturer, a surrogate who does not merely advance a particular demand for information, denunciation or confession. Rather, the victim's whole perspective is given over to that surrogate, to the extent that the only thing that matters to her is pleasing this other person who appears infinitely distant, important, inscrutable, powerful and free. The will of the torturer is thus cast as something like the source of all value in his victim's world.[15]

Such self-abnegation might be the purpose of some forms of torture, as indeed it is of some forms of slavery and brainwashing, but it is certainly not definitive of torture.

---

[15] Sussman, 'What's wrong with torture?', p. 26.

Consider victims of torture who are able to resist so that their wills are not broken. An example from the history of Australian policing is that of the notorious criminal and hard-man James Finch: 'He [Finch] was handcuffed to a chair and we knocked the shit out of him. Siddy Atkinson was pretty fit then and gave him a terrible hiding . . . no matter what we did to Finch, the bastard wouldn't talk.'[16] Again, consider the famous case of Steve Biko, who it seems was prepared to die rather than allow his torturers to break his will.[17]

Here breaking a person's will can be understood in a minimalist or a maximalist sense. This is not to say that the boundaries between these two senses can be sharply drawn.

Understood in its minimal sense, breaking a person's will is causing that person to abandon autonomous decision-making in relation to some narrowly circumscribed area of life and for a limited period.[18] Consider, for example, a thief deciding to disclose or not disclose to the police torturing him where he has hidden the goods he has stolen (a torturing practice frequently used by police in India).[19] Suppose further that he knows that he can only be legally held in custody for a twenty-four hour period, and that the police are not able to infringe this particular law. By torturing the thief the police might break his will and, against his will, cause him to disclose the whereabouts of the stolen goods.

Understood in its maximal sense, breaking a person's will involves reaching the endpoint of the kind of process Sussman describes above, i.e., the point at which the victim's will is subsumed by the will of the torturer. Winston Smith in George Orwell's *Nineteen Eighty-Four* is, as Sussman

[16]   B. Stannard, 'How we got Finch', *Bulletin*, 22 November 1988, p. 40.

[17]   S. Biko, *The Testimony of Steve Biko*, ed. M. Arnold, London: Smith, 1984, pp. 281–2. Biko was taken into custody, denied food and sleep, and kept naked in solitary confinement. However, rather than submit, he apparently attacked his torturers, leading to further physical harm. Denied medical attention, he died in transit. The implication is that he died from brain injuries in part as a consequence of severe beatings. It seems that Biko was in effect tortured to death, but apparently without giving in.

[18]   Some have suggested that torture in this minimalist sense is not really torture. For example, in policing it is referred to as the 'third degree'. Since the minimalist and the maximalist forms meet the criteria laid down here and exist on a continuum, it seems best to stay with the adopted terminology. Others can do otherwise, but if not their dispute would only be a verbal one – unless, of course, they seek to reject torture in the minimalist sense as really being torture qualitatively speaking, or to provide it with a different moral gloss.

[19]   Confessions extracted by the police are not admissible in courts in India. However, the fact that stolen goods have been retrieved obviously assists the prosecutor's case. So the police sometimes torture thieves to retrieve the stolen goods and thereby secure a conviction. See K. Dhillon, *Police and Politics in India: Colonial Concepts, Democratic Compulsions: Indian Police 1947–2002*, New Delhi: Manohar, 2005, p. 153. It goes without saying that this practice is both unlawful and immoral.

notes, an instance of the latter extreme endpoint of some processes of torture. Smith ends up willingly betraying what is dearest and most important to him, i.e., his loved one, Julia.

Moreover, there are numerous examples of long-term damage to individual autonomy and identity caused by torture, to some extent irrespective of whether the victim's will was broken. For example, some victims of prolonged torture in prisons in authoritarian states are so psychologically damaged that even when released they are unable to function as normal adult persons, i.e., as rational choosers pursuing their projects in a variety of standard interpersonal contexts such as work and family.

Given the above definition of torture, we can distinguish torture from the following practices.

Firstly, we need to distinguish torture from coercion. In the case of coercion, pressure is applied to people in order that they do what they don't want to do. This is consistent with their retaining control over their actions and making a rational decision to, say, hand over their wallets when told to do so by knife-wielding robbers. So coercion does not necessarily involve torture. Does torture necessarily involve coercion? No doubt the threat of torture, and torture in its preliminary stages, simply functions as a form of coercion in this sense. However, torture proper has as its starting point the failure of coercion, or that coercion is not even going to be attempted. As we have seen, torture proper targets autonomy itself, and seeks to overwhelm the capacity of the victims to exercise rational control over their decisions – at least in relation to certain matters for a limited period of time – by literally terrorising them into submission. Hence there is a close affinity between terrorism and torture. Indeed, arguably torture is a terrorist tactic. However, it is one that can be used by groups other than terrorists, e.g., it can be used against enemy combatants by armies fighting conventional wars and deploying conventional military strategies. In relation to the claim that torture is not coercion, it might be responded that at least some forms or instances of torture involve coercion, namely, those in which the torturer is seeking something from the victim, e.g., information, and in which some degree of rational control to comply or not with the torturer's wishes is retained by the victim. This response is plausible. However, even if the response is accepted, there will remain instances of torture in which these above-mentioned conditions do not obtain; presumably, these will not be instances of coercion.

Secondly, torture needs to be distinguished from excruciatingly painful medical procedures. Consider the case of a rock-climber who amputates a fellow climber's arm which got caught in a crevice in an isolated and inhospitable mountain area. These kinds of case differ from torture in a number of respects. For example, such medical procedures are consensual and undertaken not to break some person's will, but rather to promote his or her physical wellbeing or even to save his or her life.

Thirdly, there is corporal punishment. Corporal punishment is, or ought to be, administered only to persons who have committed some legal and/or moral offence for the purpose of punishing them. By contrast, torture is not – as is corporal punishment – limited by normative definition to the guilty; and, in general, torture, but not corporal punishment, has as its purpose the breaking of a person's will. Moreover, unlike torture, corporal punishment will normally consist of a determinate set of specific, pre-determined and publicly known acts administered during a definite and limited time period, e.g., ten lashes of the cat-o-nine-tails for theft.

Fourthly, there are ordeals involving the infliction of severe pain. Consider Gordon Liddy, the former FBI agent involved in the Watergate break-in, who reportedly held his hand over a burning candle till his flesh burnt in order to test his will. Ordeals have as their primary purpose to test a person's will but are not undertaken to break a person's will. Moreover, ordeals – as the Liddy example illustrates – can be voluntary, unlike torture.

Having provided ourselves with an analytic account of torture and distinguished torture from some closely related practices, we need to turn now to the question, what is wrong with torture?

What Is Wrong with Torture?

In terms of the above definition there are at least two things that are manifestly morally wrong with torture. Firstly, torture consists in part in the intentional infliction of severe physical suffering – typically, severe pain: that is, torture hurts very badly. For this reason alone, torture is an evil thing.

Secondly, torture of human beings consists in part in the intentional, substantial curtailment of individual autonomy. Given the moral importance of autonomy, torture is an evil thing – even considered independently of the physical suffering it involves. (And if torture involves the breaking of someone's will, especially in the maximalist sense, then it is an even greater evil than otherwise would be the case.)

Given that torture involves both the infliction of extreme physical suffering and the substantial curtailment of the victim's autonomy, torture is a very great evil indeed. Nevertheless, there is some dispute about how great an evil torture is relative to other great evils, specifically killing and murder.

Many have suggested that torture is a greater evil than killing or even murder. For example, Michael Davis claims, 'Both torture and (premature) death are very great evils but, if one is a greater evil than the other, it is certainly torture,'[20] and David Sussman says, 'Yet while there is a very strong moral presumption against both killing and torturing a human being, it seems that we take the presumption against torture to be even greater than that against homicide.'[21]

Certainly, torturing an innocent person to death is worse than murder, for it involves torture in addition to murder. On the other hand, torture does not necessarily involve killing, let alone murder, and indeed torturers do not necessarily have the power of life and death over their victims. Consider police officers whose superiors turn a blind eye to their illegal use of torture, but who do not, and could not, cover up the murder of those tortured; the infliction of pain in police cells can be kept secret, but not the existence of dead bodies.

On the moral wrongness of torture as compared to killing, the following points can be made.

Firstly, torture is similar to killing in that both interrupt and render impossible the normal conduct of human life, albeit the latter – but not the former – does so necessarily forever. But equally during the period in which a person is being tortured (and in some cases thereafter) the person's world is almost entirely taken up by extreme pain and his or her asymmetrical power relationship to the torturer, i.e., the torture victim's powerlessness. Indeed, given the extreme suffering being experienced and the consequent loss of autonomy, the victim would presumably rather be dead than alive during that period. So, as already noted, torture is a very great evil. However, it does not follow from this that being killed is preferable to being tortured. Nor does it follow that torturing someone is morally worse than killing that person.

It does not follow that being killed is preferable to being tortured, because the duration of the torture might be brief, one's will might not ultimately be broken, and one might go on to live a long and happy life; by contrast, being killed – theological considerations aside – is always 'followed by' no life whatsoever. For the same reason it does not follow that torturing a person is morally worse than killing that person. If the harm brought about by an act of torture is a lesser evil than the harm done by an act of killing, then, other things being equal, the latter is morally worse than the former.

A second point pertains to the powerlessness of the victims of torture. Dead people necessarily have no autonomy or power; so killing people is

[20] Davis, 'The moral justifiability of torture and other cruel, inhuman, or degrading treatment', p. 6.
[21] Sussman, 'What's wrong with torture?', p. 15.

an infringement of their right to autonomy as well as their right to life.[22] What of the victims of torture?

The person being tortured is for the duration of the torturing process *physically* powerless in relation to the torturer. By 'physically powerless' two things are meant: the victim is defenceless, i.e., the victim cannot prevent the torturer from torturing the victim, and the victim is unable to attack, and therefore physically harm, the torturer. Nevertheless, it does not follow from this that the victim is entirely powerless *vis-à-vis* the torturer. For the victim might be able strongly to influence the torturer's actions, either by virtue of having at this time the power to harm people other than the torturer, or by virtue of having at some future time the power to defend him- or herself against the torturer, and/or attack the torturer. Consider the clichéd example of the terrorist who is refusing to disclose to the torturer the whereabouts of a bomb with a timing device which is about to explode in a crowded marketplace. Perhaps the terrorist could negotiate the cessation of torture and immunity for himself, if he talks. Consider also a situation in which both a hostage and his torturer know that it is only a matter of an hour before the police arrive, free the hostage and arrest the torturer; perhaps the hostage is a defence official who is refusing to disclose the whereabouts of important military documents and who is strengthened in his resolve by this knowledge of the limited duration of the pain being inflicted upon him.

The conclusion to be drawn from these considerations is that torture is not necessarily morally worse than killing (or more undesirable than death), though in some instances it may well be. Killing is an infringement of the right to life and the right to autonomy. Torture is an infringement of the right to autonomy, but not necessarily of the right to life. Moreover, torture is consistent with the retrieval of the victim's autonomy, whereas killing is not. On the other hand, the period during which the victim is being tortured is surely worse than not being alive during that time, and torture can in principle extend for the duration of the remainder of a person's life. Further, according to our adopted definition, torture is an intentional or purposive attack on a person's autonomy; this is not necessarily the case with killing.[23] Finally,

---

[22] Naturally, if it is a self-defence situation or the persons to be killed are otherwise culpable, then killing them might be morally justified. Below the argument is presented for this same point in relation to torturing the culpable.

[23] For those who believe that to lose one's autonomy is a greater evil than to lose one's life and that, other things being equal, intentionally causing harm is morally worse than causing harm that is merely foreseen, there will be more cases in which torture is morally worse than killing than have been thus far admitted to. But the point is that, nevertheless, there will still be cases in which killing is morally worse than torture.

torture can in principle involve the effective destruction of a person's autonomy.

Let us now turn directly to the question of the moral justification for torture. Here we must distinguish between one-off cases of torture, on the one hand, and legalized or institutionalized torture, on the other.

The Moral Justification for One-Off Acts of Torture in Emergencies

In this section, one-off, non-institutionalized acts of torture performed by state actors in emergency situations are considered. (Such emergencies are not to be confused with *states of emergency* in the sense of the institutional and legal states of affairs declared and brought into existence by governments to deal with crises of various kinds, including terrorist attacks, and discussed in Chapter 5.) The argument is that there are, or could well be, one-off acts of torture in extreme emergencies that are, all things considered, morally justifiable. Accordingly, the assumption is that the *routine* use of torture is not morally justified; so if it turned out that the routine use of torture was necessary to, say, win the war on terrorism, then some of what is said here would not be to the point. However, liberal-democratic governments and security agencies have not even begun to exhaust the political strategies, and the military and police tactics short of the routine use of torture, available to them to combat terrorism.

Let us consider some putative examples of the justified use of torture. The first is a policing example, the second a terrorist example. Arguably, both examples are realistic.

Case Study 1: The beating

Height of the antipodean summer, Mercury at the century-mark; the noonday sun softened the bitumen beneath the tyres of her little Hyundai sedan to the consistency of putty. Her three-year-old son, quiet at last, snuffled in his sleep on the back seat. He had a summer cold and wailed like a banshee in the supermarket, forcing her to cut short her shopping. Her car needed petrol. Her tot was asleep on the back seat. She poured twenty litres into the tank; thumbing notes from her purse, harried and distracted, her keys dangled from the ignition.

Whilst she was in the service station a man drove off in her car. Police wound back the service station's closed-circuit TV camera, saw what appeared to be a heavy-set Pacific Islander with a blond-streaked Afro entering her car. 'Don't panic', a police constable advised the mother, 'as soon as he sees your little boy in the back he will abandon the car.' He did; police arrived at the railway station before the car thief did and arrested him after a struggle when he vaulted over the station barrier.

In the police truck on the way to the police station: 'Where did you leave the Hyundai?' Denial instead of dissimulation: 'It wasn't me'. It was – property stolen from the car was found in his pockets. In the detectives' office: 'It's been twenty minutes since you took the car – little tin box like that car – It will heat up like an oven under this sun. Another twenty minutes and the child's dead or brain-damaged. Where did you dump the car?' Again: 'It wasn't me.'

Appeals to decency, to reason, to self-interest: 'It's not too late; tell us where you left the car and you will only be charged with Take-and-Use. That's just a six month extension of your recognizance.' Threats: 'If the child dies I will charge you with Manslaughter!' Sneering, defiant and belligerent; he made no secret of his contempt for the police. Part-way through his umpteenth, 'It wasn't me', a questioner clipped him across the ear as if he were a child, an insult calculated to bring the Islander to his feet to fight, there a body punch elicited a roar of pain, but he fought back until he lapsed into semi-consciousness under a rain of blows. He quite enjoyed handing out a bit of biffo, but now, kneeling on hands and knees in his own urine, in pain he had never known, he finally realized the beating would go on until he told the police where he had abandoned the child and the car.

The police officers' statements in the prosecution brief made no mention of the beating; the location of the stolen vehicle and the infant inside it was portrayed as having been volunteered by the defendant. The defendant's counsel availed himself of this false-hood in his plea in mitigation. When found, the stolen child was dehydrated, too weak to cry; there were ice packs and dehydra-tion in the casualty ward but no long-time prognosis on brain damage.

(Case study provided by John Blackler,
a former New South Wales police officer.)

In this case study, torture of the car thief seems morally justifiable. Consider the following points: (1) the police reasonably believe that torturing the car thief will probably save an innocent life; (2) the police know that there is no other way to save the life; (3) the threat to life is imminent; (4) the child is innocent; (5) the car thief is known not to be an innocent – his action is known to have caused the threat to the child, and he is refusing to allow the child's life to be saved.

The classic, indeed clichéd, example used to justify torture is that of the so-called 'ticking bomb'.[24] Consider the following case.

Case Study 2: The terrorist and the ticking bomb

A terrorist group has planted a small nuclear device with a timing mechanism in London and it is about to go off. If it does it will kill thousands and make a large part of the city uninhabitable for decades. One of the terrorists has been captured by the police, and if he can be made to disclose the location of the device, then the police can probably disarm it and thereby save the lives of thousands. The police know the terrorist in question. They know he has orchestrated terrorist attacks, albeit non-nuclear ones, in the past. Moreover, on the basis of intercepted mobile phone calls and e-mails the police know that this attack is under way in some location in London and that he is the leader of the group. Unfortunately, the terrorist is refusing to talk and time is slipping away. However, the police know that there is a reasonable chance that he will talk, if tortured. Moreover, all their other sources of information have dried up. Furthermore, there is no other way to avoid catastrophe; evacuation of the city, for example, cannot be undertaken in the limited time available. Torture is not normally used by the police, and indeed it is unlawful to use it.

In this case torture also seems to be morally justifiable. Consider the following points: (1) the police reasonably believe that torturing the terrorist will probably save thousands of innocent lives; (2) the police know that there is no other way to save those lives; (3) the threat to life is imminent;

---

[24] Influentially discussed by M. Walzer, 'Political action: the problem of dirty hands', *Philosophy & Public Affairs* 2(2), 1973, 1973, pp. 160–80.

(4) the thousands about to be murdered are innocent – the terrorist has no good, let alone decisive, justificatory moral reason for murdering them; (5) the terrorist is known to be (jointly with the other terrorists) morally responsible for planning, transporting and arming the nuclear device and, if it explodes, he will be (jointly with the other terrorists) morally responsible for the murder of thousands.

If in the light of the above set of moral considerations there remains doubt that torture is justified, let us consider the following additional points. The terrorist is culpable on two counts. Firstly, the terrorist is forcing the police to choose between two evils, namely, torturing the terrorist or allowing thousands of lives to be lost. Were the terrorist to do what he ought to do, namely, disclose the location of the ticking bomb, the police could refrain from torturing him. This would be true of the terrorist even if he were not actively participating in the bombing project. Secondly, the terrorist is in the process of completing his (jointly undertaken) action of murdering thousands of innocent people. He has already undertaken his individual actions of, say, transporting and arming the nuclear device; he has performed these individual actions (in the context of other individual actions performed by the other members of the terrorist cell) in order to realize the end (shared by the other members of the cell) of murdering thousands of Londoners. In refusing to disclose the location of the device, the terrorist is preventing the police from preventing him from completing his (joint) action of murdering thousands of innocent people.[25] To this extent the terrorist is in a different situation from a bystander who happens to know where the bomb is planted but will not reveal its whereabouts, and in a different situation from someone who might have inadvertently put life at risk; rather, the terrorist is more akin to someone in the process of murdering an innocent person, and refusing to refrain from doing so.

In the institutional environment described, torture is both unlawful and highly unusual. Accordingly the police, if it is discovered that they have tortured the terrorist, would be tried for a serious crime and, if found guilty, sentenced. We will return to this issue in the following section. Here simply note that the bare illegality of their act of torture does not render it morally impermissible, given it was otherwise morally permissible. Here it is the bare fact that it is illegal that is in question. So the relevant moral considerations comprise whatever moral weight attaches to compliance with the law just for the sake of compliance with the law, as distinct from compliance for the sake of the public benefits the law

---

[25] For an analysis of joint actions see S. Miller, *Social Action: A Teleological Account*, New York: Cambridge University Press, 2001, chap. 2.

brings or compliance because of the moral weight that attaches to the moral principle that a particular law might embody. But even if it is held that compliance with the law for its own sake has some moral weight – and arguably it has none – it does not have sufficient moral weight to make a decisive difference in this kind of scenario. In short, if torturing the terrorist is morally permissible absent questions of legality, the bare fact of torture being illegal does not render it morally impermissible.

Note also that since the terrorist is, when being tortured, still in the process of attempting to complete his (joint) action of murdering thousands of Londoners, and murdering also the police about to torture him, the *post factum* legal defence of necessity may well be available to the police should they subsequently be tried for torture.[26]

Some commentators on scenarios of this kind are reluctant to concede that the police are morally entitled – let alone morally obliged – to torture the offender. How could these commentators justify their position?

Someone might claim that torture is an absolute moral wrong. On this view there simply are no real or imaginable circumstances in which torture could be morally justified.

This is a hard view to sustain, not least because we have already seen that being tortured is not necessarily worse than being killed, and torturing someone is not necessarily morally worse than killing that person. Naturally, someone might hold that killing is an absolute moral wrong, i.e., killing anyone – no matter how guilty – is never morally justified. This view is consistent with holding that torture is an absolute moral wrong, i.e., torturing anyone – no matter how guilty – is never morally justified. However, the price of consistency is very high. The view that killing is an absolute moral wrong is a very implausible one. It would rule out, for example, killing in self-defence. Let us, therefore, set it aside and continue with the view that torture, but not killing, is an absolute moral wrong.

For those who hold that killing is not an absolute moral wrong, it is very difficult to see how torture could be an absolute moral wrong, given that killing is sometimes morally worse than torture. In particular, it is difficult to see how torturing (but not killing) the guilty terrorist and saving the lives of thousands could be morally worse than refraining from torturing him and allowing him to murder thousands – torturing the terrorist is a temporary infringement of his autonomy, whereas his detonating of the nuclear device is a permanent violation of the autonomy of thousands.

By way of conclusion, it seems that the view that it is, all things considered, morally wrong to torture the terrorist should be rejected. There

---

[26] But see Luban, 'Liberalism and the unpleasant question of torture', for a contrasting view, at least in the US.

are some imaginable circumstances in which it is morally permissible to torture someone.

Let us now turn to the other argument of those opposing the moral permissibility of torture mentioned above. This is not the argument that torture is an absolute moral wrong, but rather the argument that, as Michael Davis puts it, 'For all practical purposes – and so, for moral agents like us – torture is absolutely morally wrong.'[27] The basic idea is that while torture is not an absolute moral wrong in the sense that the evil involved in performing any act of torture is so great as to override any other conceivable set of moral considerations, nevertheless, there are no moral considerations that in the real world have overridden, or ever will override, the moral injunction against torture; the principle of refraining from torture has always trumped, and will always trump, other moral imperatives. Proponents of this view can happily accept that the offenders in putative examples should be tortured, while simultaneously claiming that the scenarios in these examples are entirely fanciful ones that have never been, and will never be, realized in the real world.

It is important to stress here that the kind of scenario under discussion remains that of the one-off case of torture in an emergency situation; what is not under consideration in this section is legalized, or otherwise institutionalized, torture.

The central claim of the proponents of 'practical moral absolutes' seems to be an empirical one: ticking bomb scenarios, such as our above-described terrorist case – and other relevant one-off emergencies in which torture seems to be justified – have not happened, and will not ever happen.

The first challenge to these theorists is to offer the above case as a realistic instance of the use of morally justified torture; it is not simply a philosopher's fanciful example. Consider the recent bombings in Bali, Madrid and London – cases where, had the police caught a terrorist prior to the bombings, they may well have faced a ticking bomb scenario. In the second case study, it can be conceded that there is no guarantee that torture will succeed in saving the lives of thousands of Londoners. This is because the person tortured might not talk or he might talk too late or he might provide false or misleading information. However, it should be noted that the police *know* that the offender has committed the offence and is in a position to provide the needed information, i.e., the police know that the offender is guilty. Moreover, the information being sought is checkable: if the terrorist gives the correct location of the bomb, then the police will find it; if he does not, then they will not find it. Further, the police

---

[27]   Davis, 'The moral justifiability of torture and other cruel, inhuman, or degrading treatment', p. 11.

have no alternative methods by which to avoid the death of the innocent. Given what is at stake and given the fact that the police know the offenders are guilty, the police are, it seems, justified in the use of torture, notwithstanding a degree of uncertainty in relation to the likelihood of success.

The second point is that, practicalities notwithstanding, the proponents of 'practical moral absolutes' still need to offer a principled account of the moral limits to torture – an account of torture, so to speak, in the abstract. And these accounts could differ from one advocate of practical moral absolutes to another. For example, one advocate might accept that it would be morally permissible to torture the terrorist to save the lives of ten innocent people threatened by a non-nuclear explosive device, whereas another advocate might reject this on the grounds that ten lives are too few. What the two advocates would have in common is the belief that even the revised ticking bomb scenario involving only the death of ten innocent people is, nevertheless, a fanciful scenario that has not occurred, and will not ever occur. In short, different advocates of practical absolutism can ascribe different moral weight to different moral considerations, and we need to know what these weightings are for any given advocate. For otherwise it is extremely difficult to assess the validity or plausibility of the associated general empirical claim that in practice no act of torture has ever been, nor ever will be, morally justified. Roughly speaking, the greater the moral weight that is given by the practical moral absolutist to refraining from torture – this moral weight considered both in itself and relative to other moral considerations – the more plausible the associated general *empirical* claim becomes. On the other hand, the greater the moral weight that is given to the principle of refraining from torture, the less plausible the narrowly *moral* claims of the practical absolutist become – indeed, at the limit the practical absolutist becomes a moral absolutist *tout court*.

At any rate, the general point to be made here is that the practical moral absolutist owes us a principled account of the moral weight to be attached to refraining from torture relative to other moral considerations. For without it we are unable adequately to assess whether putative counter-examples to this position are really counter-examples or not. It is not good enough for the practical moral absolutist just to give the thumbs down to any putative counter-example that is offered.

The third general point against the practical moral absolutist is to reiterate that it has already been argued that torture is not the morally worst act that anyone could, or indeed has or will, perform. If this is correct, then it is plausible that there will be at least *some* scenarios in which one will be forced to choose between two evils, the lesser one of which is torture. Indeed, the above ticking bomb scenario is one such instance.

The Moral Justification for Legalized
and Institutionalized Torture

We have seen that there are likely to exist, in the real world, one-off emergency situations in which torture is, all things considered, the morally best action to perform. It may seem to follow that institutional arrangements should be in place to facilitate torture in such situations. However, it is perfectly consistent to oppose any legalization or institutionalization of torture, as Jeremy Waldron and David Luban have argued. They have drawn attention to the moral inconsistency and inherent danger in liberal-democratic states legalizing and institutionalizing torture, a practice that strikes at the very heart of the fundamental liberal value of individual autonomy. They have also detailed the tendency for a torture culture to develop in organizations in which torture is legalized or tolerated, a culture in which the excesses of torturing the innocent and the like take place, as in the US military detention centres in Abu Ghraib in Iraq and Guantánamo Bay in Cuba, and in the Israeli secret service (General Security Service). Nevertheless, it is useful to sketch a general argument against the legalization and institutionalization of torture. The argument is consistent with, indeed at some points it is more or less the same as, the arguments of Luban and Waldron. However, the argument has some novel elements, not the least of which is the claim that the view that torture is morally justified in some extreme emergencies is compatible with the view that torture ought not to be legalized and institutionalized.

Most of the theorists who oppose the legalization and institutionalization of torture also (at least implicitly) reject the possibility, let alone actuality, of one-off emergencies in which torture is morally justified. The argument has been put that there are, or could well be, such one-off extreme emergencies in which torture is morally justified. So the first task here is to demonstrate that these two claims are not inconsistent. Specifically, it needs to be shown that it does not follow from the fact that torture is in some extreme emergencies morally justified that torture ought to be legalized, or otherwise institutionalized. So the claim is that it is just a mistake to assume that what morality requires or permits in a given situation must be identical with what the law requires or permits in that situation. This calls for some explanation.

The law in particular, and social institutions more generally, are blunt instruments. They are designed to deal with recurring situations confronted by numerous institutional actors over relatively long periods of time. Laws abstract away from differences between situations across space and time, and differences between institutional actors across space and time. The law, therefore, consists of a set of generalizations to which the particular situation must be made to fit. Hence, if you exceed the speed limit, you are liable for a fine, even though you were only 10 kph above the speed limit, you have a superior car, you are a superior driver, there was no other traffic on the road, the road conditions were perfect, and therefore the chances of you having an accident were actually less than would be the case for most other people most of the time driving at or under the speed limit.[28]

By contrast with the law, morality is a sharp instrument. Morality can be, and typically ought to be, made to apply to a given situation in all its particularity. (This is, of course, not to say that there are not recurring moral situations in respect of which the same moral judgement should be made, nor is it to say that morality does not need to help itself to generalizations.) Accordingly, what might be, all things considered, the morally best action for an agent to perform in some one-off, i.e., non-recurring, situation might not be an action that should be made lawful. Consider the real-life example of the five sailors on a raft in the middle of the ocean and without food. Four of them decide to eat the fifth – the cabin boy – in order to survive.[29] This is a case of both murder and cannibalism. Was it morally justifiable to kill and eat the boy, given the alternative was the death of all five sailors? Perhaps not, considering that the cabin boy was entirely innocent. However, arguably it was morally excusable, and indeed the sailors, although convicted of murder and cannibalism, had their sentence commuted in recognition of this. But there was no suggestion that the laws against murder and cannibalism admit of an exception in such an extreme case; the sailors were convicted and sentenced for murder and cannibalism. Again, consider an exceptionless law against desertion from the battlefield in time of war. Perhaps a soldier is morally justifiable in deserting his fellow soldiers, given that he learns of the more morally pressing need for him to care for his wife, who has contracted some life-threatening disease back home. However, the law against desertion will not, and should not, be changed to allow desertion in such cases.

So the law and morality not only can and do diverge; indeed, sometimes they *ought* to diverge. This is the first point. The second point pertains to the nature of the sub-institution of torture within the larger military,

---

[28] F. Schauer, *Profiles, Probabilities and Stereotypes*, Cambridge, MA: Belknap Press, 2003, p. 207, argues this thesis in relation to laws and uses the speed limit as an example. Arguably, Schauer goes too far in his account of laws, and is insisting that the law is blunter than it needs to be. However, that does not affect what is being said here.

[29] Andrew Alexandra reminded me of this example.

police and correctional institutions. There is a need to begin with a few preliminary points about social institutions.[30]

Social institutions, including legal institutions and military, police and correctional organizations, have both a massive collective inertia and a massive collective momentum by virtue of the participation in them of many agents over a long time who: (a) pursue the same goals; (b) occupy the same roles and, therefore, perform the same tasks and follow the same rules and procedures; and (c) share the same culture. Accordingly, social institutions and their component organizations are like very large ocean liners that cannot slow down, speed up or change direction very easily. It follows that very careful thought needs to be given to the establishment of any additional structure of roles and associated practices that is to be woven into the fabric of the institution. For such an additional (embodied) role structure, once it becomes, so to speak, an integrated working part of the larger institution, is likely to be extremely difficult to remove; it is now a beneficiary of the inertia of the institution. Moreover, such an additional, but now integrated, role structure participates in, and influences the direction of, the institution; it is now a contributing element to the momentum of the institution.

So what can be said of the likely institutional fit between military, police and correctional institutions, on the one hand, and the sub-institution of torture, on the other? The role structure of this sub-institution consists of torturers, torturer trainers, medical personnel who assist torturers, and the like. The core practice of torture has been described in an earlier section.

It would be a massive understatement to say that historically the sub-institution of torture – whether in a lawful or unlawful form – has been no stranger to military, police and correctional institutions. Moreover, the practice of torture is endemic in many, probably most, military, police and correctional institutions in the world today, including democracies such as India and Israel. It is only in recent times and with great difficulty that torture in Australian prisons and police services, for example, has been largely eliminated, or at least very significantly reduced. The Australian, British, American and like cases are important not only because they illustrate that torture can be endemic to liberal-democratic institutions, but also because they demonstrate that liberal-democratic institutions are able – given the political will, suitable re-education and training, stringent accountability mechanisms, etc. – to combat successfully a culture of torture.

Further, there is now a great deal of empirical evidence that in institutional environments in which torture is routinely practised it has a massive impact on other practices and on moral attitudes. For example,

---

[30]   For an account of social institutions, see Miller, *Social Action*, op. cit., chap. 6.

in police organizations in which torture is routinely used, the quality of investigations tends to be low. Careful marshalling of evidence is replaced by the beating up of suspects. Again, police in organizations in which offenders are routinely tortured do not, unsurprisingly, tend to develop respect for the moral rights of offenders, suspects or even witnesses. This is entirely consistent with the excesses detailed by Luban and Waldron in the US military detention centres in Iraq and elsewhere, e.g., the Abu Ghraib scandal, and in the case of the interrogations of suspected terrorists by the Israeli secret service. Indeed, these excesses are to be expected.

And there is this further point. The prevalence of torture in numerous military, police and correctional institutions throughout the world has taken place notwithstanding that for the most part it has been both unlawful and opposed by the citizenry.

It is to be concluded from all this that for the most part military, police and correctional institutions are, *qua* institutions, very receptive to the practice of torture – even when it is unlawful – and that these institutions *qua* institutions would relatively easily incorporate the legalized sub-institution of torture; accordingly, it is very easy to legalize torture and thereby grow and develop a torture culture in military, police and correctional institutions. This does not mean that there are not important differences between, say, police services in authoritarian states and those in contemporary (though not necessarily historical) liberal-democratic states; obviously there are and we should want to keep it that way. Nor does it mean that most, or even the majority, of the individuals who occupy roles in these institutions, whether in liberal democracies or elsewhere, are necessarily receptive *qua* individuals to engaging in the practice of torture; most of them might not be. However, most of them would not be torturing people; that would be done by a distinct minority, as in fact has usually been the case even in institutions in which torture is unlawful and endemic. The question is whether or not as individuals they would initially tolerate, and finally accept, the practice of torture if it were legally and institutionally established; the suggestion is that the historical and comparative evidence is that they would, including in liberal democracies.

An additional conclusion to be drawn is that should the legalized sub-institution of torture be integrated into any of these institutions, it would be very difficult to remove and would, even in liberal democracies, have a major impact on the direction, culture and practices of these institutions. Again, this is what the historical and comparative empirical evidence tells, notwithstanding the initial and even continuing aversion of many, perhaps most, of the individuals in these institutions to torture as such. Consider the Israeli case. Limited forms of torture were legal in Israel prior to 1999, but illegal post-1999. However, evidently torture has by no means been eradicated since 1999. According to the Public Committee against Torture, reporting on the period between September 2001 and April 2003:

> The affidavits and testimonies taken by attorneys and fieldworkers . . . support the conclusions . . . [that] violence, painful tying, humiliations and many other forms of ill-treatment, including detention under inhuman conditions, are a matter of course. . . . The bodies which are supposed to keep the GSS [General Security Service] under scrutiny and ensure that interrogations are conducted lawfully act, instead, as rubberstamps for decisions by the GSS. . . . The State Prosecutor's Office transfers the interrogees' complaints to a GSS agent for investigation and it is little wonder that it has not found in even a single case that GSS agents tortured a Palestinian 'unnecessarily'.[31]

The deeper explanation for the prevalence of torture cultures and the difficulty of eradicating institutionalized torture is no doubt very complex, but presumably it consists in part in the following elements:

1   Moral docility, as opposed to physical docility, is a feature of individuals housed in, and materially dependent upon, large, hierarchical, bureaucratic organizations with strong, relatively homogeneous cultures.
2   The roles of soldier, police officer and prison warden necessarily involve the routine use of coercive, and even deadly, force against dangerous criminals, enemy soldiers or terrorists, and therefore undertaking these roles inevitably results in a degree of moral de-sensitization and a sense of moral ambiguity when it comes to torturing criminals and/or terrorists.
3   Torture is an exercise of enormous power, and power is deeply seductive to many people (and much less dangerous than shooting at armed enemy combatants or trying to arrest or subdue violent criminals).

Armed with these observations on the difference between law and morality, and on the nature of the sub-institution of torture in military, police and correctional institutions, what now can be said on the question as to whether or not to legalize and institutionalize torture in contemporary well-ordered liberal democratic states undergoing a lengthy period of attacks from terrorist organizations?

As we saw above, torture is a terrorist tactic. Indeed, arguably it is the terrorist tactic *par excellence*. Detonating bombs that kill the innocent

---

[31]   Public Committee against Torture in Israel, *Back to a Routine of Torture: Torture and Ill-treatment of Palestinian Detainees during Arrest, Detention and Interrogation (September 2001–April 2003)*, Jerusalem: Public Committee against Torture in Israel, 2003.

has come to be regarded as the quintessential terrorist tactic. But this is presumably because terrorism has implausibly come to be identified only with non-state terrorism. At any rate, the point to be made here is that torture is a terrorist tactic, and for a liberal democracy to legalize and institutionalize it, i.e., to weave the practice of torture into the very fabric of liberal-democratic institutions, would be both an inherent contradiction – torture being an extreme assault on individual autonomy – and, given what we know about the practice of torture in military, police and correctional institutions, highly damaging to those liberal-democratic institutions. It would be equivalent to a liberal democracy legalizing and institutionalizing slavery on the grounds, say, of economic necessity. Legalized and institutionalized slavery is inconsistent with liberal democracy, as is legalized and institutionalized torture. So if legalized and institutionalized slavery and/or legalized and institutionalized torture are necessary because morally required, then liberal democracy is not possible in anything other than an attenuated form. But of course neither legalized/institutionalized slavery nor legalized/institutionalized torture is morally required; quite the contrary. At best, torture is morally justified in some one-off emergencies – just as murder and cannibalism might be morally excusable in a one-off emergency on the high seas, or desertion from the field of battle might be morally justifiable given a one-off emergency back home – but absolutely nothing follows as far as the legalization/institutionalization of torture is concerned.

A final point here concerns the proposition that, absent legalized/institutional torture, *unlawful* endemic torture in the security agencies of contemporary liberal democracies confronting terrorism is inevitable. The implication here is that unless legalized, torture will become endemic in these agencies. It has already been argued that legalization/institutionalization of torture would be profoundly damaging to liberal-democratic institutions. Assume this is correct; it does not follow from this that a torture culture will not come to exist in those agencies in the context of torture being unlawful. Nor does it follow that an unlawful torture culture, indeed an unlawful sub-institution of torture, is inevitable. Here there is a tendency to use the kind of argument that is plausible in relation to, say, the prohibition of alcohol. It is better to legalize alcohol, because then it can be contained and controlled. This form of argument used in relation to torture is spurious. Consuming alcohol to excess is not morally equivalent to torture, and we do not legalize the use of alcohol in emergency situations only. Legalizing the use of torture in extreme emergencies would be much more akin to legalizing perjury in extreme situations. As with torture – and unlike alcohol – perjury is only morally justified in some extreme one-off situations.[32] However, no-one is seriously considering legalizing perjury in one-off extreme situations (at least to my knowledge), and with good reason – to do so would strike at the very heart of the legal system.

The fact is that the recent history of police, military and other organizations in liberal democracies has demonstrated that torture cultures and sub-institutions of torture can be more or less eliminated, albeit with considerable difficulty. The elimination of torture cultures and sub-institutions can only be achieved if torture is unlawful, the community and the political and organizational leadership are strongly opposed to it, police officers and other relevant institutional actors are appropriately educated and trained, and stringent accountability mechanisms – e.g., video recording of interviews, closed-circuit TV cameras in cells, external oversight bodies – are put in place. It is surely obvious that to re-introduce and indeed protect the practice of torture, by legalizing and institutionalizing it would be to catapult the security agencies of liberal democracies back into the dark ages from whence they came.

The discussion has focussed on the legalization and institutionalization of torture, where the practice of torture is understood in general terms; it ought to be now obvious why torture should not be legalized. However, some commentators, notably Alan Dershowitz, have argued that legalized torture could be justified if the torture in question was restricted to extreme emergency situations and subjected to appropriate accountability mechanisms. Specifically, Dershowitz has argued for torture warrants of the kind introduced for a time in Israel.

The notion of torture warrants is supposedly analogous to surveillance and telephone interception warrants issued to police by a magistrate or other judicial officer. The idea is that privacy is a fundamental right but it can be infringed under certain conditions, such as reasonable suspicion that the person whose privacy right is to be infringed is engaged in serious criminal activity, there is no alternative way to acquire the necessary information to convict him or her, and so on. In this kind of set-up the magistrate, not the police, makes the decision as to whether or not these conditions obtain. Consequently, the infringements of privacy rights are restricted, and subject to stringent accountability mechanisms.

However, morally speaking, torture warrants are entirely different from telephone interception or surveillance warrants. Firstly, torture is a far greater evil than the infringement of privacy. For one thing, having one's phone tapped or movements filmed is inherently much less distressing, harmful and morally repugnant than the physical suffering and loss of autonomy

---

[32] For a real-life example, see S. Miller and J. Blackler, *Ethical Issues in Policing*, Aldershot: Ashgate, 2005, p. 129.

involved in being strapped to a chair and, say, having someone drill into an unanaesthetized tooth. On the spectrum of evils, torture is closer to murder and killing than it is to the infringement of privacy. For another thing, torture is a far more dangerous practice than infringing privacy. For the degree of the infringement of privacy can be minimized: e.g., the information gained can relatively easily be kept strictly confidential by the police; moreover, there is no inherent reason for the police illicitly to widen a given infringement of privacy by breaching confidentiality. But in practice torture cannot be restricted likewise. The methods of torture and the process of torture exist on a continuum, and there is often an inherent reason to 'push the envelope' and inflict ever more severe forms of physical suffering on victims; so-called 'torture lite' becomes full-blooded, no-holds-barred torture. One of the consequences of this continuum of torture is the ever-present possibility that the victims of torture will not simply be tortured, but rather be murdered; and in point of fact numerous people have died in the course of being tortured.

Secondly, as has already been argued, there is an inherent institutional receptivity of military, police and correctional institutions to the practice of torture; a receptivity which is such that torture cultures will grow and flourish, notwithstanding Dershowitz's proposal that only tightly controlled and highly restricted forms of torture are to be legally admissible. This institutional receptivity has the consequence that inevitably large numbers of innocent people will be tortured – as happened, and continues to happen, in Israel. Indeed, even under tightly controlled and highly restricted forms of torture some innocent persons will inevitably be tortured – just as the privacy of innocent people is infringed under the existing telephone and surveillance warrant systems. Arguably, the infringement of the privacy of some – in fact, many – innocent persons is a price that we ought to be willing to pay for the sake of preventing serious crimes. However, it would be preposterous to argue that (inadvertently?) torturing numerous innocent people is a reasonable price to pay in return for the information provided by those of the tortured who are in fact guilty.

Thirdly, the information gained by wire-tapping or surveillance has in general far greater utility than that gained by means of the practice of torture – certainly by the tightly controlled and highly restricted forms of torture of the kind envisaged by Dershowitz. Indeed, it is by no means clear that the utility – in terms of saving lives (and leaving aside the costs) – of the system of legalized torture warrants will be very high. (In Israel, to repeat the example, the system does not appear to have been particularly effective.) This is so for two reasons. One reason is that torture victims typically tell the torturer whatever they think he wants to hear, e.g., they are happy to implicate others who are in fact innocent in order to bring an end to their own agony. And even in relation to desired *check-able* information there is often the problem of knowing whether or not the victim of torture is holding out or does not really know; this is espe-cially the case with hardened terrorists. So by comparison with telephone and surveillance warrants, torture warrants are likely to yield unreliable information; there is a serious question about the quality of much of the information provided under a system of torture warrants. A further rea-son to disparage the utility of torture warrants is that, again unlike tele-phone and surveillance warrants, torture warrants are to be issued only in extreme emergencies. By contrast, telephone interception and surveil-lance warrants are issued as a matter of routine, albeit only under certain (recurring) conditions. Accordingly, the volume of information capable of being provided under a system of torture warrants is extremely lim-ited. In short, over time the torture warrant system is likely only to yield an extremely small quantity of reliable information. This overall likely lack of utility of the torture warrant system *qua* institution is important to keep in mind in the context of a protracted struggle against terrorism involving ongoing loss of life on both sides. Here the torture warrant system stands in sharp contrast to telephone interception and surveillance warrant systems. Moreover, it is precisely because the set of conditions under which it is reasonable and effective to infringe privacy rights recurs that infringements of privacy rights by police can reasonably be legalized and institutionalized, e.g., by means of a warrant system. Arguably, the proponents of the torture warrant system have made the mistake of pro-posing a legal, institutional solution to what ought to be regarded as a one-off moral problem;[33] hence the inadequacy of their proposal.

At any rate, the conclusion must be that any attempt to compare tor-ture warrants to surveillance or interception warrants is entirely spurious. Torture is a very different beast.

In the light of the above three points concerning torture warrants that have just been made in the comparison between these and surveillance and interception warrants, the inevitable conclusion is that the practice of torture could not be contained under a system of legalized torture war-rants, and that the consequences of its not being contained would be horrific. Moreover, as noted above, and argued by Luban, Waldron and others, the damage to liberal institutions would be incalculable. Finally, the benefits of a system of legalized torture warrants over the longer term are likely to be slight; and certainly easily outweighed by the costs. So Dershowitz is entirely misguided in his advocacy of torture warrants. Indeed,

---

[33] A 'one-off' moral problem in this sense might in fact recur; but the point is that it will not recur often, and in any case each occurrence ought to be treated as if it were a one-off.

as repeatedly mentioned above, we have the example of Israel's use, or rather abuse, of this system to provide specific empirical evidence against the introduction of torture warrants.

So torture warrants are highly undesirable, indeed a threat to liberal-democratic institutions. Moreover, torture warrants are unnecessary. As has been argued above, there may well be one-off emergencies in which the use of torture is morally justifiable. In those cases, the relevant public officials must bite the bullet and do what is morally required, e.g., torture the terrorist to save thousands of innocent people. In such an emergency, the military or police officers involved will need to break the law on this one occasion. But in itself this is a small price to pay; and a price the police, the military and the politicians have shown themselves only too willing to pay in situations that are far from emergencies.

One final matter. What should be done to the military officer, police officer or other public official who tortures the terrorist if – after saving the city his (or her) crime is discovered? Quite clearly he should resign or be dismissed from his position; public institutions cannot suffer among their ranks those who commit serious crimes. Further, the public official in question must be tried, convicted and sentenced for committing the crime of torture.[34] Obviously, there are (to say the least) mitigating circumstances, and the sentence should be commuted to, say, one day in prison. Would public officials be prepared to act to save thousands of innocent lives if they knew they might lose their job and/or suffer some minor punishment? Presumably many would. But if not, is it desirable to set up a legalized torture chamber and put these people in charge of it?

Conclusion

This chapter has concerned a specific counter-terrorism measure, namely, torture. I have addressed the following four questions: What is torture?; What is wrong with torture?; Is torture ever morally justifiable?; and, Should torture ever be legalized or otherwise institutionalized?

I have argued that in certain extreme circumstances, the torture of a person known to be a terrorist might be morally justifiable. Roughly speaking, the circumstances are that: (1) the terrorist is in the process of completing his or her action of attempting to (say) murder thousands of innocent people by detonating a nuclear device, and is refusing to provide the information necessary to allow it to be defused; (2) torturing

---

[34] This suggestion is also made by Shue, 'Torture', p. 143.

the terrorist is necessary and sufficient to save the lives of the innocent people in question.

However, I have also argued that torture should not under any circumstances be legalized or be otherwise institutionalized. Here I invoke again the above-mentioned distinction between a morally justified one-off action and a morally justified law, or lawful institutional practice. The legalization of torture, including use of torture warrants, is unnecessary, undesirable and, indeed, a threat to liberal democratic institutions; as such, it is not morally acceptable.

7

Bioterrorism and the Dual-Use Dilemma

In the aftermath of the September 11, 2001 attacks in the US, the possibility of terrorists targeting populations in Western countries with chemical, biological, radiological and/or nuclear (CBRN) weaponry appears to be far from remote. Terrorists groups such as Al-Qaeda are known to have displayed considerable interest in acquiring CBRN weaponry. Moreover, security analysts believe they have reasonable prospects of doing so. According to Paul Wilkinson, for example, 'It is likely that there is only a very limited period (perhaps two to three years) before some elements in the Al Qaeda network succeed in acquiring viable, if only relatively crude, CBRN weaponry.'[1]

Bioterrorism, in particular, is perhaps a greater threat from non-state terrorist groups than, say, nuclear weapons of mass destruction (WMDs), given the availability of the technical knowledge necessary to produce the relevant biological agents and the feasibility of weaponization. This is not to say that there are not obstacles for would-be bioterrorists, including the dangers to themselves in handling pathogens, or to their supporters from pathogens that once weaponized and used prove unable to be contained. But it is to say that there is a non-negligible bioterrorist threat, and it is likely to increase rather than decrease.

A small number of animal, plant and human pathogens are readily obtainable from nature, and bioterrorists with minimal microbiological training could use these to inflict casualties or economic damage.

Techniques of genetic engineering have been available for some time to enhance the virulence, transmissibility, and so on, of naturally occurring

[1] P. Wilkinson, *Terrorism versus Democracy: The Liberal State Response*, 2nd edn, London: Routledge, 2006, p. xv.

pathogens. This gives rise to the possibility of terrorists getting their hands on pathogens with (say) enhanced virulence and for which there are no vaccines. Indeed, some of these techniques of enhancement are such that bioterrorists with advanced microbiological training could themselves deploy them.

Recent developments in synthetic genomics have exacerbated the problem. It is now possible to create pathogens *de novo*, i.e., to construct deadly viruses from scratch. Accordingly, in the not too distant future a would-be terrorist will no longer need to go to an inhospitable region to find a naturally occurring pathogen such as Ebola, or to steal a highly virulent and transmissible pathogen such as smallpox from one of a very small number of very secure laboratories, or even to deploy standard recombinant DNA techniques to enhance the virulence and transmissibility of some more readily available pathogen. Rather, he or she could buy a bench-top DNA synthesizer and potentially use it to assemble a specified gene sequence of a highly virulent and transmissible pathogen from readily available raw materials.

Again, this is not to say that there are not obstacles to terrorists, including the ones mentioned above, as well as the current lack of know-how of techniques of synthetic genomics amongst most cohorts of researchers and laboratory workers, and whatever safeguards exist now, e.g., the US Select Agent regulations, or can be put in place over the next few years.

The so-called 'dual-use dilemma' arises in the context of research in the biological and other sciences as a consequence of the fact that one and the same piece of scientific research sometimes has the potential to be used for evil as well as for good. Consider as an example of this kind of dilemma recent research on the mousepox virus.[2] On the one hand, the research programme on the mousepox virus should have been pursued since it may well have led to a genetically engineered sterility treatment that would have helped combat periodic plagues of mice in Australia. On the other hand, this research project should not have been pursued since it led to the creation of a highly virulent strain of mousepox and the possibility of the creation – by, say, a terrorist group contemplating a biological terrorist attack – of a highly virulent strain of smallpox able to overcome available vaccines.

A dual-use dilemma is an *ethical* dilemma, and an ethical dilemma for the *researcher* (and for those who have the power or authority to assist

[2]   R.J. Jackson, A.J. Ramsay, C.D. Christensen, S. Beaton, D.F. Hall and I.A. Ramshaw, 'Expression of mouse interleukin-4 by a recombinant ectromelia virus suppresses cytolytic lymphocyte responses and overcomes genetic resistance to mousepox', *Journal of Virology* 75(3), 2001, pp. 1205–10.

or impede the researcher's work, e.g., governments). It is an *ethical* dilemma since it is about promoting good in the context of the potential for also causing harm, e.g., the promotion of health in the context of providing the wherewithal for the killing of innocents. It is an ethical dilemma *for the researcher* not because he or she is aiming at anything other than a good outcome; typically, the researcher intends not harm but only good. Rather, the dilemma arises for the researcher because of the potential actions of *others*. Malevolent non-researchers might steal dangerous biological agents produced by the researcher; alternatively, *other* researchers – or at least their governments or leadership – might use the results of the original researcher's work for malevolent purposes. The malevolent purposes in question include bioterrorism and biowarfare.

In the recent and not so recent past, a number of governments have sought to develop weapons of mass destruction, including biological weapons, and in some cases have actually used them: e.g., the use of mustard gas by the German and British armies in the First World War; the dropping of atomic bombs on Hiroshima and Nagasaki by the US Air Force in the Second World War; the use of bioweapons, e.g. aerial spraying of plague-infested fleas during the Second World War by the Japanese military that killed thousands of Chinese civilians and military personnel; the existence of a large-scale biological weapons programme in the Soviet Union from 1946 to 1992; and the use of chemical agents against the Kurds by Saddam Hussein's regime in 1988. Indeed, it could be argued that nation-states with biowarfare programmes, rather than sub-national terrorist groups, constitute the greatest threat (not simply of engaging in biowarfare but also, simultaneously, of engaging in bioterrorism).

Moreover, there have been some high-profile 'defections' of scientists from western countries to authoritarian states with WMD programmes. For example, Dr Abdul Qadeer Khan joined and in large part established Pakistan's nuclear weapons programme after working for Urenco in the Netherlands; and Frans van Anraat (also from the Netherlands) went to Iraq to assist Saddam Hussein's WMD programme in producing mustard gas.

Further, there have been a number of acts, or attempted acts, of bioterrorism, notably by Aum Shinrikyo in Japan (they attempted to acquire and use anthrax and botulinum toxin), Al-Qaeda (they attempted to acquire and use anthrax) and the so-called 'Amerithrax' attacks (the campaign in September/October 2001 in which deadly anthrax spores were posted to a number of US addresses, resulting in the deaths of five people and the infection of seventeen others).

The expression 'dual-use dilemma' is in need of some conceptual unpacking. Here we need to introduce a number of sets of distinctions.

(1) In relation to the *purposes* (or ends) of the research, we can distinguish the following conceptual axes: (i) good/evil; (ii) military/non-military; and (iii) within the category of military purposes, the sub-categories of offensive/protective. Consider the aerosolization of a pathogen undertaken for a military purpose. The purpose in question might be offensive, e.g., biowarfare; but it might simply be protective, e.g., to understand the nature and dangers of such aerosolization in order to prepare protections against an enemy known to be planning to deploy the aerosolized pathogen as a weapon.

The categories good/evil and military/non-military do not necessarily mirror one another. Some non-military purposes are, nevertheless, evil, e.g., the supplier of a vaccine releasing a pathogen to make large numbers of people sick in order that the sick buy the vaccine against the pathogen and, thereby, increase the supplier's profits. And some military purposes might be good, e.g., the above-mentioned research on the aerosolization of a pathogen undertaken for purely protective purposes in the context of a just war. However, some of the protective research would probably yield results that could assist in the development and delivery of biological weapons.

(2) Dual-use refers to two temporally and logically distinct 'users' of the research: (i) those who initially undertake the research or use the research results for purposes intended by the original researchers (original users); and (ii) those who use the results of the work of these original researchers for some purpose other than that intended by the original researchers (secondary users). For example, the above-mentioned research on the aerosolization of a pathogen (conducted by the original users) might be used for offensive purposes by those fighting an unjust war (the secondary users).

(3) In relation to the term 'use' we can distinguish: (i) actual or potential use in accordance with the purpose for which it was designed (design-purpose); (ii) actual or potential use for some purpose other than that for which it was specifically designed. Dual-use dilemmas can involve original researchers whose purpose is a design purpose, e.g., to demonstrate how to render a vaccine against a highly transmissible pathogen ineffective. This design purpose can itself be in the service of a benevolent purpose of the original researchers, e.g., the purpose of enhancing the effectiveness of the vaccine. Alternatively, the achievement of this design purpose could be used for a malevolent non-design purpose by secondary researchers, e.g., to render the vaccine ineffective in the context of spreading the pathogen in question.

On the other hand, secondary users might build on the original research in such a way as to create, say, a new pathogen, e.g., a more virulent strain of smallpox as opposed to a more virulent strain of mousepox, in which case we might be inclined to say that they had a new design purpose (albeit a malevolent one).

(4) In relation to the *outcomes* of the research, we can distinguish: (i) intended outcomes; (ii) unintended but foreseen outcomes; and (iii) unforeseen and perhaps unforeseeable outcomes. An example of an unintended outcome is an outbreak of smallpox resulting from inadequate safety procedures in a laboratory setting. However, such accidents are not instances of the dual-use dilemma. For something to be an instance of a dual-use dilemma, both outcomes (the two horns of the dual-use dilemma) need to be (actually or potentially) intended (or at least foreseen) by someone; there needs to be two sets of (actual or potential) *users*. Naturally, an outcome might be unintended and unforeseen (even unforeseeable) by the original researcher but, nevertheless, intended by the secondary user. Thus, scientists who preserve a small number of smallpox samples for pure research purposes in the context of a policy of mandatory destruction of samples might not intend or foresee that they might be used for malevolent purposes by others, e.g., weaponized.

The dual-use dilemma is a dilemma for researchers, namely, those researchers involved in biological research that has the potential to be misused by bioterrorists, criminal organizations and governments engaged in biowarfare. It is a dilemma for researchers since, although they are not the ones misusing their biological research, nevertheless, they have a moral responsibility to minimize the likelihood that that research is, or could be, misused; after all, they are the ones who enabled the possibility of misuse of the research by undertaking the research in the first place. In relation to very high-risk research, researchers have a responsibility to ensure that it is only conducted under very stringent controls; indeed, some research is so high-risk that it ought not to be conducted at all.

The dual-use dilemma is also a dilemma for the private and public institutions, including universities and commercial firms, that fund or otherwise enable research to be undertaken. The dilemma is made more acute for university-based researchers and for universities, given their commitments to such values as academic freedom and the unfettered dissemination of research findings; and for private companies, given their commitment to free enterprise. More generally, it is a dilemma for the individual communities for whose benefit or, indeed, to whose potential detriment the research is being conducted, and for the national governments who bear the moral and legal responsibility of ensuring that the security of their citizens is provided for. Finally, in the context of an increasingly interdependent set of nation-states – the so-called 'global community' – the dual-use dilemma has become a dilemma for international bodies such as the United Nations.

The Biological Weapons Convention

Given the general threat to public health posed by transmissible pathogens, and given that biological agents can be used as WMDs in the hands of state actors, terrorist groups and criminal organizations, there is an imperative strictly to regulate the development, production, stockpiling, weaponization and use of pathogens. At the international level, a key instrument in this regard is the Biological Weapons Convention (BWC).[3]

The general aim to which the BWC is directed is, 'for the sake of all mankind, to exclude completely the possibility of bacteriological (biological) agents and toxins being used as weapons. Convinced that such use would be repugnant to the conscience of mankind and that no effort should be spared to minimize this risk.'

In accordance with Article I of the BWC,

> Each State Party to this Convention undertakes never in any circumstances to develop, produce, stockpile or otherwise acquire or retain:
>
> 1 Microbial or other biological agents, or toxins whatever their origin or method of production, of types and in quantities that have no justification for prophylactic, protective or other peaceful purposes;
> 2 Weapons, equipment or means of delivery designed to use such agents or toxins for hostile purposes or in armed conflict.

While the BWC is an important step in relation to its stated aims of prohibiting and eliminating the possibility of using biological agents as weapons, it has a number of possible loopholes and lacunae.

The BWC evidently has requirements regarding technology transfers from prohibited to non-prohibited purposes and vice versa.[4] For example, technology transfers from non-prohibited purposes, e.g., prophylactic, to prohibited, e.g. military-offensive, are prohibited under all circumstances.

---

[3] More precisely, Convention on the Prohibition of the Development, Production and Stockpiling of Bacteriological (Biological) and Toxin Weapons and on Their Destruction. (Signed at London, Moscow and Washington on 10 April 1972; entered into force on 26 March 1975; depositories – UK, US and Soviet governments.)
[4] J.P. Zanders, 'Introduction', *Minerva* 40(1), 2002, p. 9.

However, the BWC does not make a formal distinction between civilian and military purposes. Indeed, in speaking of 'protective purposes' (clause 1, above) the BWC seems to allow protective military purposes. This has the consequence that a technology transfer from civilian to military is allowable, if the latter purpose is protective and not offensive. But now an issue arises as to what counts as protective, as opposed to offensive. (See below for more on this issue.)

Moreover, the BWC does not provide for any robust verification processes: e.g., unlike the Chemical Weapons Convention (CWC) there is no international organization or national authority to verify compliance with the BWC.

Experiments of Concern

Human knowledge and understanding of the natural world is, presumably, desirable both in itself and as a means to the provision of other human goods, such as health and longevity. Moreover, human freedom, including freedom of intellectual inquiry, is agreed on all hands to be an intrinsic human good. Accordingly, there is a presumption in favour of allowing research in the biological sciences, as there is in other areas of human knowledge. In short, research in the biological sciences is morally permissible, absent special considerations in relation to specific kinds of such research. What, if any, research in the biological sciences is morally impermissible?

Research in the biological sciences undertaken for the purpose of weaponizing biological agents so that they can be used to kill or cause illness in human populations is presumably morally impermissible, whether the research in question is undertaken by state actors, (non-state) terrorist groups, criminal organizations or malevolent individuals. So much is proclaimed in the BWC, notwithstanding the fact that arguments have been used from time to time to justify the use of biological weapons in the context of a just war. It has been argued, for example, that some biological weapons are more 'humane' than some conventional weapons. It is not within the scope of this book to discuss the moral complexities arising from the use of various forms of weaponry, albeit this is an important and somewhat neglected topic. However, I note that in so far as biological weapons are a species of WMD, then there is a *general* moral objection to their use, namely, that inevitably they target civilian populations and not merely combatants. As such, they violate the so-called *ius in bello* condition of Just War Theory: the condition that, among other things, gives expression to the moral principle of civilian immunity in war.

While the principle of not deliberately targeting civilians normally applies to states, some – but obviously not all – *non-state* actors engaged in armed struggles also adhere to an analogous principle. For example, as noted in Chapter 1, for most if not all of its history the African National Congress (ANC) in its armed struggle against the apartheid government in South Africa adhered to this moral principle: military and police personnel were regarded by the ANC as legitimate targets, whereas ordinary civilians were not. On the other hand, as we have seen, terrorist groups such as Al-Qaeda violate this moral principle, as would any terrorist group using biological weapons as WMDs. Naturally, terrorist groups might use 'new generation' biological weapons that are able to target particular individuals, e.g., a biological weapon of assassination. However, use of such a biological weapon would not constitute use of a WMD.

In addition to the general concern that biological weapons may serve as weapons of mass destruction is the concern that their effects are, generally speaking, hard to predict and control; this latter feature was a central rationale behind the BWC. The fact that biological weapons are relatively inexpensive and easy to produce (in comparison with other WMDs) also means that the potential for an arms race in the context of biological weapons is especially problematic.

At any rate, let us assume here that research in the biological sciences undertaken for the ultimate purpose of using weaponized biological agents is in fact morally impermissible.

The moral problem that now arises concerns research in the biological sciences that is not undertaken *by the original researchers* for the ultimate purpose of using weaponized biological agents, but might be used by secondary researchers (or other users) for this impermissible purpose, i.e., the moral problem presented by dual-use dilemmas.

As already noted, a particularly morally problematic species of the dual-use dilemma arises in the case of research projects on biological weapons 'threat assessments'. Such research involves experimenting with weaponized pathogens so as to enable development of defensive measures.

In relation to the dual-use dilemma in the biological sciences, the approach of the US National Research Council (NRC) in its 2004 report, *Biotechnology Research in an Age of Terrorism*, is to map the range of these dual-use dilemmas by identifying and taxonomizing a set of salient 'experiments of concern'. I accept this approach in the context of our attempt to isolate the morally permissible from the morally impermissible in relation to dual-use research in the biological sciences. Moreover, it is an approach replicated (albeit extended somewhat) in a recent report prepared by the author and others for the Australian government.[5] Our first task, then, is to map the terrain of such dual-use dilemmas; hence, our recourse to experiments of concern.

According to the NRC report, 'experiments of concern' are those that would:

1 demonstrate how to render a vaccine ineffective;
2 confer resistance to therapeutically useful antibiotics or antiviral agents;
3 enhance the virulence of a pathogen or render a non-pathogen virulent;
4 increase the transmissibility of a pathogen;
5 alter the host range of a pathogen;
6 enable the evasion of diagnosis and/or detection by established methods; or
7 enable the weaponization of a biological agent or toxin.[6]

In addition, the following experiments of concern were identified in the Australian report:

8   genetic sequencing of pathogens;
9   synthesis of pathogenic micro-organisms;
10 any experiment with variole virus (smallpox);
11 attempts to recover/revive past pathogens.

Dual-Use Research: The Ethical Issues

By definition, dual-use research is morally problematic: on the one hand, such research provides benefits (at least potentially); on the other hand, there is the risk of misuse by some nation-states, terrorist groups and criminal organizations.

Broadly speaking, the most obvious benefits of research in the biological sciences of the kind in question are: the protection of human life and physical health against diseases (including novel ones), the protection of

---

[5] S. Miller and M. Selgelid, *Ethical and Philosophical Consideration of the Dual-Use Dilemma in the Biological Sciences*, Report for the Commonwealth Department of Prime Minister and Cabinet, Centre for Applied Philosophy and Public Ethics, Australian National University and Charles Sturt University, Canberra, 2006. A good deal of the material in this chapter is taken from this report.
[6] National Research Council, *Biotechnology Research in an Age of Terrorism*, Washington, DC: National Academies Press, 2004, p. 5.

existing food and water sources; and the protection of human populations against biological weapons.

By contrast, the potential burdens of such research are death and sickness caused by the use of biological agents as weapons in the hands of malevolent state actors, terrorist groups, criminal organizations and individuals.

More fine-grained analyses of the benefits and burdens of such research would elaborate on the additional kinds of benefit/burden and recipients/ bearers thereof: e.g., the economic wealth accrued by large pharmaceutical corporations and their shareholders; the economic costs of expensive, unsuccessful (or only marginally beneficial) research programmes in the biological sciences; and, more generally, the (dis)utility and (in)justice of specific allocations of resources to, and the distribution of benefits and burdens from, different research programmes in the biological sciences, e.g., the evident disutility of the large 1946–92 Soviet biological weapons programme.

Fine-grained ethical analyses of dual-use research in the biological sciences would seek to *quantify* actual and potential benefits and burdens, and actual and potential recipients/bearers of these benefits and burdens. These analyses would also identify a range of salient policy options. Each option would embody a set of trade-offs between present and future benefits and burdens, and recipients and bearers thereof. The construction of these options and the process of selection between them would consist in large part in the application of various ethical principles, including human rights principles – e.g., the right to life, freedom of inquiry, and free speech –and principles of utility and of justice. Here I note that there is no simple inverse relationship between specific benefits burdens such that, for example, any increase in security requires a reduction in scientific freedom. Rather, an increase in security might simply involve greater safety precautions and, therefore, a financial cost without any commensurate reduction in scientific freedom. At any rate, relevant benefits and burdens need to be disaggregated and subjected to individual analysis in the context of any process of determining trade-offs and selecting options.

I am not in a position to provide any such fine-grained ethical analysis here, but I will rather focus (somewhat simplistically) on a single ethical consideration that gives rise to the dilemma, namely, human health (including human life), and do so without exploring questions of which human populations or how many individual humans have benefited/ been burdened or are likely to benefit/be burdened, and so on. Viewed from this perspective the dual-use dilemma concerns human health (as a simple, unquantified human good), and the dilemma consists in the fact that research undertaken to promote human health might instead be used to destroy human health. As such, the dilemma gives rise to questions of security: what are reasonable and ethically justified forms and degrees of security in this context?

The security in question is a complex notion. It consists in part in the physical security of, for example, samples of biological agents against theft. Relatedly, security consists in part in the processes in place to ensure, for example, that the researchers themselves cannot, or will not, conduct research for malevolent purposes.

As we will see in the section following this one, security in this sense also consists in part in restrictions that might be placed on the dissemination of research findings.

Thus far I have offered a somewhat static mode of analysis of the dual-use dilemma consisting of the quantification of harms and benefits, the identification of salient options, and the selection of an option on the basis of ethical principles. However, a more dynamic, indeed creative, mode of analysis is called for.[7]

In the first place, options are not static, because well-intentioned scientists, malevolent actors and security personnel are *responsive* to the problems that they confront, including the problems provided by other actors. The response of scientists to a pathogen with enhanced virulence might be the development of a new vaccine. The response of security personnel to a new bioterrorist threat might be an enhanced regulatory system. Accordingly, the mode of analysis of the dual-use dilemma must be dynamic in character.

In the second place, ethical dilemmas are not necessarily – or even typically – to be resolved by careful calibration of the differential ethical weight that attaches to the options provided for in the dilemma. Rather, the dilemma must, if possible, be resolved by designing a new third or fourth option, i.e., by bypassing the dilemma. Consider the question of whether to disseminate dual-use research findings or not disseminate them: academic freedom versus security. Perhaps the solution is to find a third option, such as to disseminate them in a manner that will not enable the experiments in question to be replicated.

In the light of these considerations of health and security, let us address the question of the moral permissibility of dual-use research, albeit in highly general terms. Here there appear to be three separable ethical questions. Firstly, there is the ethical question as to whether or not a putative biological agent to be researched ought in fact to be eliminated

---

[7] This mode of analysis is *creative* and amounts to *designing-in* ethics. Jeroen van den Hoven has developed this notion. See, for example, J. van den Hoven, 'Computer ethics and moral methodology', *Metaphilosophy* 28(3), 1997, pp. 234–49.

(or, if already eliminated, not retrieved). Here the *possibility* of research is removed: there is no possibility of research because there is no biological agent to be researched. I have in mind the case of smallpox and the arguments in favour or against the elimination of all samples of smallpox. Secondly, there is the ethical question (or questions) arising from dual-use research in relation to a biological agent whose present and/or future existence is taken as a given: there is no intention to eliminate or not retrieve or not bring into existence the biological agent in question. For example, research to determine whether or not avian influenza could trigger a human pandemic might lead to the creation of dangerous new strains that could be used by terrorists. Such research might include work intentionally undertaken to create novel pathogens or synthesize existing ones, albeit work whose ultimate purpose was to develop, say, a vaccine against these pathogens. Thirdly, there is the ethical question of whether to undertake dual-use research for the purpose of protection against weaponized pathogens, e.g., research into the aerosolization of pathogens.

Let us now consider a couple of these ethical issues. Take research on presently existing or novel pathogens (where their present and/or future existence is accepted).

There are a number of types of experiment from our list of experiments of concern that are relevant to this question. However, the general problem here is the unintended (by the original researcher) untoward consequences of otherwise benign research. These consequences are threefold. Firstly, there is an unintended dangerous biological research outcome, e.g., a pathogen with enhanced virulence or transmissibility or at least the knowledge of how to create such a pathogen. (As we have seen, there are some *intended* dangerous research outcomes, e.g., intentional creation of vaccine-resistant strains of a disease, undertaken for, say, prophylactic purposes, e.g., to test the adequacy of a vaccine, and which have no untoward consequences.) Whether or not such an unintended and untoward outcome is possible or likely is a scientific question, best answered by biological scientists. Secondly, there is an outcome not intended by the original scientist but, nevertheless, intended by some malevolent state actor, non-state terrorist group, criminal organization or individual, e.g., the weaponization (and use as a weapon) of the pathogen that has been unintentionally created. Whether or not this outcome is possible or likely – given, say, a pathogen has already been (unintentionally) created – is a security question, best answered by security experts (with input from relevant non-security specialists such as engineers). Thirdly, there is the ultimate outcome intended by the malevolent individual or organization, namely, the public health outcome consequent on the biological attack. What the public health outcome of a given biological attack is likely to be, e.g., the extent of loss of life, is a public health question, best answered by public health experts or teams thereof (including biological scientists, medical personnel and weapons experts, but also those knowledgeable about public health resources and infrastructure).

The danger attendant upon a given dual-use research programme can be crudely quantified by determining the probability, be it low, medium or high, of a given untoward outcome, and multiplying this probability by the (quantified) disvalue (or disutility) of that outcome, e.g., in terms of the numerical loss of human life. A more fine-gained ethical analysis would explore the variety of decision making/risk-taking strategies – including the precautionary principle – that might be considered appropriate in this context.[8] Presumably, dual-use research that has a high probability of resulting in substantial loss of human life ought not to be undertaken. On the other hand, the danger attendant upon dual-use research is not the only moral consideration in play. Another important moral consideration is the (intended) benefits of the research. Clearly trade-offs need to be made between the (intended) benefits of the research and its (unintended by researchers) potential untoward outcomes. Moreover, the process of arriving at suitable trade-offs is in large part a process of moral reasoning, including the weighing of one moral consideration against another. However, as noted above, it is important to bear in mind the possibility of creative solutions that bypass the dilemma; perhaps we do not need to make the trade-offs we initially think we need to make.

The general point to be made here is that in the context of the yet to be decided grey area of dual-use research marked off by the experiments of concern, there are a complex mix of scientific, security, public health and ethical considerations in play. Moreover, the process of moral reasoning involved will require trade-offs between ethical considerations and, it is hoped, will involve the provision of creative solutions that bypass the dilemma. The result will presumably be that some putative experiments of concern will be relegated to the impermissible category and others to the permissible category, albeit in the latter case under stringent conditions of safety and security.

Consider an experiment of concern involving enhancing the virulence of a pathogen. It might be argued that if there is no evidence of a threat posed by, say, a genetically engineered strain of cowpox that attacks the immune system, then there is no reasonable justification for developing

---

[8] Roughly, this is the principle to the effect that if research might cause great harm, then, in the absence of a scientific consensus that the harm would not ensue, the research should not be pursued. See, for example, J. Weckert and J. Moor, 'The precautionary principle in nanotechnology', *International Journal of Applied Philosophy* 20(2), 2006, pp. 191–204.

such an organism.[9] No doubt, there needs to be some evidence of a threat. But this raises a number of questions: What counts as evidence? How immediate is the threat? Does the development of the more virulent pathogen constitute a greater threat than the original threat that it is supposed to protect against? Surely when a microbial threat exists only in a scientist's imagination, an experiment to create such a microbe is both unnecessary and overly risky.

There are a couple of additional points that should be stressed here. One pertains to the process of moral reasoning. I have been speaking in broadly utilitarian and consequentialist terms, e.g., using notions of future benefits/burdens, quantified loss of life, disvalue and disutility. However, some would argue that this mode of reasoning is flawed (and not only by virtue of its inherently static character – see above). For example, consequentialist reasoning is arguably one-dimensional and fails to give sufficient weight to the intrinsic moral properties of current actions, e.g., perhaps human rights of current persons override future utility. Again, there are a range of moral considerations that are absent from our discussion thus far, e.g., the human right to free inquiry, intellectual property rights (both individual and collective). Finally, there are the inherent problems described in Chapter 5 in attempting to quantify the value of human lives. I do not have the space here to unravel all these moral complexities, or to develop and defend my own favoured account of moral reasoning as it might apply to the dual-use dilemmas in question. Accordingly, I have simply sought to gesture at some of the moral considerations in play and at the general kind of process of moral reasoning that should take place.

Another point pertains to uncertainty. Proceeding in the manner of a risk assessor assumes that the probabilities of specific outcomes can realistically be determined; risk assessment is, presumably, more than mere guesswork. But the reliability of probability judgements in relation to outcomes from dual-use research in the biological sciences is, to say the least, open to question. Arguably, the possibility of the development of a vaccine-resistant strain of smallpox based on research undertaken on mousepox to develop a contraceptive for mice could not have been realistically predicted. This is, of course, not to say that attempts should not be made to foresee untoward outcomes; it is merely to caution against overconfidence in the results of such attempts. Moreover, because the actors involved in dual-use dilemmas are, as noted above, responsive to problems and to one another's actions, probability judgements need to take this into account. One way to do so is to analyse, for example, a security

[9]   S. Wright, 'Taking biodefense too far', *Bulletin of the Atomic Scientists* 60(6), 2004, pp. 58–66.

risk from bioterrorists in part in terms of a complex set of variables, including the ability, opportunity and motivation of the bioterrorists, the likely intelligence possessed by, and the likely assessment made by, the terrorists, the capacity to respond to specific forms of bioterrorist attack, the likely movements of innocent third parties at risk from specific security responses, the relevant moral principles, the rights and duties of the various actors involved, and so on.

However, what might be crucial here is the capacity to generate a creative response to the security problem thus analysed. Perhaps a focus on reducing the opportunities available to bioterrorists by establishing a licensing system for laboratories using dual-use technologies, licensing of DNA synthesizers and checks in relation to those who buy or use them are cases in point. Moreover, the developments in synthetic genomics may call for an adjustment in relation to existing security arrangements. For example, novel pathogens may escape classification under the US Select Agent regulations. Indeed, a new type of classificatory system might need to be introduced: one that makes use of functional or causal definitions of agents, instead of more traditional (non-functional, property-based) taxonomic systems.

A further ethical question arising from dual-use research pertains to weaponization. As already noted, a particularly morally problematic species of the dual-use dilemma arises in the case of research projects on biological weapons (BW). In order to develop defences against a putative BW agent, it is necessary to understand the underlying mechanisms for pathogenicity and the ways in which the biological agent may be dispersed. However, an understanding of these factors is also exactly what would be required for the development of BW.

As stated above, my assumption in this chapter is that the weaponization of pathogens for offensive military purposes is morally impermissible. Moreover, in so far as military defence is understood to include using biological weapons against an attacker (whether the attack in question is a biological attack or not), then the weaponization of pathogens for defensive military purposes – in this sense of defence – is also morally impermissible. On the other hand, research that is defensive in the sense that it serves the purpose simply of enabling combatants and civilians to *protect* themselves against a biological attack by, for example, developing early warning indicators of the presence of aerosolized novel pathogens is *prima facie* morally permissible. Let us refer to such research as research undertaken for the purpose of *protection* (as opposed to military *defence*). The problem is that such research for protective purposes might itself involve, for example, the creation of a virulent and highly transmissible novel pathogen and the weaponization of it. As such, the weaponization of pathogens for protective purpose gives rise to a dual-use dilemma of a very acute kind.

The issue resolves itself into whether or not in practice the weaponization of pathogens for protective purposes can be distinguished from the weaponization of pathogens for offensive purposes (including defensive purposes in the above adumbrated sense of that term).

Presumably, if these two conceptually distinct activities are to be distinguished in practice, then this is because there are *verifiable* differences in respect of: (i) intention or purpose; and (ii) physical properties of the weaponized pathogen.

In relation to (i), for example, if the intention is protection, then the pathogen in question will be one that some identified malevolent state or terrorist group is known to have weaponized (or it is known that they are in the process of weaponizing the pathogen).[10]

In relation to (ii), for example, if the weaponized pathogen is possessed in large quantities, i.e., quantities appropriate for a military offensive but unnecessary for research serving purely protective purposes, then it is a case of weaponization for offensive purposes. Unfortunately, recourse to quantities may not resolve this question in the case of biological agents, given that only small quantities are typically required. Also, one might expect there sometimes to be some differences in the results of research involving weapons constructed in accordance with the design purpose only of testing protections against an attack using that weapon from the results of research undertaken with the design purpose of making a successful attack using that weapon, i.e., an attack against which the enemy is not protected. For example, in the case of the former, the research result might be a protective vaccine, whereas in the case of the latter, the research result might be a weaponized pathogen that is resistant to any vaccine.

Moreover, the results of such dual-use research on the weaponization of pathogens undertaken only for protective purposes, e.g., the vaccine mentioned above, might be more likely to be disseminated; after all, it is not only one's own civilians and combatants that ought to be protected from biological attack. Or at least one would expect, other things being equal, there to be less need for secrecy in relation to such relatively benign research and a willingness on the part of those engaged in it to be subject to verification checks.[11]

[10]   Naturally, there are other evidentiary possibilities that might reach a reasonable threshold of justification in relation to protective research on weaponization: e.g., a high probability in relation to an easily weaponized, readily available pathogen that some malevolent group or other is weaponizing this pathogen.

[11]   Naturally, other things might not be equal. We might be concerned that if a malevolent state knew what our defensive capabilities were they would be more likely to develop new ways to overcome them.

Dissemination of Dual-Use Research Results

If terrorists get access to dual-use research, then they may well be in a position to weaponize virulent pathogens against which we have no immunity or vaccine and, thereby, mount a biological attack against which we have no protection. Part of the solution to this problem seems straightforward: censor scientific research in order to prevent findings being disseminated to terrorist groups. However, wholesale censorship raises a host of ethical issues, including, in the case of university-based research, academic freedom. Censorship is a clear infringement of academic freedom. Moreover, censorship might be counter-productive in the current context in which a great deal of dual-use research is already available to would-be bioterrorists; for censorship and other restrictions on academic freedom might have the effect of impeding research that would, for example, enable the development of vaccines to currently available virulent, transmissible pathogens.

In what follows I provide a brief analysis of academic freedom. Naturally, I do so in the context of the assumptions we have already made in relation to permissible and impermissible research. If a particular university-based research programme or experiment of concern is morally *impermissible* given the safety, security and health concerns outlined above, then the moral principle of academic freedom has rightly been overridden; academic freedom is an important moral value, but it is not an *absolute* value.

There are two main arguments for the principle of academic freedom. The first begins with the premise that freedom of intellectual inquiry is a fundamental human right.[12]

Thus conceived, freedom of intellectual inquiry is not an individual right of the ordinary kind. Although it is a right which attaches to individuals, as opposed to groups, it is not a right which an individual could exercise by him- or herself. Communication, discussion and inter-subjective methods of testing are social, or at least interpersonal, activities. However, it is important to stress that they are not activities which are relativized to social or ethnic or political groups; in principle, intellectual interaction can and ought to be allowed to take place between individuals irrespective of whether they belong to the same social, ethnic or political group. In short, freedom of intellectual inquiry, or at least its constituent elements, is a fundamental *human* right. Note that, being a fundamental human right, it can, at least in principle, override collective interests and goals, including organizational, and even national, economic interests and

---

[12] Material in this section is taken from S. Miller, 'Academic autonomy', in C.A.J. Coady (ed.), *Why Universities Matter*, Sydney: Allen and Unwin, 2000.

goals. This 'trumping' property of human rights is a constitutive element of liberal democracy, a form of polity the legitimacy of which is based in part on its capacity and willingness to protect human rights, including, at times, against infringements emanating from the government of the day.

If freedom of intellectual inquiry is a human right, then, like other human rights, such as the right to life and to freedom of the person, it is a right which academics as humans possess along with all other citizens. But how does this bear upon the specific institutional purpose of the university to acquire, transmit and disseminate knowledge?

Before we can answer this question we need to get clearer on the relationship between the human right freely to engage in intellectual inquiry, on the one hand, and knowledge or truth, on the other.

Freedom of intellectual inquiry and knowledge are not related simply as means to end, but also conceptually. To inquire freely is to seek the truth by reasoning. Truth is not an external, contingently connected end which some inquiries might be directed towards if the inquirer happened to have an interest in truth, rather than, say, an interest in falsity. Rather, truth is internally connected to intellectual inquiry. An intellectual inquiry which did not aim at the truth would not be an intellectual inquiry, or at least would be defective *qua* intellectual inquiry. Moreover, here aiming at truth is aiming at truth as an end in itself. (This is not inconsistent with also aiming at truth as a means to some other end.) Further, to engage in free intellectual inquiry in our extended sense involving communication with and testing by others is freely to seek the truth by reasoning with others. Intellectual inquiry in this sense is not exclusively the activity of a solitary individual.

Given that freedom of intellectual inquiry is a human right, and given the above-described relationship between intellectual inquiry and truth (or knowledge), we can now present the argument in relation to freedom of intellectual inquiry. This argument in effect seeks to recast the notion of freedom of intellectual inquiry in order to bring out the potential significance for conceptions of the university of the claim that freedom of intellectual inquiry is a human right.

1   Freedom of intellectual inquiry is a human right.
2   Freedom of intellectual inquiry is (principally) the freedom to seek the truth by reasoning with others.
3   Freedom to seek the truth by reasoning with others is a fundamental human right.

Let us grant the existence of a human right freely to pursue the truth by reasoning with others. What are the implications of this right for universities and for academics' freedom of inquiry?

Given such a right of intellectual inquiry, it is plausible to conclude that the university is simply the institutional embodiment of that moral right. In short, the university is the institutional embodiment of the right freely to seek the truth by reasoning with others.

The following claims now seem warranted.

Firstly, universities have been established as centres wherein independence of intellectual inquiry is maintained. This flows from the proposition that the university is an institutional embodiment of the moral *right* of the inquirers freely to undertake their intellectual inquiries. Universities are not, for example, research centres set up to pursue quite specific intellectual inquiries determined by their external funders. Nor should particular inquiries undertaken by academics at universities be terminated on the grounds that some external powerful group, say government, might not find the truths discovered in the course of these inquiries politically palatable.

Secondly, universities have a duty to disseminate scholarship and research to the community. Intellectual inquiry is not only a human right, it is an activity which produces external benefits. For example, knowledge is a means to other goods, including economic well-being. Accordingly, and notwithstanding the rights of academics freely to inquire, it is reasonable that, *qua* community-supported institutions, universities take on an obligation to ensure that their intellectual activities have a flow-through effect to the wider community in terms of such external benefits. Thus dissemination of research has obvious benefits to the community, including health and economic benefits.

On the view of the university under consideration, interference in the process of the free pursuit of knowledge in universities strikes at one of the fundamental purposes for which universities have been established. Such interference could not be justified, for example, on the grounds that whereas free inquiry might be necessary for the acquisition of knowledge in many instances, in some particular instance free inquiry was not leading to knowledge, and therefore in this case free inquiry could be interfered with without striking at the basic purposes of the university as an institution.

Notwithstanding the importance of the human right of intellectual inquiry and its centrality to the institution of the university, freedom of intellectual inquiry in general, and of scientific inquiry in particular, is not – as noted above – an absolute right. Specifically, it can be overridden if its exercise comes into conflict with other human rights, notably the right to life. Accordingly, if a contingency arose, such as war or a pandemic or a potential terrorist attack, then the duty of a scientist to disseminate his or her findings could well be overridden. Doubtless, in relation to most academic research, such contingencies are exceptions, and should be treated as such. Nevertheless, given the high risk to human life and health posed by misuse of research in synthetic biology and related areas, such biological research constitutes a special case. Censorship of academic research needs special justification. However, that justification is, in general terms, available in the areas in question, e.g., the high risk of misuse by terrorists of such research. Naturally, censorship of any specific research or research project will not only need some justification, it will need a *specific* justification that details the high risk of misuse of this specific research project outcome by terrorists, e.g., the research outcome is a highly virulent, easily transmissible and readily weaponized pathogen.

Earlier I noted a second argument in favour of intellectual freedom. This argument is in some respect more germane to the kind of research in the biological sciences under consideration here. It is an argument associated with the philosopher John Stuart Mill.[13]

The arguments is roughly as follows:

1   Freedom of communication is necessary for rational – including scientific – inquiry.
2   Rational – including scientific – inquiry is necessary for knowledge (including scientific knowledge).

Therefore:

3   Freedom of communication is necessary for knowledge (including scientific knowledge).

This argument is valid and premise (2) is plausible. What of premise (1)? The justification for (1) is evidently that rational (including scientific) inquiry requires a number of diverse and competing views/explanations/theories (possessed by different persons, research groups), and a substantial amount of diverse evidence for/against these view/theories/explanations (available from different sources).

This argument has considerable force and has been used in one form or another by many scientists and philosophers of science, including Karl Popper in the context of his proposed strategy of pursuing the falsification, rather than verification, of scientific theories. For our purposes here it needs to be noted that it is an instrumentalist or means/end argument for freedom of scientific inquiry. Most important, it assumes that the scientific knowledge thus gained is a human good. However, as

[13] See J.S. Mill, *On Liberty* (any edition).

the dual-use dilemma illustrates, scientific knowledge can be used for evil. To the extent that it is used for evil, the argument works against freedom of scientific inquiry: if freedom of scientific inquiry is a necessary condition for scientific knowledge, and scientific knowledge is used for evil, then freedom of scientific inquiry is morally problematic.

The upshot of our discussion of the two arguments for freedom of intellectual, including scientific, inquiry is essentially twofold. Firstly, freedom of scientific inquiry is a fundamental human right and a central component of academic freedom, but it is a right that can be overridden by other human rights, notably the right to life. Secondly, freedom of scientific inquiry is also an instrumental good and, as such, is justified to the extent that it yields knowledge that is beneficial to the human race, as opposed to knowledge that is harmful.

In the context of the dual-use dilemma in the biological sciences, these two arguments for freedom of scientific inquiry – the first argument, in particular – are sufficient to establish a presumption against censorship, but it is not clear if, and to what extent, that presumption is offset by the risks of harm attendant upon particular research programmes in the biological sciences.

While the question of censorship in relation to particular research programmes, or, at least, particular research projects, needs to be assessed on a case-by-case basis, there is, nevertheless, a general strategy that seems warranted. We saw earlier that in relation to research in the biological sciences, including synthetic biology and the like, the genie is to a large extent out of the bottle; there is already a good deal of readily available scientific research findings in the biological sciences that could be misused by terrorists. Therefore, in addition to increasing security in relation to research, what has become crucial is that well-intentioned researchers and research institutions stay ahead of bioterrorists and their fellow-travellers, scientifically speaking. Thus, if bioterrorists steal a sample of smallpox, then scientists need to have developed a vaccine; if bioterrorists come to be able to enhance the virulence of some pathogen, then scientists need to have developed an appropriate vaccine; and so on and so forth. Accordingly, the conditions conducive to the further development of research in the biological sciences need to be maintained, albeit in a context of considerably higher levels of security.

One way to square the circle and avoid the dilemma of either censoring scientific research findings or assisting terrorists in their plans to engage in bioterrorist attacks is to try to find a middle way of partial censorship, for it seems that there are important distinctions to be made in relation to dual-use publications. Some dual-use publications in the scientific literature are more directly applicable for harmful intent than others. The demonstration that a mousepox virus can be engineered for increased virulence can be directly applied to attempted enhancement of small-pox virulence; indeed, exactly the same technologies described in the publication could be used. The publication of the sequence for the 1918 influenza strain could be used to reconstruct this virus easily for harmful intent. Other publications, however, would need significant further research for them to be used for malevolent purposes. The demonstration that engineered recombinant viruses can encode genes encoding antibodies that suppress immune responses could be ultimately used for harmful intent. However, a significant amount of research would need to be undertaken before a disseminating infectious organism could be constructed. The original use of this technology was to prevent graft rejection.[14] Accordingly, we ought to develop a taxonomy of dual-use publications which at the very least should distinguish between first-tier and second-tier research: the former refers to dual-use research possessed of direct applicability for harmful intent and the latter only with indirect applicability for harmful intent. (Strictly speaking, of course, directness of applicability will be a matter of degree.) First-tier research findings might need to be censored, or presented for publication in a manner that would not enable readers to replicate the experiments in question and thereby generate dangerous pathogens and the like. While omission of (detailed description of) materials and methods from published articles will sometimes be sufficient to prevent malevolent use of dual-use discoveries, this will not always be the case. There will be many situations where the general idea of what was discovered will be critical while the materials and methods would be obvious to anyone 'skilled in the art'.

The Regulation of Dual-Use Research

In what follows I attempt to steer a middle course between a permissive approach to the regulation of research in the biological sciences that would allow research to continue (more or less) unimpeded, and one which would seek to subject it to the kind of heavy-handed, top-down, governmental regulation characteristic of nuclear research. The basic justification for my approach is in large part based on the above-made assumption that in addition to increasing security in relation to research, what has become crucial is that well-intentioned researchers and research

---

[14]   These points were made by Peter Kerr as part of his contribution to the report *Ethical and Philosophical Consideration of the Dual-Use Dilemma in the Biological Sciences* (see note 5 *supra*).

institutions stay ahead of bioterrorists and their fellow-travellers, scientifically speaking.

The regulation of dual-use research needs to take the following considerations into account:

(1) *Permissible or impermissible research:* Who is to be the decision-maker in relation to determining whether or not an instance of one of the eleven identified types of experiment of concern is permissible or impermissible? The candidates for decision-maker are: the individual researcher; the specific institution hosting the research project in question, i.e., a university, corporation or government research centre; an independent authority; and the government. In the case of the university, the decision-maker would presumably be a collegial body comprised of relevant scientists (at least).

As we saw above, freedom of inquiry is a human right that finds institutional expression in universities in the form of academic freedom. In the context of a liberal democracy, there is a presumption against governmental restriction of human rights, including in the name of protecting other human rights. Moreover, arguably progress in scientific research is importantly dependent on academic freedom, including research that enables governments to thwart would-be bioterrorists. As we have seen above, the question of whether research is morally permissible or impermissible is extremely difficult, and it is by no means obvious who the ultimate decision-maker ought to be. However, given the complex considerations and the competing interests involved, I favour an independent authority. More on this below.

(2) *Mandatory physical safety and security regulation:* Should there be regulations providing for mandatory physical safety and security of the storage, transport and physical access to samples of pathogens, equipment, laboratories, etc.? The answer is presumably in the affirmative.

In theory, the specific content of these regulations might be determined either by a government agency, an independent authority, a professional association of scientists or the specific institution hosting the research programmes in question. However, governments bear the ultimate institutional and moral responsibility for the safety and security of their citizens, including the researchers themselves, in so far as that safety and security is a matter of the physical conditions under which potentially harmful (albeit permissible) research is to be undertaken and the physical elements thereof stored, transported, etc. Accordingly, the government would at least need to be able to satisfy itself that the regulatory system, including the regulations and their enforcement mechanisms, governing the physical safety and security of dual-use experimentation are adequate.

The application of many of these regulations could be undertaken by, for example, biosafety committees operating at the institutional level, e.g., a university-based bio-safety committee. However, these committees would need in turn to be accountable to government (perhaps via an independent authority).

(3) *Licensing of dual-use technologies/techniques:* Presumably, there should be mandatory licensing of dual-use technologies/techniques/DNA synthesizers/pathogen samples, given the risks that they pose. For example, laboratories that undertake genetic engineering of pox viruses have the means to make recombinant smallpox viruses. Accordingly, only certain laboratories in the public sector and the private sector should be licensed to engage in research involving the use of certain dual-use technologies.

The establishment of a licensing authority to conduct such a licensing process would be a significant addition to the mechanisms available to contain the dangers associated with the dual-use dilemma. However, it raises a number of important questions. One set of question concerns the criteria that the licensing authority would deploy in its licensing process. Is there a presumption in favour of granting a licence, the criteria having been framed for the sole purpose of eliminating licence applicants that are manifestly unable to provide a safe and secure research environment? Are the criteria to be used to determine the issuing of licences objective and publicly available? Another set of questions pertains to the status and make-up of the licensing authority; Is it, for example, independent of government in the sense that its decisions are binding and not able to be overridden by government?

These questions are important in the context of the concerns one might have in relation to government interference with freedom of intellectual inquiry (who decides what is permissible research?) and freedom of speech/ dissemination of research findings (who decides what research findings can be disseminated and to whom?). The point is that a licensing authority could be given, at least in principle, powers that would in effect override human rights to freedom of intellectual inquiry and freedom of dissemination (and associated rights to academic freedom) by licensing, say, only government research centres.

(4) *Mandatory education and training:* Given the potential harms arising from the eleven identified types of experiments of concern, it is clear that some process of education and/or training for relevant researchers and other personnel is called for. There is a question as to the precise content of such education and training. However, at the very least those working in laboratories would need to have received safety and security

training in relation to the physical safety and security of the storage, transport and physical access to samples of pathogens, equipment, laboratories, etc. In addition, there is a need to ensure that editors and others responsible for the dissemination of potentially harmful information are aware of the issues in relation to dual-use research findings. In short, some forms of mandatory education and/or training are justified. What the precise content of such education/training programmes ought to be, and who ought to be responsible for their provision, remain open questions. However, it is an institutional and moral responsibility of government to ensure that minimal training/education programmes in relation to potentially harmful dual-use research and dissemination of dual-use research findings are being provided (even if not by government itself).

(5) *Mandatory personnel security regulation:* Physical safety and security of a research environment, including access by non-authorized persons, e.g., potential thieves, is one thing; however, personnel security in relation to researchers, e.g., background checks, screening of researchers in relation to any history of mental illness, political affiliations with extremist groups, etc., is quite another. Doubtless it is prudent, indeed it is a moral requirement, that access to virulent pathogens be disallowed to a researcher diagnosed as a psychopath or to a known member of a terrorist organization. On the other hand, other things being equal, government officials prying into the lives of university students enrolled in degrees in the biological sciences is an unwarranted intrusion of civil liberties. Here, as elsewhere, the devil is in the details, and there is a need for specific policies to be framed in the light of a range of human rights, academic and scientific considerations as well as security concerns.

One way forward here might be to develop a system of security checks for personnel working in licensed laboratories but (absent special considerations) not for other research personnel.

(6) *Censorship/constraint of dissemination:* As we have seen above, the question of whether research findings ought to be freely disseminated, censored or their dissemination in some lesser way restricted is an extremely difficult issue and it is by no means obvious who the ultimate decision-maker ought to be. Freedom of speech and freedom of dissemination of knowledge are human rights that find institutional expression in universities in the form of academic freedom; that said, academic freedom has less moral weight than the right to life, other things being equal. On the other hand, arguably progress in science is importantly dependent on academic freedom, including progress in research findings that might serve to protect human life, e.g., vaccines against highly virulent pathogens.

A relevant important distinction here is that made above between first-tier and second-tier dual-use research. For example, first-tier research findings might need to be disseminated in such a way that anyone being informed of these findings would not be able to replicate the experiments that enabled the results reported in the findings.

An Independent Authority

One option that seeks to deal with many of the above issues involves the establishment of an authority that is independent of both the research institutions (universities, corporations and government research centres) and government. This independent authority would comprise scientists, health experts, security experts (including those with the highest feasible level security clearance) and ethicists.

This independent authority would have ultimate decision-making powers in relation to both the conduct of dual-use research and the dissemination of dual-use research findings. Moreover, it might also constitute the above-mentioned independent authority issuing licences to laboratories in relation to dual-use technologies (and providing for personnel security). Other things being equal, decisions of this independent authority would not be able to be overridden by government. Naturally, other things might not be equal. For example, the decisions of the independent authority would have to comply with laws enacted by government; to this extent it would be accountable to government.

In addition, this independent authority might have an accountability role on behalf of government in relation to the application of government regulations in respect of physical safety and security and dual-use education and training. Its determinations in these respects would not be final; rather, these determinations would have the status of advice to government.

Under this arrangement, researchers might be required to submit any research proposals falling within categories of concern to Institutional Biosafety Committees (IBCs) for review; and they would be required to submit any research findings which end up falling within categories of concern to IBCs after the fact (i.e., if a relevant dual-use discovery is unexpectedly made). In cases where sufficient dangers of experimentation or of information dissemination are foreseen, the IBCs will refer the studies to the independent authority for determination.

It is important to note that even under this form of meta-regulation, the independent authority would have the power to intervene at any lower level, including overturning decisions at the lower level and auditing the work of the IBCs. In effect, this independent body would have the ultimate authority to determine what was permissible or impermissible dual-use research, and to determine whether and in what form dual-use research findings could be disseminated.

In addition to the research screening process described above, a national code of scientific conduct would be developed by the independent authority. The code would include the requirement that any research or research findings that fall within the categories of experiments of concern be reported by scientists to IBCs or other institutional ethics committees for determination. The code of conduct would be legally binding and apply to those working in industry as well as academia.

The establishment of an independent authority involves a decision-making body embodying both the scientific and security expertise required for rigorous analysis of the security risks of research and of publication.

The code of conduct would help to ensure that any research falling within the category of types of experiments of concern will be sent for adjudication by those with increasing levels of expertise in comparison with that of the (ordinary, educated) researcher – i.e., IBCs and ethics committees (whose members receive advanced training) and the independent authority (whose members have the highest degree relevant expertise and which contains members with a combination of different forms – i.e., scientific and security – of expertise) in cases where the former committees conclude this is called for.

Because ultimate decision-making authority in problematic cases will not lie in the hands of either the individual researcher or the individual institution (or collegial committee of scientists, in the case of universities), problems regarding bias and conflicts of interest will be addressed. If the independent authority is appropriately constituted, then it is less likely that its decisions would be biased either towards the promotion of science and freedom of inquiry/expression (in the case of a university-based authority), towards financial profits (in the case of a commercial firm) or towards the promotion of security (in the case of a purely governmental authority).

Finally, the two-tiered screening procedure would ensure a degree of efficiency: the independent authority would make determinations only in a fraction of cases, since IBCs would make determinations in the bulk of cases.

Conclusion

In this final chapter I have turned to the matter of the potential use of WMDs by terrorists and, more specifically, to the so-called 'dual-use dilemma' confronting both researchers in the biological sciences and governments and policymakers. Techniques of genetic engineering are available to enhance the virulence, transmissibility, and so on, of naturally occurring pathogens such as Ebola and smallpox; indeed, recent developments in synthetic genomics enable the creation of pathogens *de novo*. The unfortunate consequence of these scientific developments is that the means are increasingly available to enable terrorists to launch bioterrorist attacks on populations whom they consider to be enemies. Accordingly, there is a dual-use dilemma: on the one hand, research in the biological sciences can, and does, do a great deal of good, e.g., by producing vaccines against viruses; on the other hand, the results of such research can potentially be used by terrorists to cause enormous harm by, for example, the weaponization of infectious diseases against which there is no vaccine.

I have attempted to steer a middle course between a permissive approach to the regulation of research in the biological sciences that would allow research to continue (more or less) unimpeded, and one which would seek to subject it to the kind of heavy-handed, top-down, governmental regulation characteristic of nuclear research. The justification for my approach is in part based on the assumption that the genie is to a large extent out of the bottle and that, therefore, in addition to increasing security in relation to research, what has become crucial is that well-intentioned researchers and research institutions stay ahead of bioterrorists and their fellow-travellers, scientifically speaking. Thus, if bioterrorists steal a sample of smallpox, then scientists need to have developed a vaccine; if bioterrorists come to be able to enhance the virulence of some pathogen, then scientists need to have developed an appropriate vaccine; and so on. Accordingly, the conditions conducive to the further development of research in the biological sciences need to be maintained, albeit in a context of greater levels of security.

I recommend, among other things, the setting up of an independent authority, mandatory physical safety, education and personnel security procedures, the licensing of dual-use technologies and various censorship provisions.

Bibliography

Alexandra, A., 'Political pacifism', *Social Theory and Practice* 29(4), 2003.

Allhoff, F., 'Terrorism and torture', *International Journal of Applied Philosophy* 17(1), 2003.

Benn, S.I., *A Theory of Freedom*, Cambridge: Cambridge University Press, 1988.

Bergen, P.L., *Holy War Inc.: Inside the Secret World of Osama bin Laden*, New York: Free Press, 2001.

Berman, P., *Terror and Liberalism*, New York: Norton, 2004.

Biko, S., *The Testimony of Steve Biko*, ed. M. Arnold, London: Smith, 1984.

Bok, S., *Secrets: Concealment and Revelation*, Oxford: Oxford University Press, 1982.

Bottomley, S. and Bronitt, S., *Law in Context*, 3rd edn, Sydney: Federation Press, 2006.

Bowden, M., *Killing Pablo: The Hunt for the World's Greatest Outlaw*, London: Atlantic Books, 2001.

Bronitt, S. and Stellios, J., 'Sedition, security, and human rights: "unbalanced" law reform in the war on terror', *Melbourne University Law Review* 30(3), 2006.

Bryett, K., Harrison, A. and Shaw, J., *An Introduction to Policing: The Role and Function of Police in Australia*, vol. 2, Sydney: Butterworths, 1993.

Chomsky, N., *Power and Prospects: Reflections on Human Nature and the Social Order*, Sydney: Allen and Unwin, 1996.

Coady, C.A.J., 'Defining terrorism', in I. Primoratz (ed.), *Terrorism: The Philosophical Issues*, New York: Palgrave Macmillan, 2004.

Coady, C.A.J., 'Terrorism, just war and supreme emergency', in C.A.J. Coady and M. O'Keefe (eds), *Terrorism and Justice: Moral Argument in a Threatened World*, Melbourne: Melbourne University Press, 2002.

Coady, C.A.J. and O'Keefe, M. (eds), *Terrorism and Justice: Moral Argument in a Threatened World*, Melbourne: Melbourne University Press, 2002.

Cohen, S., *Visions of Social Control: Crime, Punishment and Classification*, Cambridge: Polity, 1985.

Cooper, D.E., 'Collective responsibility', *Philosophy* 43, 1968.

David, S.R., 'If not combatants, certainly not civilians', *Ethics & International Affairs* 17(1), 2003.

Davis, K.C., *Discretionary Justice: A Preliminary Inquiry*, Baton Rouge: Louisiana State University Press, 1969.

Davis, M., 'The moral justifiability of torture and other cruel, inhuman, or degrading treatment', *International Journal of Applied Philosophy* 19(2), 2005.

Delattre, E., *Character and Cops: Ethics in Policing*, Washington, DC: American Enterprise Institute, 1994.

Dershowitz, A.M., *Why Terrorism Works: Understanding the Threat, Responding to the Challenge*, Melbourne: Scribe Publications, 2003.

Dhillon, K., *Police and Politics in India: Colonial Concepts, Democratic Compulsions: Indian Police 1947–2002*, New Delhi: Manohar, 2005.

Dworkin, R., *Taking Rights Seriously*, Cambridge, MA: Harvard University Press, 1977.

Fisk, R., *The Great War for Civilisation: The Conquest of the Middle East*, London: HarperCollins, 2005.

French, P.A., *Collective and Corporate Responsibility*, New York: Columbia University Press, 1984.

Gilbert, M., 'Collective guilt and collective guilt feelings', *Journal of Ethics* 6(2), 2002.

Gilbert, P., *New Terror, New Wars*, Edinburgh: Edinburgh University Press, 2003.

Goodin, R.E., *What's Wrong with Terrorism?* Cambridge: Polity, 2006.

Graham, K., *Practical Reasoning in a Social World: How We Act Together*, Cambridge: Cambridge University Press, 2002.

Greenberg, K. (ed.), *Al Qaeda Now: Understanding Today's Terrorists*, Cambridge: Cambridge University Press, 2005.

Griffin, J., 'First steps in an account of human rights', *European Journal of Philosophy* 9(3), 2001.

Haubrich, D., 'September 11, anti-terror laws and civil liberties: Britain, France and Germany compared', *Government and Opposition* 38(1), 2003.

Haydar, B., 'The ethics of fighting terror and the priority of citizens', *Journal of Military Ethics* 4(1), 2005.

Hewitt, C., *The Effectiveness of Anti-Terrorist Policies*, Lanham, MD: University Press of America, 1984.

Hill, R.S., *Policing the Colonial Frontier: The Theory and Practice of Coercive Social and Racial Control in New Zealand, 1767–1867*, Wellington: New Zealand Department of Internal Affairs, 1986.

Honderich, T., *After the Terror*, Edinburgh: Edinburgh University Press, 2002.

Joustra, T.H.J., *Radicalisation in Broader Perspective*, The Hague: National Coordinator for Terrorism, 2007.

Kant, I., *Groundwork of the Metaphysics of Morals*, New York: Cambridge University Press, 1998.

Kapitan, T., 'Terrorism in the Arab–Israeli conflict', in I. Primoratz (ed.), *Terrorism: The Philosophical Issues*, London: Palgrave Macmillan, 2004.

Kasher, A. and Yadlin, A., 'Military ethics of fighting terror: an Israeli perspective', *Journal of Military Ethics* 4(1), 2005.

Keane, F., *Season of Blood: A Rwandan Journey*, London: Viking, 1995.

Khatchadourian, H., 'Counter-terrorism: torture and assassinations', in G. Meggle (ed.), *Ethics of Terrorism and Counter-Terrorism*, Frankfurt: Ontos Verlag, 2005.

Khatchadourian, H., 'Is political assassination ever morally justified?', in H. Zellner (ed.), *Assassination*, Cambridge, MA, Schenkman, 1974.

Kimmerling, B., *Politicide: Ariel Sharon's War against the Palestinians*, London: Verso, 2003.

Kleinig, J. (ed.), *Handled with Discretion: Ethical Issues in Police Decision Making*, Lanham, MD: Rowman and Littlefield, 1996.

Knight, A., *Beria: Stalin's First Lieutenant*, Princeton: Princeton University Press, 1995.

Lackey, D., 'Assassination, responsibility and retribution', in H. Zellner (ed.), *Assassination*, Cambridge, MA: Schenkman, 1974.

Luban, D., 'Liberalism and the unpleasant question of torture', *University of Virginia Law Review* 91(6), 2005.

Luban, D., 'The war on terrorism and the end of human rights', *Philosophy and Public Affairs Quarterly* 22(3), 2002.

Lynch, A. and Williams, G., *What Price Security? Taking Stock of Australia's Anti-Terror Laws*, Sydney: University of New South Wales Press, 2006.

Machan, T.R., 'Exploring extreme violence (torture)', *Journal of Social Philosophy* 21(1), 1990.

McKendrick, B. and Hoffmann, W. (eds), *People and Violence in South Africa*, Cape Town: Oxford University Press, 1990.

Mackey, S., *The Reckoning: Iraq and the Legacy of Saddam Hussein*, London: W.W. Norton, 2002.

Mavrodes, G.I., 'Conventions and the morality of war', *Philosophy & Public Affairs* 4(2), 1975.

May, L., *The Morality of Groups: Collective Responsibility, Group-Based Harm, and Corporate Rights*, Notre Dame, IN: University of Notre Dame Press, 1987.

May, L., 'Vicarious agency and corporate responsibility', *Philosophical Studies* 43(1), 1983.

May, L., *War Crimes and Just War*, Cambridge: Cambridge University Press, 2007.

Meggle, G. (ed.), *Ethics of Terrorism and Counter-Terrorism*, Frankfurt: Ontos Verlag, 2005.

Mendez, J.E., 'Torture in Latin America', in K. Roth and M. Worden (eds), *Torture: Does It Make Us Safer? Is It Ever OK?* New York: New Press, 2005.

Mill, J.S., *On Liberty*, New York: Norton, 1975.

Miller, A., *Miller's Court*, New York: Houghton Mifflin, 1982.

Miller, S., 'Academic autonomy', in C.A.J. Coady (ed.), *Why Universities Matter*, Sydney: Allen and Unwin, 2000.

Miller, S., 'Civilian immunity, forcing the choice and collective responsibility', in I. Primoratz (ed.), *Civilian Immunity in War*, New York: Oxford University Press, 2007.

Miller, S., 'Collective responsibility: an individualist account', in P.A. French (ed.), *Midwest Studies in Philosophy: Collective Responsibility* 30, 2006.

Miller, S., *Investigative Ethics*, Oxford: Blackwell, forthcoming.

Miller, S., 'Is torture ever morally justified?', *International Journal of Applied Philosophy* 19(2), 2005.

Miller, S., *Issues in Police Ethics*, Wagga Wagga, Australia: Keon Publications, 1996.

Miller, S., 'Judith Jarvis Thomson on killing in self-defence', *Australian Journal of Professional and Applied Ethics* 3(2), 2001.

Miller, S., 'Just War theory: the case of South Africa', *Philosophical Papers* 19(2), 1990.

Miller, S., 'Killing in self-defence', *Public Affairs Quarterly* 7(4), 1993.

Miller, S., 'On the morality of waging war against the state', *South African Journal of Philosophy* 10(1), 1991.

Miller, S., 'Osama bin Laden, terrorism and collective responsibility', in C.A.J. Coady and M. O'Keefe (eds), *Terrorism and Justice: Moral Argument in a Threatened World*, Melbourne: Melbourne University Press, 2002.

Miller, S., 'Privacy and the Internet', *Australian Computer Journal* 29(1), 1997.

Miller, S., *Social Action: A Teleological Account*, Cambridge: Cambridge University Press, 2001.

Miller, S., 'Terrorism and collective responsibility', in G. Meggle (ed.), *Ethics of Terrorism and Counter-Terrorism*, Frankfurt: Ontos Verlag, 2005.

Miller, S., 'Terrorism and collective responsibility: response to Narveson and Rosenbaum', *International Journal of Applied Philosophy* 18(2), 2005.

Miller, S., 'Torture', in E.N. Zalta (ed.), *The Stanford Encyclopedia of Philosophy (Spring 2006 Edition)*, <http://plato.stanford.edu/archives/spr2006/enteries/torture/>

Miller, S., 'Torture and terrorism', *Iyyun: The Jerusalem Philosophical Quarterly* 55, 2006.

Miller, S. and Blackler, J., *Ethical Issues in Policing*, Aldershot: Ashgate, 2005.

Miller, S., Roberts, P. and Spence, E., *Corruption and Anti-Corruption*, Saddle River, NJ: Prentice Hall, 1995.

Miller, S. and Selgelid, M., *Ethical and Philosophical Consideration of the Dual-Use Dilemma in the Biological Sciences*, Report for the Commonwealth Department of Prime Minister and Cabinet, Centre for Applied Philosophy and Public Ethics, Australian National University and Charles Sturt University, Canberra, 2006.

Miller, S. and Selgelid, M., 'Ethical and Philosophical Consideration of the Dual-Use Dilemma in the Biological Sciences', *Science and Engineering Ethics*, December 2007.

Miller, S., Sen, S., Mishra, P. and Blackler, J., *Ethical Issues in the Policing of India*, Hyderabad: National Institute for Policing, 2007.

Mohamedou, Mohammad-Mahmoud Ould, *Understanding Al-Qaeda: The Transformation of War*, London: Pluto Press, 2007.

Murphy, J.G., 'The killing of the innocent', *Monist* 57(4), 1973.

National Research Council, *Biotechnology Research in an Age of Terrorism*, Washington, DC: National Academies Press, 2004.

Narveson, J., 'Pacifism and terrorism: why we should condemn both', *International Journal of Applied Philosophy* 17(2), 2003.

Neyroud, P. and Beckley, A., *Policing, Ethics and Human Rights*, Cullompton, UK: Willan Publishing, 2001.

Primoratz, I. (ed.), *Civilian Immunity in War*, New York: Oxford University Press, 2007.

Primoratz, I., 'Terrorism in the Israeli–Palestinian conflict: a case study in applied ethics', *Iyyun: The Jerusalem Philosophical Quarterly* 55, 2006.

Primoratz, I. (ed.), *Terrorism: The Philosophical Issues*, New York: Palgrave Macmillan, 2004.

Primoratz, I., 'What is terrorism?', in I. Primoratz (ed.), *Terrorism: The Philosophical Issues*, New York: Palgrave Macmillan, 2004.

Public Committee against Torture in Israel, *Back to a Routine of Torture: Torture and Ill-treatment of Palestinian Detainees during Arrest, Detention and Interrogation (September 2001–April 2003)*, Jerusalem: Public Committee against Torture in Israel, 2003.

Risen, J., *State of War: The Secret History of the CIA and the Bush Administration*, New York: Free Press, 2006.

Rosenbaum, A.S., 'On terrorism and the just war', *International Journal of Applied Philosophy* 17(2), 2003.

Said, E., *Orientalism*, New York: Vintage Books, 1979.

Saikal, A., *Islam and the West: Conflict or Cooperation?* London: Palgrave, 2003.

Schauer, F., *Profiles, Probabilities and Stereotypes*, Cambridge, MA: Belknap Press, 2003.

Sen, S., *Law Enforcement and Cross Border Terrorism*, New Delhi: Concept Publishing, 2005.

Shue, H., *Basic Rights: Subsistence, Affluence, and US Foreign Policy*, 2nd edn, Princeton: Princeton University Press, 1996.

Shue, H., 'Torture', *Philosophy & Public Affairs* 7(2), 1978.

Simpson, P., 'Violence and terrorism in Northern Ireland', in I. Primoratz (ed.), *Terrorism: The Philosophical Issues*, New York: Palgrave Macmillan, 2004.

Smith, M.L.R., *Fighting for Ireland: Military Strategy of the Irish Republican Movement*, London: Routledge, 1995.

Stannard, B., 'How we got Finch', *Bulletin*, 22 November 1988.

Stein, Y., 'By any name illegal and immoral', *Ethics & International Affairs* 17(1), 2003.

Sussman, D., 'What's wrong with torture?', *Philosophy & Public Affairs* 33(1), 2005.

Thomson, J.J., 'Self-defence', *Philosophy & Public Affairs* 20(4), 1991.

Townshend, C., *Terrorism: A Very Short Introduction*, Oxford: Oxford University Press, 2002.

van den Hoven, J., 'Computer ethics and moral methodology', *Metaphilosophy* 28(3), 1997.

Waldron, J., 'Torture and positive law: jurisprudence for the White House', *Columbia Law Review* 105(6), 2005.

Walzer, M., *Just and Unjust Wars: A Moral Argument with Historical Illustrations*, New York: Basic Books, 1977.

Walzer, M., 'Political action: the problem of dirty hands', *Philosophy and Public Affairs* 2(2), 1973.

Whittaker, D.J. (ed.), *The Terrorism Reader*, 2nd edn, London: Routledge, 2003.

Wilkins, B.T., *Terrorism and Collective Responsibility*, London: Routledge, 1992.

Wilkinson, P., *Terrorism versus Democracy: The Liberal State Response*, 2nd edn, London: Routledge, 2006.

Wilson, F. and Ramphele, M., *Uprooting Poverty: The South African Challenge*, Cape Town: University of Cape Town Press, 1988.

Weber, M., 'Politics as a vocation', in H. Gerth and C. Wright Mills (eds), *From Max Weber: Essays in Sociology*, London: Routledge, 1991.

Weckert, J. and Moor, J., 'The precautionary principle in nanotechnology', *International Journal of Applied Philosophy* 20(2), 2006.

Wellman, C., 'On terrorism itself', *Journal of Value Inquiry* 13(4), 1979.

Wright, S., 'Taking biodefense too far', *Bulletin of the Atomic Scientists* 60(6), 2004.

Zanders, J.P., 'Introduction', *Minerva* 40(1), 2002.

Zellner, H. (ed.), *Assassination*, Cambridge, MA: Schenkman, 1974.

Index